U0037397

綠野仙蹤

The Wonderful Wizard of Oz

中英對照雙語版

L·法蘭克·包姆—著

VIVIANWANG—插畫

盛世教育—譯

笛藤出版

目　次

綠野仙蹤

Contents

The Wonderful Wizard of Oz

綠野仙蹤

第 1 章

龍捲風來了

接著發生了一件怪事。
房子旋轉了兩三圈後慢慢升上天空，
桃樂絲覺得自己好像坐在氫氣球上。

桃樂絲和亨利叔叔以及他的妻子艾姆嬸嬸住在廣闊的堪薩斯草原中部。亨利叔叔是農民，他用手推車從好幾英里以外的地方運木材來建房子，房子很小，可以說是家徒四壁。這間小房子裡只有一個生鏽的爐子、一個櫥櫃、一張桌子、三、四張椅子和擺在不同角落的大小兩張床：一張是亨利叔叔和艾姆嬸嬸的，一張是桃樂絲的。房子沒有閣樓，也沒有地窖，只有房子正中央的地板上有個暗門，可以通往一個叫做「避風窖」的小地洞，萬一颳起橫掃一切的大龍捲風，全家人就可以順著一架梯子躲進又小又黑的洞裡。

桃樂絲站在門口四處眺望，觸目所及只有灰色大草原，其他什麼也看不見，既沒有樹，也沒有房子阻礙這片平坦的鄉野向四面八方延伸至天邊。太陽炙烤著耕犁過的土地，將它變成灰色一片，一條條裂縫蜿蜒在上面。草也不再是綠色的了，太陽將它們的長葉炙烤成與土地一樣的顏色。即使那曾經粉刷過的房子也在日曬雨淋之下褪了色，如今房子的油漆已經剝離，和周遭的一切一樣是黯淡的灰色。

艾姆嬸嬸初來這裡住下的時候，還是個年輕漂亮的少婦，如今風吹日曬也改變了她的模樣。曾經閃爍在眼裡的光芒不見了，只剩下沉重的灰色；臉頰和嘴唇的粉紅不見了，也是灰色的。她面容憔悴，形色枯槁，臉上也不再有笑容。當桃樂絲這個孤兒第一次來到艾姆嬸嬸身邊時，這小女孩的笑聲傳到她耳朵裡，著實嚇了她一跳，她甚至驚呼了一聲，並將手按在自己的胸口。她看著這個小女孩，很驚訝任何事都能讓桃樂絲笑。

亨利叔叔從來不笑。他從早到晚辛勤勞動，絲毫不知道什麼叫快樂。他也是灰色的，灰色的鬍鬚、灰色粗糙的長靴，他看起來莊嚴肅穆，甚少開口。

　　帶給桃樂絲歡笑的是托托，也正是托托，讓桃樂絲沒有成長為和她周遭事物一樣的灰色。托托不是灰色的，牠是一隻小黑狗，有著如絲絨般滑順的長毛，一雙黑色的小眼睛在牠滑稽有趣的小鼻子之間快樂地眨著。托托整天都在玩，桃樂絲陪著牠一起玩，她非常喜歡牠。

　　然而，今天她們沒有玩。亨利叔叔坐在門檻上，焦慮不安地望著比平常更灰的天空。桃樂絲也抱著托托站在門口看著天空。而艾姆嬸嬸正在洗碗。

　　遙遠的北方傳來了風的哀號，亨利叔叔和桃樂絲看到野草在風暴來襲前如波浪般起伏。此刻南方的天空傳來了一陣急劇的呼嘯聲，一轉眼，只見那裡的草也掀起了波浪，不斷向前湧。

　　亨利叔叔突然站了起來。

　　「艾姆，龍捲風來了！」他向他的妻子喊道，「我去看看那些牲畜。」於是他跑到那些關著牛和馬的小圈棚裡。

　　艾姆嬸嬸放下手邊的工作，跑到了門口，她馬上就知道危險逼近了。

　　「桃樂絲，快！」她喊道，「快跑去地窖！」

　　托托從桃樂絲的懷裡一躍而出，躲到了床底下，這小女孩跑過去，想要抓住牠。艾姆嬸嬸害怕極了，打開地洞的門，順著梯子爬下去，躲進了狹小黑暗的地洞裡。

桃樂絲終於抓住了托托，打算跟著嬸嬸躲到地洞去，但是才跑到半路，房子便隨著一陣尖銳的呼嘯聲劇烈地晃動起來，桃樂絲難以站穩，一下子跌坐在地上。

　　接著發生了一件怪事。

　　房子旋轉了兩三圈後慢慢升上天空，桃樂絲覺得自己好像坐在氫氣球上。

　　南北方的風暴在房子所在的地方會合，讓這裡成為龍捲風的中心。龍捲風的中心是平靜的，但四周的強大氣壓使房子越升越高，直到龍捲風頂部，並在那停了一下，接著又被帶往幾英里之外，如同拿起一根羽毛般輕而易舉。

　　這時，天色暗了下來，四周的風朝著桃樂絲怒吼，但她發現自己正輕鬆的乘風飛行。除了一開始旋轉了幾圈，以及房子偶爾嚴重地傾斜之外，她覺得自己好像被放在搖籃裡的嬰孩，被輕柔地搖動著。

　　托托不喜歡那樣，牠狂吠著，在房子裡跑來跑去，一下往這，一下往那；而桃樂絲只是安靜地坐在地上，等著看會發生什麼事。

　　有一次，托托離地洞的門太近而掉了進去，起初桃樂絲還以為牠不見了，但很快地就看到托托的一隻耳朵從洞裡冒了出來，巨大的氣壓撐住了托托，牠才沒有掉下去。她爬到洞口，抓住托托的耳朵，把牠拉進房子裡，然後關上地洞的活板門，以免再出事。

　　時間慢慢地過去了，桃樂絲漸漸不再害怕，但她覺得很寂寞，風又如此大聲地咆嘯著，她幾乎都要聾了。起初，她還擔心如果房子倒塌，她會不會被壓扁，不過幾個小時過去了，沒有可怕的事情發生，於是她不再擔憂，開始靜下心來，等待即將發生的事情。最後，她從搖搖晃晃的地板爬到床上，托托跟了過去，躺在她身旁。

不管房子多晃，也不管風如何呼嘯不停，桃樂絲閉上雙眼，很快地進入了夢鄉。

第 2 章

遇見芒奇金人

正當她站在那裡，熱切地望著這片陌生
而美麗的景色時，她發現有一群她生平
見過最奇怪的人正朝她走來。

一陣突如其來的劇烈震動驚醒了桃樂絲，如果不是躺在柔軟的床上，她或許就受傷了。事實上，這個震動讓她屏住了呼吸，心裡納悶著究竟發生了什麼事。托托用牠那冰冷的小鼻子，觸碰著她的臉頰，低沉地哀號著。桃樂絲坐了起來，發現房子已經不再移動，天色也不再昏暗了，明亮的陽光透過窗戶照了進來，灑滿了整間房子。她從床上跳了下來，打開門，托托則跟在她的後面。

小女孩看著自己的周圍，發出了驚訝的叫聲，面對著眼前奇妙的景色，她的雙眼睜得越來越大。

一陣龍捲風把房子輕輕地（以龍捲風來說）放到了這片不可思議的美景之中。到處都點綴著可愛的草地還有雄偉的大樹，上面結滿了甘甜的果實。每一邊的斜坡上都長滿了耀眼奪目的花朵，鳥兒們披著燦爛美麗的羽毛，在樹林及灌木叢中翩翩飛舞，吟唱著歌曲。不遠處有一條小溪閃閃發亮地冒著泡，沿著綠色的堤岸湍急地流動著，發出潺潺的流水聲，讓這個生活在乾燥又灰暗的草原上太久的小女孩雀躍不已。

正當她站在那裡，熱切地望著這片陌生而美麗的景色時，她發現有一群她生平見過最奇怪的人正朝她走來。他們不像她過去見到的大人那麼高大，但也不矮。事實上，他們看起來跟桃樂絲一樣高（她比同年齡的孩子高大），儘管從外表上看起來比她大了好多歲。

他們總共三男一女，所有人都穿著古怪的衣服，頭上戴著圓形尖頂的帽子，帽沿上繫著小鈴鐺，在他們走動時總會發出甜美的叮噹聲。三個男人的帽子是藍色的，小個子女人的帽子是白色的，她身上穿著一件白袍，褶邊從肩上垂下來，上面點綴著小星星，在陽光下像鑽石般閃閃發亮。三個男人穿著和他們的帽子一樣顏色的藍色衣裳，腳上穿著擦得亮晶晶的靴子，靴子的尖端有一圈深藍色。桃樂絲心想，這些男人和亨利叔叔差不多年紀，因為其中兩個留著鬍子。小個子女人明顯更老一些，她的臉上長滿了皺紋，頭髮幾乎全白，走路的姿態也有幾分僵硬。

桃樂絲站在門口，當這幾個人靠近這棟房子的時候，他們停了下來，相互耳語著，好像不敢再靠近一步。不過那個小個子女人走到了桃樂絲面前，深深地鞠了躬，親切和藹地說道：「最高貴的魔法師，歡迎來到芒奇金國。非常感謝您殺死了東方的邪惡女巫，把我們從奴役之中解放了出來。」

桃樂絲驚訝地聽她說著這番話。為什麼這個小個子女人要稱呼她為「魔法師」，還說她殺死了東方的邪惡女巫？桃樂絲是個天真無邪又善良的小女孩，一陣龍捲風把她帶到了遠離故鄉好幾英里之外的地方，她這一生中從沒有殺過任何人。

但是那個小個子女人正熱切地等著她回話，因此桃樂絲支支吾吾地說：「謝謝，不過一定有什麼地方搞錯了，我沒有殺過人啊。」

「但是你的房子殺了人，」那個小個子女人笑著回答她說，「結果是一樣的。你看！」她指了指房子的一個角落，接著說，「她的兩隻腳尖都從木板下伸出來了。」

桃樂絲看了一眼，驚慌失措地輕輕叫了一聲。房子底下的大橫樑果真壓著兩隻腳，伸直了的腳尖上穿著一雙銀鞋。

「噢，天哪！天哪！」桃樂絲叫道，慌張地緊握著雙手，「肯定是房子壓到她了。我們該怎麼辦？」

「什麼都不用做。」小個子女人平靜地說。

「她是誰？」桃樂絲問道。

「她就是我說的東方邪惡女巫。」小個子女人回答道，「這麼多年來，她一直奴役著芒奇金人，讓他們夜以繼日地為她工作。現在，他們全都自由了，並且要感謝您的救命之恩。」

「芒奇金人是誰？」桃樂絲問。

「他們是居住在由邪惡女巫統治的東方領土中的百姓。」

「那你是芒奇金人嗎？」桃樂絲問道。

「不，我是他們的朋友。儘管我住在北方，芒奇金人看見東方女巫死了之後，迅速地稍了信給我，我就立刻趕到這裡。我是北方女巫。」

「噢，天哪！」桃樂絲叫道，「你真的是女巫嗎？」

「是啊，是真的，」小個子女人回答，「但我是個善良的女巫，人們都喜歡我，我不像統治這裡的邪惡女巫那麼強勢，不然我早就讓這裡的人們重獲自由了。」

「可是，我以為所有的女巫都是惡毒的。」小女孩說道，面對真正的女巫，她不免有些害怕。

「噢，不，你這麼想可就大錯特錯了，整個奧茲國裡只有四個女巫。其中兩個分別住在北方和南方，她們都是善良的女巫。這是真的，因為我就是其中一個，肯定不會錯。另外兩個分別住在東方和西方，她們的確是邪惡的女巫。但現在其中一個已經被你殺死了，整個奧茲國就只剩下一個邪惡女巫了，就是住在西方的那個。」

桃樂絲沉思了片刻之後說：「可是艾姆嬸嬸跟我說過，女巫們很早以前就已經全死光了。」

「艾姆嬸嬸是誰？」小個子女人問。

「她是我的嬸嬸，住在堪薩斯州，我就是從那裡來的。」

北方女巫低下了頭，看著地面，似乎在思考著什麼，之後她抬起頭來說道：「我不知道堪薩斯州在哪裡，因為我從沒有聽說過這個地方。但是請你告訴我，那個地方文明化了嗎？」

桃樂絲回答說：「噢，是的。」

「那就說得通了。我相信在文明化的地方確實沒有女巫或巫師，也沒有魔法師。但是奧茲國一直都沒有文明化，因為我們與世界上的其他地方相互隔絕。所以在我們中間還有女巫和巫師。」

「巫師是什麼樣的人？」桃樂絲問。

「奧茲就是個大巫師，」女巫壓低了聲音回答道，「我們所有人聯合起來都不及他厲害。他就住在翡翠城裡。」

桃樂絲還想問其他問題，但是就在此時，一直默默站在一旁的芒奇金人大聲喊了起來，同時指著邪惡女巫躺著的角落。

　　「怎麼了？」小個子女人問道。她往那邊一看，笑了起來。原來那個死掉的女巫的腳已經消失得無影無蹤，除了一雙銀鞋之外，什麼都沒有留下。

　　「她都已經一把年紀了，」北方女巫解釋道，「太陽一曬很快就灰飛煙滅了。這就是她的下場。不過那雙銀鞋已經是你的了，穿上吧。」她走到那邊，撿起那雙鞋子，拂去上面的灰塵，然後遞給桃樂絲。

　　「這雙銀鞋可是東方女巫的驕傲，」其中一個芒奇金人說，「這雙鞋有某種魔力，但是我們一直都不知道是什麼魔力。」

　　桃樂絲把這雙鞋拿進房子裡，放在桌子上，然後又跑出來走到芒奇金人的面前，說道：

　　「我想要回到我叔叔嬸嬸身邊，因為我知道他們肯定會擔心我。你們能幫我找到回去的路嗎？」

　　芒奇金人和女巫先是面面相覷，然後又看了看桃樂絲，最後搖了搖頭。

　　「離這裡不遠的東方，」一個芒奇金人說道，「有一個大沙漠，沒有人能活著穿越。」

　　「南方也是如此，」另一個芒奇金人說，「因為我就住在那裡，

18

親眼看到過。南方是奎德林人的地盤。」

第三個芒奇金人說：「我聽說，西方也一樣有個大沙漠。那裡住著溫基人，被西方邪惡女巫統治著，如果你經過她那邊，她會把你抓去當奴隸。」

「北方是我的家，」小個子女人說道，「它的邊界也是一片圍繞著奧茲國的沙漠。親愛的，我想你得和我們住在一起了。」

聽到這番話，桃樂絲哭了起來，因為在這群奇怪的人中間，她感到很寂寞。她的眼淚似乎讓熱心的芒奇金人感到了悲傷，他們立刻拿出手帕，開始擦眼淚。至於小個子的老婦人，她摘下了自己的帽子，把尖頂頂在自己的鼻尖上，同時一本正經地數著：「一、二、三」，剎那間，這頂帽子變成一塊石板，上面寫著一行大大的粉筆字：「讓桃樂絲去翡翠城」。

小個子老婦人把這塊石板從她的鼻子上拿了下來，唸著上面的字，並且問道：「親愛的，你的名字叫桃樂絲是嗎？」

「是的。」小女孩擦乾了眼淚，抬起頭回答道。

「那麼，你必須去翡翠城，奧茲可能會幫助你。」

「翡翠城在哪裡呢？」桃樂絲問道。

「就在這個國家的中心，奧茲統治著那裡，就是我跟你提起的那個大巫師。」

小女孩憂心忡忡地問道：「那他是好人嗎？」

　　「他是個善良的巫師。但我並不知道他是不是一個好人，因為我從沒見過他。」

　　桃樂絲問：「我該怎麼去他那裡呢？」

　　「你必須走路過去。這是一段漫長的路程，要經過一個時而讓人愉悅、時而黑暗到令人害怕的地方。不過，我會使出自己所有的魔法來幫助你，讓你不會受到傷害。」

　　「你能跟我一起去嗎？」小女孩望著小個子女人祈求著，此時這個人已經是她唯一的朋友了。

　　「不，我不能這麼做，」她回答道，「但是我會給你一個吻，只要是被北方女巫吻過的人，就沒人敢傷害他了。」

　　她走近桃樂絲，在她的額頭上輕輕地吻了一下。很快地，桃樂絲就發現，被她親吻過的地方留下了一個又圓又亮的印記。

　　「去翡翠城的路全都是用黃磚鋪砌而成的，」女巫說，「因此你絕對不會迷路。當你找到奧茲的時候，不用怕他，只要把你的故事告訴他，求他幫助你就行了。再見了，親愛的孩子。」

　　三個芒奇金人也深深地向她鞠躬，並祝福她一路順風，之後他們就穿過樹林走了。女巫友善地、微微向桃樂絲點了點頭，用左腳跟轉了三圈，立刻就消失了，托托對此大吃一驚，當女巫消失的時候，牠還在後面大聲地吠著，因為剛才女巫站在旁邊的時候，牠嚇得根本不敢吭聲。

　　不過桃樂絲知道她是一個女巫，所以早就已經料到她會用這種方式離開，因此絲毫不覺得驚訝。

第 3 章

拯救稻草人

正當桃樂絲認真地注視著稻草人那張被畫出來的奇怪面孔時,她驚訝地發現稻草人的一隻眼睛正慢慢地對她眨動著。

就只剩下桃樂絲獨自一人了，她覺得肚子有點餓，於是走到櫥櫃旁，給自己切了幾片麵包，抹了一點奶油。她還分托托吃了一些，又從架子上拿了一個木桶，來到小河邊，舀了些清澈發亮的溪水。托托跑進了樹林，對著那些蹲在樹上的鳥兒吠著。桃樂絲跑過去抓住托托，她發現樹上結滿了美味芳香的果實，於是就摘了一些，正好可以拿來當早餐。

然後她又回到房子裡，和托托一起喝了清涼的溪水，準備動身前往翡翠城。

桃樂絲只有一件可以更換的洋裝，碰巧洗乾淨了，掛在床邊的衣帽鉤上。這是一件藍白格紋的棉質洋裝，因為洗了好多次，藍色已經褪得差不多了，但這件衣服仍然非常漂亮。小女孩仔細地洗了把臉，穿上這件乾淨的格紋洋裝，戴上粉紅色的遮陽帽。她拿起一個小籃子，裡面裝滿了從櫥櫃裡拿來的麵包，又在上面蓋了一塊白布。之後她低頭看了看自己的腳，發現自己穿的鞋子又舊又破。

她說：「托托，這雙鞋子肯定走不了多少路。」托托抬起頭來，那雙黑色的小眼睛望著她的臉，搖晃著尾巴，說明牠聽懂了她說的話。

這時候，桃樂絲看到了那雙放在桌子上的銀鞋，那原本是東方女巫的鞋子。

「不知道這雙鞋子合不合我的腳，」她對托托說，「如果要走很長一段路的話，這雙鞋正好派得上用場，這種鞋子不容易磨破。」

　　她脫下舊皮鞋，穿上了那雙銀鞋，大小剛剛好，就像是為她訂做的一樣。

　　最後她提起了籃子。

　　「托托，走吧，」她說，「我們要去翡翠城，請求偉大的奧茲告訴我們該如何回堪薩斯州。」

　　她關上門，上了鎖，小心翼翼地把鑰匙放進衣服口袋。就這樣，桃樂絲開始了這趟旅程，托托則認真地跟在她後面。

　　這附近有好幾條路，不過她很快就找到了那條用黃磚鋪成的路。沒花多久時間，她就輕鬆地踏上了通往翡翠城的路，她的銀鞋走在堅硬的黃色路面上，發出悅耳動聽的聲音。陽光閃耀，鳥兒歡唱，一個小女孩突然被一陣龍捲風把自己從故鄉吹到了一片陌生的土地上，桃樂絲似乎不像人們想像的傷心難過。

　　一路上，她驚訝地發現周圍的景色是如此漂亮。道路兩旁豎著整齊的圍牆，漆著講究的藍色，圍牆外面是一大片豐收的穀物和蔬菜。很顯然地，芒奇金人都是優秀的農夫，才能有這麼好的收成。偶爾，在她路過房子的時候，人們會跑出來看她，對她深深地鞠躬，目送她離開。因為所有人都知道是她殺死了邪惡女巫，是她解放了他們，讓他們不再被人奴役。芒奇金人的房子長得非常奇怪，每一幢都是圓的，上面有個大圓頂。所有房子都被漆成了藍色，因為在這片東方國度上，大家最喜歡的顏色就是藍色。

　　夜幕降臨，此時桃樂絲已經走了很長一段路，感到疲憊不堪，她開始擔心起自己該在哪裡過夜。她來到一棟比較大的房子前，房子前面的綠草地上，許多男男女女正在跳舞。五個小提琴手盡情地、大聲地拉奏著曲子，人們笑著、唱著。旁邊的一張大桌子上擺著美味的水果和糕點，還有許多好吃的東西。

人們親切地向桃樂絲問好，還邀請她跟他們一起吃晚飯，在這裡過夜。這戶人家是芒奇金這片區域中最富有的，他的朋友們聚集在這裡，一起慶祝他們從邪惡女巫的統治中重獲自由。

桃樂絲吃了一頓豐盛的晚餐，這家的男主人親自招待她，這個人的名字叫波奎。晚飯之後，桃樂絲坐在一張有靠背的長椅上，看大家跳舞。

當波奎看見她那雙銀鞋的時候說：「你肯定是個大魔法師吧！」

「為什麼？」小女孩問道。

「因為你穿著一雙銀鞋，而且還殺死了邪惡女巫。還有，你穿著白色的長袍，只有女巫和魔法師才穿白色的衣服。」

「我的衣服是藍白格子的，」桃樂絲一邊說，一邊撫平了衣服上的皺褶。

「你穿那種衣服很好看，」波奎說，「藍色是芒奇金人的顏色，白色是女巫的顏色，因此我們知道你是一個友善的女巫。」

對於這一點，桃樂絲不知道該如何回答才好，因為所有人似乎都以為她是女巫，她自己則是非常清楚，她不過是個普通的小女孩，被一陣龍捲風吹到了這個奇怪的地方罷了。

　　當她看跳舞看累了的時候，波奎帶著她走進房子，替她安排一個房間，裡面放著一張漂亮的床，床單是用藍布做的，桃樂絲躺在上面，托托則蜷縮在她旁邊的藍色小毯子上，一直熟睡到天亮。

　　她吃了一頓豐盛的早餐，看著一個芒奇金的小嬰兒跟托托一起玩，並拉著托托的尾巴，又叫又笑，把桃樂絲逗得開心極了。在所有人眼中，托托是那麼地令人感到好奇，因為他們從沒有見過小狗。

　　小女孩問：「到翡翠城還有多遠？」

　　「我不知道，」波奎一本正經地回答道，「因為我從沒有去過那裡。若沒什麼事情，人們都儘量離奧茲遠遠的。不過這裡距離翡翠城還有很長的一段路，得花上好幾天的時間。我們這個地方富饒又快樂，但是你必須經過一些貧瘠又危險的地方，才能到達旅程的目的地。」

　　這番話讓桃樂絲增添了幾分憂愁，但是她知道，只有偉大的奧茲才能幫助她回到堪薩斯州，因此她勇敢地下定決心，絕不回頭。

　　她跟她的朋友們告別，然後再次沿著黃磚路動身。走了好幾英里之後，她心想應該停下來休息一下，於是爬到路邊的圍牆上坐了下來。圍牆之外是一大片稻田，在不遠處，她看見了一個稻草人，被高高地插在竹竿上，防止鳥兒靠近已經成熟的稻子。

　　桃樂絲用手托著下巴，若有所思地凝視著稻草人。它的頭是一個塞滿了稻草的麻布袋，上面畫著眼睛、鼻子和嘴巴。它戴著破舊的藍色尖帽子，這頂帽子原本是屬於某個芒奇金人的。它穿著破破爛爛、褪了色的藍衣服，衣服裡面也塞滿了稻草。它腳上套著一雙舊舊的藍色布靴子。這裡的每一個人穿的都是這種靴子。它被高高地掛在稻草稈上，背後撐著一根竹竿。

正當桃樂絲認真地注視著稻草人那張被畫出來的奇怪面孔時，她驚訝地發現稻草人的一隻眼睛正慢慢地對她眨動著。剛開始，她還以為是自己弄錯了，因為在堪薩斯州，稻草人從來都不會眨眼睛。但是這時候，這個傢伙卻友好地向她點了點頭。於是她爬下圍牆，向它走了過去，與此同時托托繞著竹竿邊跑邊吠。

「你好啊。」稻草人聲音沙啞地說。

「是你在說話嗎？」小女孩驚訝地問。

「當然囉，」稻草人回答道，「你好嗎？」

「我很好，謝謝你」。桃樂絲禮貌地回答，「你好嗎？」

「我覺得不舒服，」稻草人微笑著說，「整天被插在這裡嚇走烏鴉，太讓人厭倦了。」

桃樂絲問：「你不能從那上面下來嗎？」

「不能，因為這根竹竿插在我的背上。如果你願意幫我拔掉，我會非常感謝你。」

桃樂絲伸出雙手，把稻草人從竹竿上舉起來，因為裡面塞的都是稻草，所以非常輕。

「真謝謝你，」當稻草人坐在地上的時候，他說，「我覺得自己就像得到了新生。」

對此，桃樂絲感到很困惑，聽一個稻草人說話，看著他鞠躬，還在自己身旁走來走去，她覺得這一切聽起來十分詭異。

「你是誰？」稻草人一邊伸著懶腰、打著哈欠，一邊問道，「要去什麼地方？」

「我叫桃樂絲，」小女孩說，「要去翡翠城，請求偉大的奧茲送我回堪薩斯州。」

「翡翠城在哪裡？」他又問道，「奧茲又是誰？」

「什麼，連你也不知道嗎？」她驚訝地回答。

「不知道，真的，我什麼都不知道。你看，我是用稻草做成的，因此我根本沒有腦袋。」他傷心地回答道。

「噢，」桃樂絲說，「我真替你感到難過。」

他問：「你覺得如果我和你一起去翡翠城的話，奧茲會給我一個腦袋嗎？」

「我不敢肯定，」她回答，「但是如果你願意的話，可以跟我一起去。即使奧茲沒有給你腦袋，你也不會比現在更糟」。

「那倒是，」稻草人說。「你看，」他很有自信地接著說，「我的雙手、雙腳和身體都是稻草填塞而成的，但我並不介意，因為我不會受傷。如果有人踩我的腳或用針紮我都沒關係，因為我感覺不到痛。但是我不願意被人叫傻瓜，如果我的腦袋裡塞的一直是稻草，而非像你一樣是頭腦的話，我又要怎麼知道所有的事呢？」

「我理解你的心情，」小女孩說，她真心替他感到難過，「如果你跟我一起去，我會求奧茲盡力幫助你的。」

「謝謝你！」他感激地回答。

他們回到了路上，桃樂絲幫助他翻過圍牆，然後順著去翡翠城的黃磚路繼續向前走。

剛開始，托托並不喜歡和這個新朋友一起。牠把稻草人嗅了一圈，好像懷疑稻草裡一定有個老鼠窩，還經常很不友善地對著稻草人亂吠。

「別理托托，」桃樂絲對她的新朋友說，「牠不會咬人的。」

「噢，我不害怕，」稻草人回答，「牠不會咬傷稻草的。讓我來幫你提那個籃子吧。我不在乎，因為我不會累。我跟你說一個秘密，」他一邊向前走，一邊繼續說，「在這個世界上，我只害怕一樣東西。」

「是什麼？」桃樂絲問，「是那個做出你的芒奇金農夫嗎？」

「不，」稻草人回答，「是燃燒的火柴。」

第 4 章

穿過森林的路

「如果這條路通往森林，一定也可以帶
我們走出去，」稻草人說，「既然翡翠
城就在路的另一頭，那麼不管這條路帶
我們去哪，我們都必須一直走下去。」

幾個小時之後，道路開始變得崎嶇不平，越來越難走了，稻草人時常被黃磚絆倒。有的地方黃磚已經碎了，或是不見了，留下一個個洞穴，托托跳了過去，桃樂絲繞了過去。至於稻草人，因為他沒有腦袋，就筆直地向前走，結果就踩進了洞裡，整個身子摔倒在堅硬的磚頭上。不過他從來都不會受傷，桃樂絲把他扶了起來，然後讓他重新站直；而他則為自己的小災難感到好笑，然後繼續跟著桃樂絲走。

這裡的農田並不像遠在後面的農田那樣得到細心的耕種。這裡的房子很少，果樹也寥寥無幾。他們越往前走，鄉村就變得越陰暗荒涼。

中午時分，他們在一條靠近小溪的路旁坐了下來，桃樂絲打開籃子，拿出一些麵包，分了一片給稻草人，不過被他拒絕了。

「我永遠不會感到饑餓，」他說，「這是一件讓我覺得幸運的事，因為我的嘴巴只是畫出來的，如果在上面挖個洞，我就能吃東西了，但是這麼一來，那些塞在裡面的稻草就會跑出來，會破壞我腦袋的形狀。」

桃樂絲立刻發現他說得沒錯，因此她只是點了點頭，繼續吃麵包。

「跟我說說你的事吧，還有你的故鄉。」稻草人在桃樂絲吃完午飯後對她說。於是她對他說了所有關於堪薩斯州的事，告訴他那裡的每樣東西有多麼灰暗，龍捲風又是如何把她帶到了這個奇妙的奧茲國度。

　　稻草人仔細地聽著，然後說：「我不明白為什麼你想要離開這個美麗的地方，回到那個乾燥又灰暗的堪薩斯州。」

　　「因為你沒有腦袋啊，」小女孩回答說，「不管我們的家鄉有多麼淒涼灰暗，我們這些血肉做成的人都喜歡住在那裡，而不是其他地方，儘管非常漂亮。任何地方都比不上自己的家鄉。」

　　稻草人嘆了一口氣。

　　「我當然不能理解，」他說，「如果你們的腦袋裡也像我這樣塞滿了稻草，你們或許就都住在這個美麗的地方了，到時候堪薩斯州就沒人住了。你們有腦袋，對堪薩斯州來說是件很幸運的事。」

　　「我們休息的時候，你能說個故事給我聽嗎？」小女孩問。

　　稻草人用責備的目光看著她，回答說：「我的生命如此短暫，我實在不知道有什麼故事可以說。我還是前天才被做出來的。在那之前，我完全不知道這個世界上發生了什麼事。幸運的是，在農夫做出我的頭之後，他做的第一件事就是給我畫了耳朵，因此我聽到了接下來發生的事情。當時，他身旁還有另一個芒奇金人，我聽到的第一句話就是這個農夫說：『你覺得這兩隻耳朵畫得怎麼樣？』

　　另一個回答：『畫得不夠直。』

　　『沒關係，』農夫說，『反正都是耳朵。』這話說得倒是沒錯。

　　『現在我要畫眼睛了。』農夫說。於是他替我畫了右眼，不一會兒他就畫完了，我發現自己正帶著十足的好奇心打量著他，看著在我周圍的每一樣東西，因為這是我看到這個世界的第一眼。

『那隻眼睛真是漂亮啊，』另一個芒奇金人看著農夫說道：『藍色很適合用來畫眼睛。』

『我想我應該把另一隻眼睛畫得更大些。』農夫說。當第二隻眼睛畫完之後，我就看得比剛才更清楚了。接著，他又給我畫了鼻子和嘴巴。但是我沒辦法說話，因為那時候我還不知道嘴巴能做什麼。我興致盎然地看著他們做出我的身體、雙手跟雙腳。最後，當他們裝上我的腦袋的時候，我覺得非常驕傲，因為我以為自己是個很棒的人。

『這傢伙肯定能一下子就嚇跑烏鴉的，』農夫說，『他看起來就像真的人。』

『哎呀，他本來就是個人嘛。』另外一個人說。我非常認同他的話。農夫把我夾在他的手臂下，帶到稻田裡，把我插在一根很高的竹竿上，就是你遇見我那裡。很快地，農夫和他的朋友就離開了，把我獨自一個人丟在那裡。

我不喜歡就這樣被拋下，因此我試著走在他們後面，但是我的腳根本構不著地，於是我就被迫插在那根竹竿上。這種生活真是孤單，因為我剛剛才被做出來，根本沒有事情可以想。許多烏鴉和鳥類飛到稻田裡，牠們一看見我立刻就飛走了，以為我是一個芒奇金人，這倒讓我挺高興的，我覺得自己是一個非常重要的人。不久之後，一隻老烏鴉飛向了我，仔細打量我一番之後，牠站在我的肩膀上說：『那個農夫竟然想用這種笨拙的方法愚弄我。不管是哪隻有常識的烏鴉，都看得出來你不過是用稻草做的。』說完，牠跳到我的腳上，盡情地吃起穀粒來。其他的鳥兒發現我並沒有傷害牠們，也都飛過來吃穀粒，因此不一會兒，我身邊就圍了一大群鳥。

我很傷心，因為這說明了我不是一個稱職的稻草人，不過那隻老烏鴉安慰我說：『如果你的腦袋裡裝的是腦袋，你就會跟他們一樣稱職了，甚至會比他們更有能耐。不管是烏鴉還是人，只有腦袋是這世上唯一有價值的東西。』

烏鴉飛走之後，我想了又想，決定要努力找一個腦袋。很幸運地，你來了，把我從竹竿上拔了下來，照你先前所說的，我相信等我們到了翡翠城，偉大的奧茲一定會給我一個腦袋的。」

「但願如此，」桃樂絲真誠地說道，「你似乎很渴望得到它。」

「噢，是啊，我渴望極了，」稻草人回答道，「知道自己是個笨蛋的感覺真難受！」

小女孩說：「好吧，我們走吧。」她把籃子交給稻草人。

這時候，路邊已經沒有了圍牆，土地也沒有開墾。臨近黃昏時，他們來到了一片大森林之中，那裡的樹木非常高大茂密，樹枝交錯遮掩了黃磚鋪成的路。因為樹枝掩蓋了陽光，樹下幾乎是一片黑暗，但是這兩位旅人並沒有停下腳步，走進了森林。

「如果這條路通往森林，一定也可以帶我們走出去，」稻草人說，「既然翡翠城就在路的另一頭，那麼不管這條路帶我們去哪，我們都必須一直走下去。」

綠野仙蹤

桃樂絲說：「這件事大家都知道。」

「當然，所以我也知道，」稻草人回答說，「如果這需要動腦袋才想得到，那我永遠都說不出來。」

大概一小時之後，太陽下山了，他們在黑暗中跟蹌地走著。桃樂絲完全看不見東西，但托托可以，因為某些狗可以在黑暗中看得非常清楚。而稻草人說他自己也能看得像白天一樣清楚。於是她拉著稻草人的手，設法走得穩當些。

「如果你看見了房子，或是任何可以過夜的地方，」她說，「你一定要告訴我，因為在黑暗中走路很不舒服。」

不一會兒，稻草人就停下了腳步。

「我看見我們左手邊有一間小房子，」他說，「是用木頭和樹枝蓋的。我們要過去嗎？」

「要，當然要了」小女孩回答，「我真的好累了。」

於是稻草人帶她穿過了樹林，來到了那間小木屋，桃樂絲走了進去，在角落裡找到了一張用枯葉鋪成的床。她立刻躺了上去，很快就睡著了，托托則躺在她的身旁。稻草人永遠都不會疲倦，他站在另一個角落，耐心地等待黎明到來。

第 5 章

拯救錫樵夫

他的頭、手和腳全都連接在他的身上，
但是他卻站在那裡一動也不動，好像完
全不能動彈似的。

當桃樂絲醒來時，陽光從樹林間灑了進來，托托早就已經跑到了外面，追逐著圍繞著它的鳥兒和松鼠。桃樂絲坐了起來，看了看四周，發現稻草人仍舊耐心地站在那個角落等待著。

「我們該走了，去找水。」她對稻草人說。

「為什麼要找水呢？」他問。

「水可以拿來洗臉，洗掉一路上的灰塵，還可以拿來喝，乾麵包就不會卡在我的喉嚨了。」

「血肉之軀肯定很不方便，」稻草人認真地說，「你們必須睡覺、吃飯、喝水。但是無論如何，你們有腦袋，可以正確地思考問題，就算有再多的煩惱也是值得的。」

他們離開了小屋，穿過了樹林，最後找到了一小灘清澈的泉水，桃樂絲在那裡喝了點水，洗了把臉，吃了點麵包。她發現籃子裡所剩的麵包已經不多，幾乎只夠給自己和托托撐一天。因此，小女孩非常感謝稻草人，因為他什麼都不用吃。

當她吃完早飯，正準備走回到黃磚路上的時候，忽然從附近傳來了一聲低沉的呻吟，把她嚇了一跳。

她膽怯地問道：「那是什麼聲音？」

「我想不出來，」稻草人回答說，「不過我們可以過去看看。」

就在這時候，又傳來了一陣呻吟，這個聲音似乎是從他們背後傳來的。他們轉過身，往樹林裡走了幾步，這時候桃樂絲發現樹叢中有樣東西在陽光的照耀下閃閃發亮。她跑到那個地方，突然停下了腳步，驚叫了起來。

原來有一棵大樹被砍掉了一半，而在這棵樹的旁邊站著一個全身用錫片做成的人，手中還高舉著一把斧頭。他的頭、手和腳全都連接在他的身上，但是他卻站在那裡一動也不動，好像完全不能動彈似的。

桃樂絲驚訝地注視著他，稻草人也是一臉驚訝，而托托則激動地吠著，在錫樵夫的腿上咬了一口，卻咬疼了自己的牙齒。

「是你在呻吟嗎？」桃樂絲問道。

「是的，」錫樵夫回答說，「就是我，我已經在這裡叫喚一年多了，可是都沒有人聽見，或是過來幫我。」

「我可以幫上忙嗎？」桃樂絲溫柔地詢問，錫樵夫憂愁的聲音打動了她。

「去拿一個油罐，然後在我身體的各個關節上點油。」他回答，「這些地方已經嚴重生鏽了，害得我根本動彈不得。只要給我上點油，我馬上就能活動了。你可以在我小屋的架子上找到一個油罐。」

桃樂絲立刻跑回小屋，找到了油罐，然後跑回來，焦急地問：「你的關節在哪裡？」

「先給我的脖子上點油。」錫樵夫回答。於是桃樂絲往他脖子

43

上了點油，因為實在鏽得太厲害了，稻草人扶著錫樵夫的頭，輕輕地左右搖晃，直到那顆頭可以自由活動，接著錫樵夫靠自己就能轉動腦袋了。

「現在，給我手臂上的那些關節上點油。」他說。於是，桃樂絲又給那些關節上了些油。稻草人則小心翼翼地彎曲著錫樵夫的手臂，直到生了鏽的手臂可以靈活運動，像新生的手一樣才停了下來。

這個錫樵夫心滿意足地嘆了口氣，放下那把斧頭。

「真是舒服極了，」他說，「自從我生鏽之後，我就一直把這斧頭高舉在空中。我終於把它放下來了，真是開心。現在，只要你再給我腿上的關節上油，我就可以恢復正常了。」

於是他們替他的腿添上了油，直到他可以自由自在地走動為止。錫樵夫再三地對他們的救命之恩表示感謝，他似乎是個很有禮貌的人，十分懂得感激。

「如果你們沒有出現，我可能就要一直站在這裡了，」他說，「你們真的救了我一命。你們怎麼會來這裡呢？」

「我們要去翡翠城拜訪偉大的奧茲，」桃樂絲回答說，「我們在你的小屋裡過了一夜。」

「你們為什麼要去拜訪奧茲？」他問。

「我想讓他送我回堪薩斯州，稻草人想求奧茲給他一個腦袋。」她回答。

　　錫樵夫似乎沉思了一會，然後說道：「你覺得奧茲會給我一顆心嗎？」

　　「這個，我想應該會吧，」桃樂絲回答，「這就像給稻草人一個腦袋一樣輕而易舉。」

　　「這倒是沒錯，」錫樵夫回答說，「這樣的話，如果你們同意我加入你們的隊伍，我也想去翡翠城，請求奧茲幫幫我。」

　　「那就走吧。」稻草人熱心地說。桃樂絲也表示很樂意有他的陪伴。於是錫樵夫扛起他的斧頭，和他們一起穿過樹林，踏上了黃磚路。

　　錫樵夫要求桃樂絲把油罐放在她的籃子裡。他說：「我如果淋到雨又會生鏽，因此我非常需要這個油罐。」

　　有了新夥伴的加入真是件幸運的事。因為在他們再次啟程之後沒多久，就來到了一個樹木和枝葉濃密叢生的地方，那裡的路完全被樹枝擋住了，一般人根本過不去。不過錫樵夫熟練地揮舞著斧頭，砍著樹枝，很快地就為他們清出了一條路。

　　桃樂絲一邊走路一邊全神貫注地思考，沒有注意到稻草人跌進了洞裡，滾到了路邊。他不得不叫她，好讓她過去把他扶起來。

　　「你為什麼不繞過洞走過來呢？」錫樵夫問道。

　　「我不知道呀，」稻草人高興地回答說，「你看，我的腦袋裡裝的都是稻草，所以我才要去奧茲那裡，請他給我一個腦袋。」

「噢，我明白了，」錫樵夫說，「但是，腦袋畢竟不是這個世界上最美妙的東西。」

「那你有腦袋嗎？」稻草人問。

「沒有，我的腦袋也是空的，」錫樵夫回答說，「從前我有腦袋也有心，但是用過這兩樣東西之後，我寧願只要一顆心。」

「那又是為什麼呢？」稻草人問。

「等我把我的故事告訴你之後，你就會明白了。」

於是，當他們穿越這片樹林的時候，錫樵夫講起了故事：「我是一個樵夫的兒子，父親在樹林砍伐樹木，以賣木柴為生。當我長大後，也成了一個樵夫。後來我父親去世了，就由我照顧著年邁的母親，直到她也去世。之後，我下定決心準備結婚，不再獨自一個人生活，這樣我就不會孤獨寂寞了。

有一個芒奇金女孩，她長得非常漂亮，很快地我就愛上她了。至於她，也答應我，等我賺到足夠的錢為她造一棟更好的房子以後就嫁給我，因此我比以往更加辛勤地工作。但是這個女孩跟一個老太婆住在一起，這個老太婆不願把她嫁給任何人，因為她非常懶惰，想讓這個女孩一直跟她住，幫她煮飯、做家事。於是這個老太婆就去找東方邪惡女巫幫忙，並且答應她，如果她能阻止這門婚事，就給她兩隻羊和一頭牛。因此邪惡女巫就在我的斧頭上施了魔法。有一天，當我使勁全力砍樹的時候，因為我急切地想要造好新房，儘快迎娶那位女孩，結果那把斧頭突然就滑了出去，砍斷了我的左腿。

　　剛開始，這件事似乎是個天大的不幸，因為我知道，只有一條腿的人是沒辦法成為一個好樵夫的。所以我去錫匠那裡，請他用錫片替我做了一條新腿。等我習慣了這條腿之後，我就可以熟練地工作了。但是我的行為惹怒了東方邪惡女巫，因為她答應了那個老太婆，要阻止我娶那位漂亮的芒奇金女孩。當我重新開始砍樹的時候，斧頭又滑了出去，砍斷了我的右腿。我又去找那個錫匠，他又用錫片給我做了一條腿。在那之後，這把被施了魔法的斧頭又相繼砍斷了我的手臂，但是我並沒有心灰意冷，用錫片做成的雙手代替了它們。這時候，邪惡女巫就讓那把斧頭滑出去，砍掉了我的腦袋，起初我還以為自己完蛋了。但是那個錫匠碰巧路過這裡，他又用錫片替我做了一顆新的頭。

　　當時我以為自己已經打敗了那個惡女巫，而且比以往更加辛勤地工作，但是我根本沒想到我的敵人竟會如此殘忍，她想出了一個新方法來毀滅我對美麗的芒奇金女孩的愛。她讓我的斧頭再次滑了出去，剛好劃過我的身體，把我砍成了兩半。那個錫匠又一次過來幫助了我，替我做了一副錫製身軀，用一個個關節把我那錫製的雙手雙腳以及腦袋連接在一起，因此我又能像從前那樣活動自如了。但是，唉！我現在沒有心了，因此失去了對芒奇金女孩的愛，根本不在乎自己能不能娶到她，我想她應該仍然和那個老太婆住在一起，等著我去娶她吧。

　　在陽光下，我的身子閃閃發光，對此我感到了無比的自豪，現在我再也不擔心斧頭是否會從手中滑落，因為它已經傷害不到我了。唯一危險的就是我的關節會生鏽。不過我在自己的小屋裡藏了一個油罐，不管什麼時候，只要有需要，我就給自己上點油。可是有一天，我忘記給自己上油，還被暴風雨淋濕，在我意識到這個危險之前，我的關節已經生鏽了，然後就一直等待，直到你們來幫助我。經歷這樣的事情著實讓人覺得害怕，但是，在這一年裡，我站在這裡，讓我有時間去思考：我最大的損失就是失去了自己的心。當我沉浸在戀愛中時，我是這世界上最幸福的人；但是沒有人會喜歡一個沒有心的人，因此我下定決心要去求奧茲給我一顆心。如果他給了，我就回到那位芒奇金女孩的身邊，娶她為妻。」

錫樵夫的這個故事讓桃樂絲和稻草人聽得津津有味，這時候，他們才知道錫樵夫為什麼如此急切地想要得到一顆嶄新的心。

「儘管如此，」稻草人說，「我還是想要腦袋，而不是一顆心，因為一個笨蛋即使有了心，也不知道該拿它來做什麼。」

「我還是想要一顆心，」錫樵夫回應道，「因為有了腦袋並不會讓人覺得幸福，而幸福是這世上最美好的事物。」

桃樂絲什麼也沒有說，因為她不知道這兩位朋友誰說得對。她心想只要能夠回到堪薩斯州，回到艾姆嬸嬸的身邊，不管錫樵夫有沒有心，不管稻草人有沒有腦袋，又或是他們每個人都得到了自己想要的東西，這些都不關她的事。

最令她擔心的是麵包已經快要吃完了，她和托托再吃上一頓，這個籃子就要空了。當然，錫樵夫和稻草人肯定什麼都不用吃，但是她既不是錫做的，也不是稻草做的，只有吃飽了，她才能活下去。

第 6 章

膽小的獅子

面對著這個敵人，小托托吠了起來，朝
獅子的方向跑去，而這隻大野獸張大了
嘴巴想要咬這隻小狗。

桃樂絲和她的同伴們一直行走在這片濃密的樹林之中。雖然這條路依舊鋪著黃磚，但是地上卻覆蓋著許多樹上掉下來的枯枝敗葉，走在上面非常不方便。

在這一帶的樹林中，幾乎見不到小鳥，因為牠們喜歡陽光明媚的空曠田野；但是一些藏匿於樹林之中的野獸不時會發出低沉的嚎叫聲。這些聲音嚇得小女孩的心臟怦怦跳，因為她不知道這是什麼東西。不過托托知道，牠緊緊地靠在桃樂絲身邊，甚至沒有吠。

小女孩問錫樵夫說：「我們還要走多久才能出得了這片森林呢？」

「我也不是很清楚，」他回答道，「因為我從沒有去過翡翠城。不過，在我小時候，我父親去過那裡。他說那是一段漫長的旅程，儘管愈靠近奧茲居住的地方就愈美麗，卻要經過一個非常危險的地方。不過只要我有油罐，就什麼都不怕，而且任何東西都無法傷害稻草人，你的額頭上還留有善良女巫吻過的印記，它會保護你不受任何傷害的。」

「但是托托呢？」小女孩憂心忡忡地說道，「什麼東西能保護牠呢？」

「如果牠遇到了危險，我們會保護牠。」錫樵夫回答道。

正當他說出這句話的時候，森林裡傳來了一個可怕的怒吼聲。緊接著，一隻大獅子跳到了路中間。牠用爪子一揮，稻草人就滾到了路邊；隨後牠用尖銳的爪子襲擊錫樵夫，但是讓牠驚訝的是儘管錫樵夫摔倒在路上，一動也不動地躺在那，身上卻沒有任何傷痕。

面對這個敵人，小托托吠了起來，朝獅子的方向跑去，而這隻大野獸張大了嘴巴想要咬這隻小狗。桃樂絲擔心托托會被咬死，於是奮不顧身地衝上前去，用盡全力拍打著獅子的鼻子，同時大聲喊道：「你怎麼敢咬托托！你應該為你自己感到羞愧，像你這麼大的一隻野獸，居然咬一隻這麼可憐的小狗！」

「我沒有咬牠。」獅子一邊說，一邊用爪子摩擦被桃樂絲打過的鼻子。

「可是你想要咬牠，」桃樂絲反駁道，「你只是個巨大的膽小鬼。」

「我知道，」獅子說著，羞愧地低下了頭，「我一直都知道這個缺點。但是我又能怎麼辦呢？」

「我不知道。可是你自己想想看，你竟然襲擊一個用稻草填塞而成的可憐稻草人！」

「他是個稻草人嗎？」獅子吃驚地問道，牠看著桃樂絲扶起稻草人，讓他站直，然後又輕輕地拍著他，讓他恢復了原貌。

「他當然是稻草人了。」桃樂絲回答，仍然非常憤怒。

「難怪他這麼輕易就摔了出去，」獅子說道，「看著他打轉的樣子確實令我驚訝。另外一個也是用稻草做的嗎？」

「不，」桃樂絲說，「他是錫片做的。」說著，她又過去扶起了錫樵夫。

「難怪他幾乎磨鈍了我的爪子，」獅子說，「當我的爪子抓住錫片的時候，我感到背脊發涼。那隻小傢伙又是誰，你為什麼對牠這麼溫柔？」

「牠是我的狗，叫托托。」桃樂絲回答。

「那牠是用錫片做的，還是用稻草紮的？」獅子問。

「都不是。牠是……是……是隻有血有肉的狗。」小女孩說。

「啊！牠長得真稀奇，現在看起來還真的是非常小呢。除了我這樣的膽小鬼，誰都不會想要咬這樣一個小東西的。」獅子傷心地說。

「你為什麼會變成膽小鬼呢？」桃樂絲驚訝地注視著這頭大野獸問道，因為牠的體形有一匹小馬那麼大。

「這是一個謎，」獅子回答說，「我想是天生的吧。森林中的野獸都理所當然地覺得我非常勇敢，因為不管在什麼地方，獅子都被奉為萬獸之王。我知道只要自己咆哮一聲，所有的動物都會受到驚嚇，避開我所走的路。每當遇到人的時候，我都非常害怕，但是只要我對著人吼叫一聲，他就會拼了命地逃跑。如果有大象、老虎或熊來跟我一較高下，我就逃跑，我就是這樣一個膽小鬼。但是只要一聽到我的吼聲，牠們就會儘快逃離，當然，我也會放牠們一馬。」

「但是這樣是不對的。萬獸之王不該是膽小鬼。」稻草人說。

「我知道，」獅子一邊回答，一邊用尾巴端尖擦去眼中的淚水，「這是我最大的悲哀，讓我的生活非常不開心。因為每次我遇到危險，我的心就會跳得飛快。」

「可能是你有心臟病吧。」錫樵夫說。

「或許是吧。」獅子說。

「如果你真有心臟病，」錫樵夫接著說道，「那你應該開心才對，因為那就說明你有心。至於我，我沒有心，所以我不會有心臟病。」

「也許是吧，」獅子若有所思地說道，「如果我沒有心，那我就不會是膽小鬼了。」

「那你有腦袋嗎？」稻草人問道。

「我想應該有的。我從來都沒有見過它。」獅子回答說。

「我要去偉大的奧茲那裡，求他給我一個腦袋，」稻草人說，「因為我的腦袋裡面塞的都是稻草。」

「我去求他給我一顆心。」錫樵夫說。

「我去求他送我和托托回堪薩斯州。」桃樂絲跟著說道。

「你們覺得奧茲會給我勇氣嗎？」膽小的獅子說道。

「就像給我腦袋一樣簡單。」稻草人說。

「或者像給我心一樣。」錫樵夫說。

「或者像送我回堪薩斯州一樣。」桃樂絲說。

「那麼，如果你們不介意的話，我想跟你們一起去，」獅子說，「我的生活簡直令人無法忍受，因為我一點勇氣都沒有。」

「非常歡迎，」桃樂絲回答，「因為你可以幫我們嚇走其他野獸。在我看來，如果牠們這麼容易就被你嚇跑，那麼牠們肯定比你更膽小。」

「牠們的確很膽小，」獅子說，「但是那並不會讓我變得更勇敢。只要我知道自己是個膽小鬼，我就開心不起來。」

於是這一小群夥伴又開始了他們的旅程，獅子雄赳赳氣昂昂地走在桃樂絲身邊。剛開始，托托並不喜歡這個新同伴，因為牠無法忘記自己差點被這隻獅子的血盆大口咬得粉碎的情景，但是過了一會兒之後，托托就變得自在多了，此時，牠已經和這隻膽小的獅子變成了好朋友。

這一天接下來的時間裡，一路上都沒有發生特別危險的事。不過有一次，錫樵夫踩到了一隻在路上爬的甲蟲，殺死了這個可憐的小生命。這讓錫樵夫感到非常傷心，因為他總是小心翼翼地不去傷害任何生命。因此在他繼續向前趕路的同時，他流下了幾滴傷心的淚水。這些眼淚慢慢地從他的臉上流下來，流到了他下巴的連接處，那個地方就生鏽了。過了一會兒，當桃樂絲問他問題的時候，錫樵夫連嘴都張不開了，因為他的上下顎已經因為生鏽緊緊地閉著。這讓錫樵夫驚慌失措，對著桃樂絲指手畫腳地做著手勢，想讓她救救自己，可是桃樂絲根本不知道這是什麼意思，獅子也一臉困惑，不知道發生了什麼事情。不過稻草人從桃樂絲的籃子裡拿出了油罐，給錫樵夫的下巴加了些油，片刻之後，錫樵夫又能像從前一樣說話了。

「這真是給了我一個教訓，」他說，「走路的時候要先看清楚再踏出步伐。因為如果我再踏死一隻小蟲子，我肯定又會哭的，我一哭下巴就會生鏽，到時就說不出話了。」

因此他看著路面，小心翼翼地走著。他看見一隻小螞蟻艱難地爬著，為了不傷害它，錫樵夫就跨了過去。錫樵夫非常明白，因為他沒有心，因此要特別留意，絕不能殘忍或無情地對待任何東西。

「你們都有心。」他說，「可以指引著你們行動，永遠都不會犯錯。但是我沒有，所以必須非常謹慎。等到奧茲給我心之後，我就不用這麼擔心了。」

第 7 章

前往偉大的奧茲國

獅子對桃樂絲說：「我們完了，牠們肯定會用尖利的爪子把我們撕成碎片的。不過，你還是躲在我後面吧，只要我還活著，我就會跟牠們搏鬥到底。」

那天夜裡，他們不得不露宿在森林中的一棵大樹底下，因為附近沒有房子。那棵樹非常高大，枝繁葉茂，可以幫他們擋住露水。錫樵夫用他的斧頭砍了一大堆木柴，桃樂絲點起了一堆柴火取暖，同時驅散了她的寂寞感。她和托托吃著最後一點麵包，不知道明天的早餐該吃什麼。

獅子說：「如果你願意，我可以去森林裡替你抓一隻鹿。你們的口味那麼特別，喜歡吃煮熟的食物，你可以用火把牠烤了，明天就有一頓非常美味的早餐。」

「不！拜託你別這麼做！」錫樵夫懇求道，「如果你殺死了一隻可憐的鹿，我肯定會哭的，到時我的下巴又要生鏽了。」

不過獅子還是跑進了森林中，給自己找晚餐去了。誰也不知道牠吃了什麼，因為牠什麼都沒說。稻草人找到了一棵長滿堅果的果樹，他用桃樂絲的籃子裝了滿滿一籃的堅果，在之後的一段時間裡，桃樂絲就不用挨餓了。她心裡想著稻草人真是體貼周到，但是看見這可憐的傢伙摘堅果時那笨拙的樣子，她忍不住哈哈大笑。他那稻草填塞而成的手如此笨拙，而堅果又那麼小，因此掉在地上的堅果跟籃子裡的一樣多。可是稻草人並不在乎自己要花多少時間才能裝滿這個籃子，因為這可以讓他離那堆營火遠遠的，他擔心火星鑽進他的稻草裡，把自己燒個精光。所以他遠遠地離開那堆火，只有在桃樂絲躺下睡覺的時候，他才走過去在她的身上蓋了些乾樹葉。這些樹葉讓她感到舒適和溫暖，一覺到天亮。

天亮之後，小女孩在一條潺潺流動的小河邊洗了把臉，然後他們一行人又開始向翡翠城出發了。

對於這幾個旅行者來說，這一天真是個多事的日子。他們走了不到一個鐘頭，就看見前面有一條非常寬闊的壕溝橫在路上，把他們眼前的森林分成了兩半。這是一條極其寬闊的壕溝。當他們躡手躡腳地爬到溝邊向下望時，發現這條溝非常深，而且在壕溝下面還有許多嶙峋的巨大石塊。壕溝的兩邊非常陡峭，沒有人可以爬得下去，一時看來，他們的旅程似乎必須到此為止了。

「我們該怎麼辦呢？」桃樂絲失望地問。

「我什麼辦法也想不出來。」錫樵夫說。獅子抖動著蓬鬆的鬃毛，似乎在思考著什麼。

不過稻草人說：「我們肯定是飛不過去的，也沒辦法爬到壕溝下面，如果我們跳不過去，就必須停在這裡了。」

「我想我跳得過去。」在仔細地估量完壕溝的寬度之後，膽小的獅子說。

「那我們就沒問題了，」稻草人回答，「你可以一個個把我們全都背過去。」

「好，那我試試看，」獅子說，「誰要先過去呢？」

「我，」稻草人鄭重地說，「因為，如果你跳不過這條壕溝，桃樂絲可能會摔死，而錫樵夫可能會摔到下面的石頭上，造成嚴重的凹痕。但是如果我坐在你背上，就用不著擔心那些問題了，因為即使摔下去了，也完全不會傷害到我。」

「我自己都非常怕會掉下去，」膽小的獅子說，「但是我想除了嘗試之外，也別無他法了。所以你就騎上我的背，我們來試試看吧。」

於是稻草人坐到獅子的背上，這隻大獅子走到壕溝旁，蹲了下來。

「你為什麼不先助跑，然後再跳過去呢？」稻草人問。

「因為我們獅子不會這麼跳。」牠回答，然後縱身一跳，飛向空中，平安地落到對面。看著獅子這麼輕而易舉就跳了過去，大家都非常高興。稻草人從牠背上下來之後，獅子又跳回壕溝這邊。

桃樂絲心想著下一個就是她了，於是抱著托托，爬上獅子的後背，一隻手緊緊地抓住他的鬃毛。接著就像飛在空中一樣，她還來不及回想，就已經平安到達對面。獅子又跳了回去，把錫樵夫背了過來。然後他們全都坐了下來，讓獅子好好休息一下，這幾次劇烈的跳動已經讓他氣喘吁吁，就像一隻跑了很長一段路的狗似地喘著氣。

他們發現這一邊的森林非常濃密，看上去陰森而黑暗。等到獅子休息完之後，他們又沿著黃磚路出發了，每個人心中都暗自地發出疑問：他們到底能不能走出這片森林，再度見到明媚的陽光？沒過多久，他們聽到樹林深處傳來了奇怪的聲音，這又增添他們心中的不安。獅子悄悄地對他們說卡力達就住在這一區。

「卡力達是什麼？」小女孩問。

「牠們是一種恐怖的怪獸，身體像熊，頭像老虎，」獅子回答說，

62

「牠們的爪子大而鋒利，可以毫不費勁地把我撕成兩半，就像我殺死托托那麼簡單。我非常怕牠們。」

「我一點都不意外你會害怕，」桃樂絲回答說，「牠們肯定是非常可怕的野獸。」

正當獅子想要回話的時候，他們眼前突然又出現了一道壕溝。不過這道壕溝很深、很寬，獅子立刻就知道自己這次跳不過去。

於是他們坐下來商量該怎麼辦，經過認真思考後，稻草人說：

「壕溝旁邊有一棵大樹，如果錫樵夫能夠砍倒這棵樹，讓它橫倒在壕溝的另一邊，那麼我們就能輕易地走過去了。」

「這是最棒的辦法，」獅子說，「我們都要懷疑你的腦袋裡裝的不是稻草，而是真正的大腦了。」

錫樵夫立刻動手，他的斧頭非常鋒利，很快地那棵樹就幾乎被砍倒。然後獅子用他那強而有力的前腿頂住樹幹，用盡全力推著這棵樹。大樹慢慢地傾斜了，砰的一聲倒躺在壕溝上，樹梢上的枝幹落在壕溝的另一邊。

正當他們出發走過這座怪異的樹橋時，一聲尖銳的咆哮使得所有人都抬起頭來張望，只見兩頭長著虎頭熊身的大野獸向他們跑過來，讓他們驚恐萬分。

「牠們就是卡力達！」膽小的獅子說著開始顫抖起來。

「快跑！」稻草人大聲叫道，「我們快點過去。」

於是桃樂絲抱著托托跑在最前面，錫樵夫緊緊尾隨，稻草人也緊跟在後。獅子雖然非常害怕，但是仍舊轉過身來，面對著卡力達，發出一聲洪亮又可怕的怒吼。桃樂絲被嚇得尖叫起來，稻草人向後退了一步，甚至連那兇猛的野獸也停了一會兒，驚訝地看著獅子。

可是當牠們發現自己比獅子還要高大，而且想到牠們有兩隻，而獅子只有一隻時，牠們又繼續向前衝。獅子穿過了這棵樹，轉過身去看看牠們想要幹什麼。那兩頭兇猛的野獸毫不遲疑也跨上了這棵樹。獅子對桃樂絲說：「我們完了，牠們肯定會用尖利的爪子把我們撕成碎片的。不過，你還是躲在我後面吧，只要我還活著，我就會跟牠們搏鬥到底。」

「等等！」稻草人叫道，剛才他一直在想最佳的解決之道，這時候，他讓錫樵夫砍斷靠近他們這一邊的樹梢。錫樵夫立刻揮動起斧頭，正當這兩頭卡力達快要衝過來的時候，這棵樹轟的一聲，連這兩頭醜陋的、咆哮著的野獸一同掉進了壕溝，落在底部那些鋒利的石塊上，摔得粉身碎骨。

「好了，」膽小的獅子一邊說，一邊深深地吸了一口氣，放下了心中的不安，「看來我們還能再活得久一點了，真是讓人開心啊，因為死亡肯定是一件非常痛苦的事。那些野獸真是嚇死我了，我的心到現在還怦怦跳呢。」

「唉，」錫樵夫卻傷心地說道，「我倒希望自己能有一顆怦怦跳的心。」

這個危險使得這些旅行者更加急切地想要走出這片森林。他們走得太快，桃樂絲開始感到了疲倦，只好騎在獅子的背上。讓他們頗為欣喜的是，他們越往前走，樹林就變得越稀疏。到了下午，他們面前突然出現了一條寬闊的河流，河水湍急地流動著。在河的另外一邊，他們可以看見一條黃磚路穿過了一個美麗的地方。綠茵茵的草地上點綴著燦爛的鮮花，路的兩旁全是掛滿鮮果的果樹。他們非常高興能看到眼前這個美好的地方。

「我們要怎麼過河呢？」桃樂絲問道。

「很簡單，」稻草人回答，「只要錫樵夫替我們做一個木筏，我們就能到對岸去了。」

於是錫樵夫揮動斧頭，砍倒幾棵小樹，準備做出木筏。就在他為此忙碌的時候，稻草人發現岸邊的一棵樹上結滿了新鮮的水果。桃樂絲開心極了，因為她這一整天除了堅果之外什麼都沒吃，於是她吃了一頓豐盛的水果大餐。

但是做木筏是件費時的差事，即使是像錫樵夫這樣手腳勤快、不知疲倦的人，也無法在天黑前做出來。因此，他們在樹下找了一個舒適的地方，一覺睡到第二天早上。桃樂絲夢見了翡翠城，還有善良的魔法師奧茲，一下子就把她送回家。

第 8 章

致命的罂粟花田

那裡有黃色的、白色的、藍色的、紫色
的大花朵。除此之外，還有一大簇一大
簇猩紅色的罌粟花，色彩如此豔麗，讓
桃樂絲看得眼花繚亂。

第二天早晨，我們這一小群旅行者醒了，重新振作了精神，心中充滿了希望。桃樂絲像個公主似的吃著從河邊的樹上摘來的桃子和梅子當早餐。他們的身後是一片黑暗的森林，雖然他們在那裡遭遇了許多危險，不過總算是平安地走出來了。而此時在他們眼前的，是一個可愛而又充滿陽光的地方，似乎在召喚著他們去翡翠城。

當然，眼前這條寬廣的河流仍舊把他們和這片美麗的地方分隔開來，幸虧木筏就快要完成了，錫樵夫又砍來了一些木頭，用木樁把它們牢牢地釘在一起，然後他們就準備出發了。桃樂絲手裡抱著托托，坐在木筏的中間。膽小的獅子踏上木筏時，這條木筏嚴重傾斜，因為牠又大又重。不過稻草人和錫樵夫站在另一邊，讓木筏平穩了下來。他們各自拿著一根長長的木竿，撐著木筏穿過這條河。

剛開始他們非常順利，但是，當他們到河中央的時候，湍急的河流把木筏沖到了下游，使他們離黃磚路越來越遠。同時，河水也變得非常深，長木竿已經觸不到河底了。

「真是太糟了，」錫樵夫說，「如果沒辦法上岸，我們就要被帶到西方邪惡女巫的地盤了，她會對我們施展妖術，讓我們成為她的奴隸。」

「那我就得不到腦袋了。」稻草人說。

「我就得不到勇氣了。」膽小的獅子說。

「我就得不到心了。」錫樵夫說。

「我永遠也回不去堪薩斯州了。」桃樂絲說。

　　「我們一定要盡全力去翡翠城。」稻草人接著說。他使勁撐著長木竿，可是木竿卻牢牢地插在了河底的淤泥中，他還來不及拔出或丟掉木竿，木筏就被河水沖走了。可憐的稻草人就這樣被插在河中間的木竿上。

　　「再見了！」他朝著夥伴們喊著。他們為失去稻草人而感到傷心，錫樵夫開始哭了起來，不過幸虧他記得自己會生鏽，就用桃樂絲的圍裙把眼淚擦乾了。

　　當然，這件事對稻草人來說實在是令人遺憾。

　　「現在的我比遇見桃樂絲時更糟了，」他想，「那時，我被插在稻田裡的竹竿上，不管怎麼樣，我還能扮成人類嚇嚇烏鴉，但是一個被插在河中央木竿上的稻草人肯定是毫無用處的。我恐怕永遠得不到腦袋了！」

　　木筏順著河水往下漂，可憐的稻草人離他們越來越遠。這時獅子說：

　　「我們必須想點辦法救救自己。我想我可以游到岸邊，把木筏拖在後面，只是你們要緊緊拉住我的尾巴。」

　　於是獅子跳進了水裡，當牠使盡全力向岸邊遊去的時候，錫樵夫則是緊緊地拉著牠的尾巴。雖然獅子的體型高大威猛，這仍是一項艱巨的任務。但是不久後，他們就被拖出了這股急流。桃樂絲拿起錫樵夫的長木竿，讓木筏朝岸邊去。

　　最後，他們終於到達了岸邊，踏上那片碧綠的草地。此時他們都已精疲力盡，也很清楚那股急流已經把他們帶往離通往翡翠城的黃磚路很遠的地方了。

正當獅子躺在草地上，讓太陽曬乾身體的時候，錫樵夫問道：「現在我們該怎麼辦？」

「我們必須想辦法回到那條路上。」桃樂絲說。

「最好的辦法就是沿著河岸往回走，一直到那條黃磚路為止。」獅子說。

因此，在他們休息完畢之後，桃樂絲提起她的籃子，他們一夥人開始沿著綠意盎然的河岸走回到河水沖走他們的地方。這是個可愛的地方，百花齊放、果實纍纍，明媚的陽光讓他們心曠神怡，若不是為可憐的稻草人感到傷心難過，他們一定會非常快樂。

他們用最快的速度向前趕路，桃樂絲只停下過一次，摘了一朵漂亮的花。過了一會，錫樵夫大聲叫道：「快看！」

所有人都朝河裡望去，只見稻草人停在河中央的那根木竿上，神情非常寂寞、悲傷。

「我們可以用什麼辦法救他呢？」桃樂絲問道。

獅子和錫樵夫全都搖了搖頭，不知道該怎麼辦。於是，他們就坐在岸邊，愁眉苦臉地望著稻草人。這時候一隻鸛鳥飛過，看見了他們，於是就停在岸邊休息。

「你們是誰？要去哪裡？」鸛鳥問。

「我叫桃樂絲，」小女孩回答道，「他們是我的朋友，錫樵夫和膽小的獅子，我們要去翡翠城。」

「你們走錯路了。」鸛鳥一邊說著，一邊扭動著修長的脖子，敏銳地打量著這群奇怪的人。

「我知道，」桃樂絲回答說，「只是我們少了一個稻草人，正想著該怎麼把他救回來。」

「他在哪裡？」鸛鳥問道。

「就在這條河裡。」小女孩回答說。

「如果他不是太大太重的話，我可以替你們把他救出來。」鸛鳥說道。

「他一點都不重，」桃樂絲急切地說道，「因為他是用稻草紮成的。如果你能把他救回來，我們會永遠感謝你的。」

「好，那我就試試看，」鸛鳥說，「但是，如果我發現他太重載不動的話，我就會重新把他丟回河裡的。」

於是這只大鸛鳥飛向空中，來到水面上，飛到了抱著木竿的稻草人那裡。然後鸛鳥用它那碩大的爪子抓住稻草人的手臂，把他拖到空中，飛回了岸邊。桃樂絲、獅子、以及錫樵夫和托托都坐在那裡。

當稻草人發現自己又回到了朋友們的身邊時高興極了，他和所有人擁抱了一遍，甚至還擁抱了獅子和托托。在他們向前趕路時，他每走一步，就唱一句：「托─德─列─德─噢！」他感覺開心極了。

「我還擔心自己要永遠留在那條河當中了呢，」稻草人說，「但是那隻熱心的鸛鳥救了我，如果我能得到腦袋，我會再去找那隻鸛鳥，做些好事報答牠。」

「沒什麼，」鸛鳥說，牠飛到他們旁邊，「我一直都很喜歡幫助那些有困難的人。不過現在我得走了，我的孩子們還在巢裡等我呢。祝你們能找到翡翠城，希望奧茲會幫助你們。」

「謝謝你。」桃樂絲回答，然後善良的鸛鳥就飛到空中，一下子就消失不見了。

他們一邊向前走，一邊聽著豔麗的鳥兒歌唱，看著滿山遍野可愛的花爭相開放。那裡有黃色的、白色的、藍色的、紫色的大花朵。除此之外，還有一大簇一大簇猩紅色的罌粟花，色彩如此豔麗，讓桃樂絲看得眼花繚亂。

當小女孩呼吸著這些花朵的芳香時，問道：「這些花是不是很漂亮？」

「我想是吧，」稻草人回答說，「等我有了腦袋之後，或許會更喜歡它們。」

「如果我有了心，我應該會喜歡它們。」錫樵夫接著說道。

「我一直都非常喜歡花，」獅子說，「它們看起來雖然孱弱無力，但是在這森林之中，沒有比這更鮮豔的花朵了。」

這時候他們面前出現了越來越多猩紅色的大罌粟花，其他花朵則愈來愈少，不一會兒他們發現自己來到了大片罌粟花海。如今，人人都知道，當這種花大量地集中在一起時，它們的氣味會變得非常濃郁，任何人聞過之後就會昏昏欲睡。如果這個沉睡的人沒有遠離這種花的香氣，就會永遠地睡著。但是桃樂絲並不知道，也沒有遠離這些到處生長的豔麗紅色花朵，因此，很快她的眼皮就變得沉重起來，她覺得自己必須坐下來休息一下，睡個覺。

不過錫樵夫並沒有讓她睡覺。

「我們必須快點趕路，在天黑之前回到黃磚路上。」他說。稻草人也對此表示贊同，因此他們一直不停地趕路，直到桃樂絲再也堅持不住。她的眼睛不由自主地閉了起來，她忘記自己身在何處，倒在這片罌粟花叢中，一轉眼就睡著了。

「我們該怎麼辦？」錫樵夫問道。

「如果我們把她丟在這裡，她會死的，」獅子說，「這些花的氣味會殺了我們所有人。我的眼睛幾乎都快睜不開了，那隻狗已經睡著了。」

獅子說得沒錯，托托已經倒在牠的小主人旁邊。不過因為稻草人和錫樵夫並非血肉之軀，所以這些花的香氣並沒有讓他們感到不適。

「快跑，」稻草人對獅子說道，「儘快逃離這片致命的花園。

我們會帶小女孩一起走，可是如果你睡著了，你那麼大，我們可抬不動。」

於是獅子振作精神，使盡全力向前跑，不一會兒就消失在他們眼前。

「我們用手搭成一把椅子，抬著她走。」稻草人說。於是他們抱起托托，把牠放在桃樂絲的膝上，然後用手搭成一把椅子，手臂當做扶手，抬著這個熟睡的女孩，穿過這片花叢。

他們一直不停地向前走，這一大片圍繞著他們的致命罌粟花就像永無邊際似的沒有盡頭。他們沿著彎曲的河流向前走，最後遇到了他們的朋友獅子，他躺在罌粟叢中酣睡著。這些花的香氣如此強烈，最終這隻龐然大物也只能放棄，在距離罌粟花田盡頭不過一步之差的地方倒了下來。在他們面前，芳香的青草在美麗的綠草地上隨風擺動著。

「我們什麼也幫不了牠，」錫樵夫傷心地說道，「牠實在太重了，我們根本抬不動牠，只能讓牠永遠睡在這裡。最後，牠或許會在夢中找到勇氣。」

「真讓人難過，」稻草人說，「對於一隻這樣膽小的獅子來說，牠的確是一個很好的同伴。不過我們還是繼續往前走吧。」

他們抬著這個睡著的小女孩，遠離那片罌粟花田，來到河邊一個美麗的地方，防止她再聞到那些花朵散發的毒素。他們輕輕地把她放在柔軟的草地上，等待著清風把她吹醒。

第 9 章

田鼠女王

「只是一隻小田鼠！」這個小傢伙忿忿
不平地叫了起來，「什麼！我可是女王，
所有田鼠的女王！」

「**現**在我們應該離那條黃磚路不遠了，」稻草人站在小女孩身旁說道，「我們走過的路已經差不多跟被流水沖走的一樣多了。」

錫樵夫正想要回應，卻聽到一聲低沉的怒吼，他轉過頭去（他的頭活動起來還是相當靈活的），看見一隻奇怪的野獸躍過草地直奔他們而來。那是一隻碩大的黃色野貓，錫樵夫心想牠一定是在追捕什麼東西，因為牠那雙耳朵緊緊地貼在頭的兩側，嘴巴張得很大，露出兩排可怕的牙齒，一雙血紅的眼睛像燃燒著的火球一般閃閃發光。當這隻大野貓跑近之後，錫樵夫發現跑在牠前面的是一隻灰色的小田鼠。錫樵夫雖然沒有心，但是他仍舊知道，大野貓想要殺死一隻對人無害的小動物是不對的。

於是錫樵夫舉起斧頭，當大野貓往自己身邊跑過的時候，他迅速地劈了下去，將那隻大野貓砍成兩半，貓的頭從貓身上掉了下來，滾到錫樵夫的腳邊。

此刻，那隻死裡逃生、重獲自由的田鼠停了下來，慢慢地走到錫樵夫跟前，用非常短促而尖銳細小的聲音說道：

「噢，謝謝你！非常感謝你救了我的命。」

「請別這麼說，」錫樵夫回答道，「我沒有心，所以要特別留心幫助需要幫助的朋友，哪怕只是一隻小田鼠。」

「只是一隻小田鼠！」這個小傢伙忿忿不平地叫了起來，「什麼！我可是女王，所有田鼠的女王！」

「啊，真的嗎？」錫樵夫說，同時鞠了躬。

「所以，你救了我的命不但是立了大功，而且非常勇敢。」田鼠女王接著說。

這時，有好幾隻田鼠擺動著小腿，用最快的速度跑了過來，當牠們看見自己的女王之後，紛紛喊著：

「啊，女王陛下，我們還以為您會被殺掉呢！您是怎麼從那隻大野貓手中逃脫的？」他們全都深深地向女王鞠躬，簡直像是用頭站在地上。

「是這位古怪的錫樵夫殺死了大野貓，救了我的性命。所以，從今以後你們必須服侍他，順從他的意思。」田鼠女王說道。

「遵命！」田鼠們用尖銳的聲音異口同聲地回答，然後全往四面八方跑開。原來是因為托托睡醒後，看見有那麼多田鼠圍在自己身邊，便欣喜若狂地吠了起來，跳進田鼠群中。以前在堪薩斯州的時候，托托總是喜歡追趕老鼠，覺得這沒什麼壞處。

但是錫樵夫卻捉住了這隻小狗，緊緊地把牠抱在懷裡，與此同時，他召喚著田鼠們：「回來！回來！托托不會傷害你們。」

聽到這話，田鼠女王便從下面的草叢裡探出頭來，膽怯地問：「你確定牠不會咬我們嗎？」

「我不會讓牠咬你們的，」錫樵夫說，「不用擔心。」

於是田鼠們又一個個地爬了回來，而托托也沒再吠叫了，儘管牠仍舊想從錫樵夫的手臂中掙脫出來，若不是知道錫樵夫是用錫片做的，說不定還會咬他呢。最後，最大隻的田鼠開口了。

「我們可以做什麼來報答您對女王的救命之恩呢？」牠問。

「我不知道。」錫樵夫回答。

但是稻草人（他一直想要動腦思考，可惜他腦袋裡裝的都是稻草）立刻說：「對了，你們可以去救我們的朋友——膽小的獅子，他正睡在罌粟花田裡。」

「獅子！」田鼠女王大聲叫道，「哎呀，牠會把我們全吃掉的。」

「噢，不會，」稻草人鄭重地說，「這隻獅子是一個膽小鬼。」

「牠自己是這麼說的，」稻草人回答說，「牠絕對不會傷害我們的朋友。如果你們能幫忙救牠出來，我保證牠會友好地對待你們的。」

「那就好，」女王說，「我們相信你。但是我們該怎麼救牠呢？」

「這裡大部分的田鼠都是您的子民，並且願意服從您的命令嗎？」

「是的，有好幾千隻呢。」女王回答說。

「那麼請把牠們全都召集到這裡，越快越好，讓每隻田鼠都帶一條長繩子過來。」

田鼠女王轉過身來對著牠的隨從，要求牠們立刻把所有的子民全都召集過來。他們一聽到命令就迅速地往四面八方跑開了。

「現在，」稻草人對錫樵夫說，「你得去河邊砍一些樹來，然後造一輛載獅子用的車子。」

錫樵夫立刻就跑到樹林裡，開始工作起來。沒過多久，他就用樹幹造出了一輛木車，他削掉樹幹上的所有枝葉，用木釘把樹幹全都釘在一起，將大樹的樹幹分段做成四個輪子。錫樵夫又迅速又熟練，在田鼠們陸續到來之前，他已經做好了車子，等著他們。

好幾千隻田鼠從四面八方趕來：有大田鼠、小田鼠、不大不小的田鼠；每一隻的嘴裡都銜著一根繩子。就在這個時候，桃樂絲從她悠長的睡夢中醒了過來，睜開了眼睛。她發現自己躺在草地上，身邊還圍繞著成千上萬隻田鼠，膽怯地注視著她，心中滿是訝異。不過稻草人把來龍去脈全都告訴了她，然後轉向令人敬畏的小田鼠說道：

「請讓我向你介紹田鼠女王。」

桃樂絲莊重地點了點頭，女王行了個屈膝禮，然後，牠和小女孩變成了非常好的朋友。

這時候，稻草人和錫樵夫開始用田鼠們帶來的繩子，把田鼠們跟車子綁在一起。繩子的一端繞在每一隻田鼠的脖子上，另一端綁在車子上。當然，車子本身比任何一隻拉著它的田鼠大上一千倍。但是當所有的田鼠都套上繩子後，牠們輕而易舉地就能拉動這輛車了。即使稻草人和錫樵夫坐在上面，這些奇特的小馬也能快速地將這輛車拉到獅子熟睡的地方。

獅子的身體非常笨重，牠們費盡一番工夫才把牠搬上車。接著女王便急忙命令牠的子民們開始拉車，因為牠擔心田鼠們在罌粟花田裡停留太久也會昏睡過去。

　　雖然這些小動物數量眾多，但是剛開始牠們也很難拉動這輛沉重的車子。不過有錫樵夫和稻草人在後面推著，車子順利地動了起來。很快地，牠們就把獅子從罌粟花田拉到綠草地上，獅子終於能呼吸到甜美清新的空氣，而不是罌粟花散發出來的有毒香氣了。

　　桃樂絲上前迎接他們，真心誠意地感謝小田鼠們救出了自己的朋友。她很喜歡這隻大獅子，所以非常開心牠被救了出來。

　　然後，田鼠們從車子上卸下繩子，穿過草地，回牠們的老家去了。田鼠女王最後一個離開。

　　「如果你們還有什麼需要，」牠說，「就到田裡來呼喚一聲，我們聽到後，就會跑出來幫助你們的。再見！」

　　「再見！」他們齊聲回答。當田鼠女王離開時，桃樂絲緊緊地抱著托托，不讓牠去追趕田鼠女王，以免讓女王受到驚嚇。

　　田鼠女王離開之後，他們就坐在獅子旁邊等牠醒過來。稻草人從附近的樹上摘了許多水果，給桃樂絲當午餐。

第 10 章

城門守衛

在他們前面，那條黃磚路的盡頭，是一
扇高大的城門，全都鑲著翡翠，在陽光
的照耀下閃爍著光芒，即使是稻草人那
雙畫出來的眼睛，也被照射得頭暈目眩。

因為膽小的獅子躺在罌粟花田中的時間太長，一直呼吸著致命香氣，所以過了很久牠才醒過來。但是當牠張開雙眼，從車子上滾下來，發現自己還活著時，真是高興極了。

「我使盡全力向前跑，」牠坐起來，打著哈欠說，「但是那些花的香氣太強烈了，我根本抵擋不住。你們是怎麼把我救出來的？」

於是他們跟牠說起了田鼠，說牠們是如何勇敢地把牠從死亡中救出來。膽小的獅子笑著說：

「我一直以為自己是個龐然大物，令人害怕，可是就連花朵這麼小的東西都會要了我的命，而就連田鼠這麼的小動物都能救我，這一切可真是奇怪啊！不過，朋友們，我們現在要怎麼辦呢？」

「我們必須繼續往前走，重新找到那條黃磚路，」桃樂絲說，「然後才能去翡翠城。」

因此，等獅子完全清醒，重新振作之後，他們一行人就又開始了旅程，十分愜意地走在柔軟清新的草地上。沒花多少時間，他們就來到了那條黃磚路，重新往奧茲居住的翡翠城出發。

此時路變得非常平坦又整潔，周圍的景色也很怡人，這幾位旅行者很慶幸能夠把那片森林遠遠地拋在後頭，遠離陰沉的樹蔭中所遇到的眾多危險。他們又看到了築在路邊的圍牆，不過這些圍牆都被漆成了綠色。他們走進一間住著一位農夫的小屋子，那間小屋子一樣被漆成了綠色。這個下午，他們經過了很多這樣的房子，有時候房子裡的人會跑出來看他們，似乎有問題想要問，但是沒有一個人敢走近他們，也沒有一個人跟他們說話，因為他們都非常害怕那隻大獅子。這裡的居民都穿著翠綠色的漂亮衣服，頭上戴著像芒奇金人那樣的尖頂帽子。

「這裡一定就是奧茲國了，」桃樂絲說，「我們已經越來越靠近翡翠城了。」

「是啊，」稻草人回答，「這裡所有東西都是綠色的，就像在芒奇金人的國家裡，他們喜愛藍色一樣。但是這裡的人似乎不像芒奇金人那麼友善，我們恐怕找不到地方過夜了。」

「我要吃點其他東西，不能總是吃水果，」小女孩說，「我想托托也差不多餓了。到了下一戶人家我們就停下來，跟那裡的住戶商量一下吧。」

當他們來到一座不大不小的農舍前面時，桃樂絲鼓起勇氣走上前去敲門。

一位婦人開了條門縫，剛好可以探出頭來，說：「孩子，你想做什麼，為什麼跟一隻大獅子在一起？」

「如果您允許的話，我們想在這裡借住一晚，」桃樂絲回答道，「這隻獅子是我的朋友，也是我的夥伴，牠絕不會傷害您的。」

「牠很溫馴嗎？」婦人把門稍微開大了一點問道。

「是的，」小女孩說，「而且非常膽小，所以牠應該更怕你。」

婦人想了想，又偷看了一眼獅子，然後，她說：「那好吧，如果情況屬實，你們就進來吧，我先幫你們準備晚飯，然後再找個地方讓你們睡一覺。」

　　於是他們全都走進了房子，房間裡除了婦人以外，還住著兩個小孩和一個男人。那個男人的腿受了傷，躺在一張放在角落的床上。他們看見這樣一群奇怪的人，都感到很詫異，在婦人忙著擺放桌子的時候，那男人問道：

　　「你們幾個要去哪裡？」

　　「去翡翠城，」桃樂絲說，「拜訪偉大的奧茲。」

　　「噢，真的嗎！」男人大聲叫道，「你們確定奧茲會接見你們嗎？」

　　「為什麼不呢？」桃樂絲回答說。

　　「聽說他從來不讓任何人接近他。我去過翡翠城很多次，那是一個美妙的地方。但是我從來都沒有得到允許去見偉大的奧茲，我也不知道有誰見過他。」

　　「他從不出門嗎？」稻草人問道。

　　「從來沒有。他每天都坐在皇宮中寬敞的大殿裡，即使是侍從們也從沒見過他。」

　　「那他長什麼樣子呢？」小女孩問。

「那可就難說了，」這個人沉思著說道，「你知道，奧茲是一個偉大的魔法師，他可以隨心所欲地變成自己希望的樣子。因此有人說他像一隻鳥，有人說他像一頭大象，也有人說他像一隻貓。而對於另一些人來說，他的樣子是一個美麗的仙子，是一個善良的精靈，又或是任何他喜歡的樣子。但是沒有一個人可以說出真正的奧茲是誰，以及他本來長怎樣。」

「那真是奇怪，」桃樂絲說，「但是我們必須見到他，不管什麼方法都要嘗試一下，不然我們就白走這一趟了。」

「你們為什麼想要見可怕的奧茲呢？」這個人問道。

「我想請他給我一個腦袋。」稻草人急切地說道。

「噢，這種事情奧茲可以輕易辦到的，」這個人肯定地說，「他有許多腦袋，用都用不完。」

「我想請他給我一顆心。」錫樵夫說。

「那也難不倒他，」這個人繼續說道，「奧茲有一大堆心，各種大小、各種形狀的都有。」

「我想請他給我一點勇氣。」膽小的獅子說。

「奧茲在他的大殿裡藏著一大鍋勇氣呢，」這個男人說，「為了不讓它們跑掉，他用一個金色的蓋子蓋著。他會很樂意給你一點的。」

「我想請他送我回堪薩斯州。」桃樂絲說。

「堪薩斯州在什麼地方？」男人驚訝地問道。

「我也不知道，」桃樂絲傷心地回答說，「但那是我的家鄉，我肯定有這個地方。」

「可能是吧。奧茲是無所不能的，所以我想他會為你找到堪薩斯州的。但是，首先你們必須要見到他，那是一件非常困難的事情，因為這位偉大的魔法師不喜歡接見任何人，他總是我行我素。可是你想要什麼呢？」這個人問托托。托托只是搖了搖尾巴，說來奇怪，托托竟然不會說話。

這時候，婦人招呼他們說晚飯準備好了，於是他們在桌子旁圍坐下來，桃樂絲吃了一些可口的燕麥粥，一碟炒蛋和一盤精緻的白麵包，盡情享受她的晚餐。獅子也吃了一些燕麥粥，但是牠並不喜歡，說這粥是用燕麥做的，而燕麥是給馬吃的，不是給獅子吃的。稻草人和錫樵夫什麼都沒吃。托托把所有東西都吃了一遍，牠很高興又吃到了一頓美味的晚餐。

吃完晚飯，婦人就給桃樂絲準備了一張床睡覺，托托睡在她的旁邊，獅子守著她的房門，這樣她就不會被人打擾。稻草人和錫樵夫一整夜都安靜地站在角落裡，當然他們不用睡覺。

第二天早晨，太陽一出來，他們就上路了。不一會兒，他們就看見一道綠光閃耀在他們前面的天空中。

「那一定就是翡翠城了。」桃樂絲說。

他們越往前走，那道綠光就變得越明亮，看來他們總算是走近旅行的目的地了。不過他們一直到了下午才來到高大的城牆外面。城牆又高又厚，漆著明亮的綠色。

在他們前面，那條黃磚路的盡頭，是一扇高大的城門，全都鑲著翡翠，在陽光的照耀下閃爍著光芒，即使是稻草人那雙畫出來的眼睛，也被照射得頭暈目眩。

城門旁邊裝著一個門鈴，桃樂絲按了一下按鈕，聽到裡面傳來一陣清脆的叮噹聲。接著那扇高大的城門慢慢打開了，他們全都走了進去，發現自己置身於一間拱形的房子之中，四周的牆上裝飾著無數個閃閃發光的翡翠。

在他們面前站著一個身材跟芒奇金人差不多的小矮人，他全身上下，從頭到腳都穿著綠色，甚至連他的皮膚都透露著一種淺綠。在他的旁邊有一個綠色的大箱子。

這個人看見了桃樂絲和她的同伴，問道：「你們來翡翠城有什麼事情嗎？」

「我們想拜見偉大的奧茲。」

聽到這一回答，這個人感到非常驚訝，坐下來仔細地想了想。

「已經有很多年沒有人跟我說要見奧茲大人了，」他疑惑不解地搖了搖頭說，「他的法力無邊，令人生畏，如果你們只是因為一件無聊或愚蠢的事情而打擾這位偉大聰明的魔法師，他可能會發怒，立刻要了你們的命。」

「但我們並不是為了愚蠢或是無聊的事情才來的，」稻草人回答說，「這件事情非常重要。而且我們聽說奧茲是一位善良的魔法師。」

「確實是這樣，」這個綠色的矮人說道，「他將翡翠城管理得有條不紊。但是對於那些不誠實的人，或因為好奇而想接近他的人，他就會變得非常恐怖，從來都沒有人敢請求見他一面。我是城門守衛，既然你們要求拜見偉大的奧茲，我就必須把你們帶去他的宮殿。但是首先你們必須戴上眼鏡。」

「為什麼？」桃樂絲問說。

「因為你們要是不戴眼鏡，翡翠城燦爛的光芒就會讓你們的眼睛失明。即便是住在這個城裡的居民也得一天到晚戴著眼鏡。眼鏡全都被鎖起來了，奧茲在這座城剛建好的時候就下了這道命令，只有我這個掌管鑰匙的人，可以打開這個鎖。」

他打開了那個大箱子，桃樂絲看到裡面裝滿了各種尺寸的眼鏡。每副眼鏡都裝著綠色的鏡片。城門守衛給桃樂絲找了一副適合她的眼鏡替她戴上。眼鏡上有兩條金絲帶，緊緊地繫在她的後腦勺上，用一把小鎖鎖起來。那把鑰匙就掛在城門守衛的脖子上。戴上眼鏡之後，桃樂絲就不能隨意地把它摘下來了，不過，她當然也不想被翡翠城的光芒灼瞎雙眼，因此她什麼也沒說。

然後，這個人也幫稻草人、錫樵夫和獅子戴上了眼鏡，甚至連小托托也不例外，所有眼鏡都用一把小鎖鎖著。

接著，城門守衛給自己也戴上了眼鏡，告訴他們說他準備帶他們進宮。他從牆上的釘子上拿下一把巨大的金鑰匙，打開了另外一扇門，他們都跟著這個人穿過那扇門，走進翡翠城。

第 11 章

神奇的翡翠城

「如果你希望我用我的魔法送你回到你
的家鄉，那麼首先你必須為我做點事情。
你先幫我，我再幫你。」

雖然桃樂絲和她的朋友們都戴著綠色的眼鏡，但是在一開始，這座奇妙城市的光芒還是讓他們眼花繚亂。街道兩旁全都是用綠色的大理石建造的漂亮房子，到處都鑲嵌著閃閃發亮的翡翠。他們走在一條同樣用綠色大理石鋪砌而成的人行道上，街道連接處也是一排排緊密鑲嵌的翡翠，在明亮的陽光下燦爛地閃爍著光芒。每一扇窗戶上的玻璃都是綠色的，即便是這座城市的天空也散發著綠色，一道道太陽光也被染成了綠色。

在街上有許許多多行人：男人、女人和小孩，他們全都穿著綠色的衣服，連皮膚也是淺綠色的。他們都用好奇的眼光打量著桃樂絲和她帶領的那群奇怪的朋友們，當他們看見獅子的時候，所有的小孩都躲到了媽媽的背後，沒有人和他們說話。街道上有許多琳琅滿目的店鋪，桃樂絲發現店裡的所有東西都是綠色的。有綠色的糖果，綠色的爆米花，以及各式各樣的綠鞋子、綠帽子和綠衣服。在另一個地方，有人在賣綠色的檸檬汽水，當小孩買汽水的時候，她發現他們付的錢也是綠色的。

這裡似乎沒有馬，也沒有任何動物。人們推著綠色的小貨車運送貨物。每個人看起來都非常快樂、滿足、幸福。

城門守衛帶領著他們走過街道，最後來到了位於市中心的一座高大的建築物前，這就是偉大的魔法師奧茲的宮殿。門前站著一個士兵，穿著綠色的制服，留著一撮綠色的長鬍子。

「這裡有幾位客人，」城門守衛對他說，「他們想要拜見偉大的奧茲。」

「進去吧，」士兵回答說，「我給你們通報一聲。」

於是，他們走進宮殿，被帶到了鋪著綠色地毯，擺放著鑲嵌翡翠的綠色傢俱的大房間裡。走進房間之前，士兵讓他們在綠色的腳踏墊上把鞋底擦乾淨。等他們全都坐下之後，他彬彬有禮地說道：

「你們先在這裡休息一下，我去大殿門前向奧茲通報說你們來了。」

他們等了很長的時間。最後當士兵回來時，桃樂絲問道：「你見到奧茲了嗎？」

「噢，沒有，」士兵回答說，「我從沒見過他。他坐在帷幔後面，我跟他說話，把你們的意思轉告給他。他說，既然你們的欲望如此強烈，他允許你們去見他，但是，你們必須一個個進去，而且每天只能見一個。因此你們得在宮中待上好幾天了，我會帶你們去看看房間，經過了長途的跋涉，你們可以好好休息一下。」

「謝謝你，」小女孩回答，「奧茲真是個大好人。」

這時候，士兵吹響了綠色的哨子，立刻就有一位穿著漂亮綠色絲綢長袍的年輕女孩走進房間。她有著可愛的綠頭髮和綠眼睛，她一面向桃樂絲深深地鞠躬，一面說：「請跟我來，我帶你去你的房間。」

於是桃樂絲和他的朋友們告別，除了托托，她把托托抱在懷裡，跟著綠衣女孩穿過七條走廊，爬上三座樓梯，最後來到了前殿的一個房間。這是世界上最可愛的小房間，裡面擺著一張柔軟舒適的床，上面鋪著綠色綢緞的床單以及綠色天鵝絨的被褥。房間的中央有一個小噴水池，一股股綠色香水噴向空中，落在一個雕刻精美的綠色大理石盆子裡。窗戶上擺了一些嬌豔的綠色花朵，窗戶旁邊還有一個書架，上面放了一排綠色小書。當桃樂絲有空翻開這些書時，發現裡面都是些奇怪的綠色圖片，這些圖片非常有趣，令她發笑。

在一個衣櫥裡放著許多用絲綢、錦緞和天鵝絨做成的綠色衣服，而且這些衣服全都合桃樂絲的身。

「就把這裡當自己家吧，不用拘束，」綠衣女孩說，「如果有什麼需要就按這個鈴。明天早上奧茲會派人來召見你。」

她把桃樂絲獨自留在房裡，然後回去找其他人。她也把他們領到各自的房裡，每個人都發現自己住在皇宮中非常愜意的房間裡。當然，這樣的禮貌周到，對稻草人來說完全是浪費了。因為當他發覺自己獨自一人待在房間的時候，他只是傻傻地站在門口，等待著天亮。他一躺下來就沒辦法休息，而且也無法閉上眼睛，因此一整個晚上，他就凝視著房間角落的一隻小蜘蛛織著牠的網，好像這根本不是這世上最舒適的房間。錫樵夫還記得自己血肉之軀時的情景，因此他習慣地躺在床上，但是睡不著，於是整夜上上下下地運動關節，確保它們保持良好的狀態。獅子寧願睡在森林中用枯樹葉鋪成的床上，也不願被關在房間裡。不過牠很聰明，不會讓這件事困擾自己，因此牠跳上床去，像一隻貓似的蜷縮起來，馬上就睡著了。

第二天早上吃過早餐後，綠衣女孩去接桃樂絲，替她穿上一件綠色錦緞做的最漂亮的衣裳。桃樂絲又加了一條綠綢圍裙，在托托的脖子上繫了一條綠絲帶。然後她們動身前往偉大奧茲的大殿。

一開始，她們來到了一個大廳，那裡有許多宮廷中的貴婦和紳士，全都穿著華麗的衣服。這些人沒什麼事情可做，只是彼此閒聊著。每天早上，他們都會在大殿外面等候著，儘管他們從沒有得到允許可以拜見奧茲。當桃樂絲走進去的時候，他們都好奇地注視著她，其中一個人輕聲地問道：

「你真的要去拜見可怕的奧茲嗎？」

「當然，」小女孩回答說，「只要他願意見我。」

「噢，他會見你的，」那個替她傳信給魔法師的士兵說，「儘管他不喜歡有人請求拜見他。起初他確實非常生氣，還說你是從哪來的，就讓我把你送回那裡去。之後他又問我你的長相，當我提到你腳上的銀鞋子時，他對此產生了極大的興趣。最後，我又跟他說了你額頭上的記號，他就決定讓你見他了。」

就在這時，響起了一陣鈴聲，綠衣女孩對桃樂絲說：「來信號了，你必須一個人去大殿。」

綠衣女孩打開一扇小門，桃樂絲大膽地走了進去，她發現自己來到了一個奇妙的地方。這是一間寬敞的圓形房子，上面是高聳拱形的屋頂，四周的牆壁、天花板和地板全都用大塊的翡翠緊密地接著。屋頂的中間是一盞大燈，亮得像太陽一樣，照得翡翠閃耀著神奇的光芒。

但是最讓桃樂絲感興趣的是房子正中央的那把大理石的綠色寶座。它的形狀像一把椅子，也跟其他的東西一樣閃耀著光芒。椅子上有一顆巨大的頭顱，沒有身體或是四肢支撐著它。這顆頭上沒有頭髮，不過有一雙眼睛、一個鼻子和一張嘴巴，比世上最高的巨人的頭大很多。

正當桃樂絲好奇而恐懼地凝視著這顆頭時，那雙眼睛慢慢轉動起來，用尖銳而堅定的眼神注視著她。然後那張嘴巴也動了起來，桃樂絲聽到一個聲音說道：「我是奧茲，偉大而可怕的奧茲。你是誰？為什麼要來找我？」

從這顆碩大的頭顱中發出的聲音並不像桃樂絲想的那麼可怕，於是她鼓起了勇氣回答：

「我是桃樂絲，渺小而溫順的桃樂絲。我找你是想請你幫忙。」

那雙眼睛若有所思地注視著她，足足過了一分鐘，那聲音才說：

「你那雙銀鞋是從哪裡來的？」

「我的房子掉下來，壓死了東方邪惡女巫，這雙鞋就是從她那裡拿來的。」桃樂絲回答說。

「你額頭上的印記又是從哪裡來的？」這個聲音繼續說道。

「這是北方善良女巫在跟我告別時吻我之後留下的，她讓我來找你。」小女孩說。

那雙眼睛再次用銳利的眼神注視著她，看出小女孩說的都是真話。於是奧茲問：「你希望我做些什麼？」

「送我回堪薩斯州，我的艾姆嬸嬸和亨利叔叔就住在那裡，」她誠懇地回答，「儘管你的國土風景如畫，但是我並不喜歡。我離開家鄉那麼久了，艾姆嬸嬸一定很擔心我。」

這雙眼睛眨了三下，朝上望了望天花板，又朝下看了看地面，它們奇怪地轉動著，似乎把房間的角落都看了一遍。最後它們又看著桃樂絲。

「我為什麼要幫你？」奧茲問道。

「因為你是強者，而我是弱者；因為你是一個偉大的魔法師，而我只是一個無助的小女孩。」

「但是你殺死了東方邪惡女巫，這已經非常強大了。」

「那是碰巧發生的，」桃樂絲單純地回答道，「不是刻意的。」

「那麼，」這個頭顱說，「我現在答覆你。你沒有權利要求我送你回堪薩斯州，除非你做一件事回報我。在這片國土中，每個人都要為自己得到的東西付出代價。如果你希望我用我的魔法送你回到你的家鄉，那麼首先你必須為我做點事情。你先幫我，我再幫你。」

「我要為你做什麼事？」小女孩問。

「殺死西方的邪惡女巫。」奧茲回答。

「可是我辦不到。」桃樂絲大吃一驚，尖叫了起來。

「你殺死了東方女巫，穿上了這雙帶有巨大魔力的銀鞋。如今這片土地上就只剩下一個邪惡女巫了。只要你能告訴我她已經死了，那我就送你回堪薩斯州。但是在這之前，我不能幫你。」

小女孩開始哭了起來，她失望極了。那雙眼睛又眨了眨，焦急地看著她，這位偉大的奧茲似乎覺得只要她願意，就能夠幫助他。

「我從來都不曾主動殺死過任何人，」她嗚咽著說道，「就算我願意，我又該如何殺死邪惡女巫呢？像你這樣偉大而可怕的人都無法親自殺死她，你又怎麼能指望我辦到呢？」

「我不知道，」那顆頭顱說，「但這就是我給你的答覆，只要邪惡女巫不死，你就再也見不到你的叔叔和嬸嬸了。記住，那是個邪惡女巫──非常邪惡──她應該被殺死。你走吧，在你完成這個任務之前，不要再來見我。」

桃樂絲滿臉愁容地離開了大殿，回到獅子、稻草人和錫樵夫那裡，他們都等著聽奧茲對她說了些什麼。

「我沒希望了，」桃樂絲傷心地說道，「在我殺死西方邪惡女巫之前，奧茲是不會送我回家的。可是這件事我永遠都做不到。」

她的朋友們也感到非常難過，但是也沒有辦法幫助她。於是桃樂絲回到自己的房間，躺在床上，一個人哭泣，直到不知不覺地睡著。

第二天早晨，綠鬍子士兵來找稻草人，他說：

「跟我來，奧茲要接見你。」

於是稻草人跟著他走進了大殿，他在那裡看見一位美麗動人的小姐坐在翡翠寶座上，她穿著綠色的絲綢薄紗，飄逸的綠色長髮上戴著一頂寶石皇冠。她的肩膀上長著一對翅膀，色彩豔麗，非常輕盈，即便是最輕微的氣息拂動，也會使它們擺動起來。

稻草人盡可能優雅地向那位美麗的小姐鞠躬，而那位小姐溫柔地注視著他，說道：

「我是奧茲，偉大而可怕的奧茲。你是誰？為什麼要來找我？」

此時此刻，稻草人驚訝不已，他原本以為會見到桃樂絲所說的那顆巨大的頭顱。不過他非常勇敢地回答說：

「我只是個用稻草填塞而成的稻草人，所以我沒有腦袋。我來找你，是想求你把我腦袋中的稻草換成一個腦袋，這樣我就能跟你國土上的任何人一樣正常了。」

「我為什麼要幫你做這件事呢？」這位小姐問。

「因為你聰明而強大，除了你之外，任何人都幫不了我。」稻草人回答。

「如果沒有報酬，我是從來都不會給予恩惠的。」奧茲說，「但是最多我只能這麼答應你，如果你能為我殺了西方邪惡女巫，我就賞賜你最聰明的腦袋，讓你成為全奧茲國最最聰明的人。」

「我以為你已經讓桃樂絲去殺死那個女巫了。」稻草人驚訝地說。

「我是這麼說過。我不在乎是誰殺死了女巫。但是只有等她死了，我才能滿足你的願望。你走吧，在你可以得到那個渴望已久的腦袋之前，不要再來找我。」

稻草人滿面憂傷地回到他朋友們的身邊，把奧茲說過的話全都告訴了他們，桃樂絲得知這位大巫師不是她所看見的巨大頭顱，而是一位美麗的小姐，這讓她大吃了一驚。

稻草人說：「不管怎樣，她也跟錫樵夫一樣需要一顆心。」

第二天早晨，綠鬍子士兵來找錫樵夫，他說：

「奧茲要召見你。跟我來。」

於是錫樵夫跟著他來到了大殿。他不知道自己將要見到的奧茲是一位漂亮的小姐，還是一顆頭顱，不過他希望是一位漂亮小姐。「因為，」他自言自語說，「如果是一顆腦袋的話，我想我肯定得不到心，因為連腦袋自己都沒有心，所以它肯定不會知道我的感受。但如果是一位漂亮的小姐，我就可以苦苦哀求她給我一顆心，據說小姐全都是心地善良的。」

但是當錫樵夫走進大殿的時候，他看到的既不是腦袋，也不是小姐，因為奧茲變成了一隻最最可怕的野獸。牠幾乎有一隻大象那麼大，那把綠色的翡翠寶座似乎都無法承載它的重量了。這只野獸的頭像犀牛，但是它的臉上卻有五隻眼睛，身上長出五條長臂，還有五條細長的腿。全身上下覆蓋著羊毛狀濃密的毛，再也想像不出比這更可怕的怪物了。在那一刻，幸好錫樵夫沒有心，要不然他的心早就因為恐懼而怦怦跳個不停了。不過他只是錫樵夫，雖然非常失望，卻絲毫不害怕。

「我是奧茲，偉大而可怕的奧茲！」野獸說道，那聲音就像是在怒吼，「你是誰？為什麼要來找我？」

「我是個樵夫，用錫片做成的，所以我沒有心，無法得到愛情。我請求你給我一顆心，可以讓我像其他人一樣。」

「我為什麼要這麼做呢？」野獸問道。

「因為我請求你，只有你才能滿足我的請求。」錫樵夫說道。

奧茲聽到這一回答，低沉地咆哮了一聲，粗魯地說道：「如果你真的想要一顆心，你必須自己得到它。」

錫樵夫問：「怎麼得到呢？」

「幫助桃樂絲殺死西方邪惡女巫，」野獸回答說，「只要這個女巫一死，你就可以來找我，我會把全奧茲國中最大、最仁慈、最充滿愛的心給你。」

錫樵夫愁眉苦臉地回到他朋友們那裡，跟他們說起自己看到的那頭可怕的野獸。他們全都對大巫師可以變出那麼多樣子而感到萬分驚訝。獅子說：

「如果我去拜見他時，他變成了一隻野獸，我就發出最大的吼聲，恐嚇他，讓他答應我所有的請求。如果他變成了漂亮的小姐，我就假裝撲到她身上，強迫她答應我的請求。如果他變成了一個大頭，他會向我求饒，因為我會讓那顆頭在房間到處滾來滾去，直到他答應給我們想要的東西。所以，朋友們，樂觀點，一切都會順利的。」

第二天早晨，綠鬍子士兵帶著獅子來到大殿裡，讓他進去拜見奧茲。

獅子立刻跳進那扇門，向四周看了一眼，牠驚訝地發現在寶座前的是一顆火球，熊熊燃燒著，火光四射，獅子幾乎無法直視。剛開始牠還以為奧茲遇上了火災，被這顆火球燒死了。但是，當牠試著靠近一點時，那火球酷熱難擋，燒到了牠的鬃毛，於是牠全身顫抖地爬回到靠近門口的地方。

這時候，火球裡傳來一個低沉而平靜的聲音，說道：

「我是奧茲，偉大而可怕的奧茲。你是誰？為什麼要來找我？」

獅子回答說：「我是一隻膽小的獅子，什麼東西都害怕。我來這裡是想求你給我一些勇氣，讓我成為名副其實的萬獸之王，就像人們稱呼我的那樣。」

「我為什麼要給你勇氣呢？」奧茲問道。

「因為在所有魔法師中，你是最最偉大的，只有你有能力實現我的請求。」

這時候，火球更加猛烈地燃燒了起來。那聲音說：「只要你能向我證明，邪惡女巫已經死了，到時候我就會給你勇氣。但是，只要那邪惡女巫還活著，你就只能當一隻膽小的獅子。」

對於這番話，獅子感到非常生氣，卻又無言以對。牠默默地站在那裡，盯著那顆火球。火球變得越來越熱，因此牠只能掉頭轉身衝出房間，牠很高興地看到朋友們都在等牠，牠把自己跟魔法師的可怕會面告訴了他們。

「現在我們該怎麼辦？」桃樂絲遺憾地說。

「我們就剩一條路可走了，」獅子回答說，「去溫基人的故鄉，找到邪惡女巫，然後殺死她。」

「但是如果我們殺不死她呢？」小女孩說。

「那我就永遠沒有勇氣了。」獅子說。

「那我就永遠沒有腦袋了。」稻草人接著說道。

「那我就永遠沒有心了。」錫樵夫說。

「那我就永遠看不見艾姆嬸嬸和亨利叔叔了。」桃樂絲說著又哭了起來。

「小心！」綠衣女孩喊道，「眼淚會掉在你那件綠緞長袍上，會把衣服給弄髒的。」

於是桃樂絲擦乾了眼淚說：「我想我們得試試看，但是我很清楚，我真的不想為了再見到艾姆嬸嬸而殺害任何人。」

「我跟你一起去,可是我太膽小,不敢殺那個女巫!」獅子說。

「我也去,」稻草人鄭重地說道,「可是我是個笨蛋,肯定幫不上什麼忙。」

「即便是一個女巫,我也無心去傷害她,」錫樵夫說,「但是,如果你去,我當然會跟你一起去。」

因此他們決定第二天就出發。錫樵夫用一塊綠色的磨石把他的斧頭磨得鋒利,還替自己身上的所有關節添了油。稻草人替自己塞了一些新鮮稻草,桃樂絲幫他重新畫了眼睛,讓他可以看得更清楚一些。那位非常和善的綠衣女孩將桃樂絲的籃子裝滿了美味的食物,還在托托的脖子上繫了一條綠色的絲帶,上面綁著一個小鈴鐺。

他們很早就上床睡覺,一直酣睡到天亮。皇宮後院的一隻綠公雞咕咕叫,一隻生下綠色蛋的母雞咯咯叫,喚醒了他們一群人。

第 *12* 章

尋找邪惡女巫

雖然西方的邪惡女巫只有一隻眼睛，那
隻眼睛卻像望遠鏡一樣可以看到任何地
方。因此，當她坐在城堡門口，偶然地
向四周眺望時，就看見了桃樂絲睡在草
地上，她的朋友們全都圍繞在她身旁。

那個綠鬍子士兵帶著他們穿過大街小巷，把他們送到城門守衛的地方。城門守衛摘下了他們的眼鏡，放回到那個大箱子裡，然後，又彬彬有禮地為這幾位朋友打開了城門。

「哪一條路可以到西方的邪惡女巫那裡？」桃樂絲問道。

「那裡沒有路，」城門守衛回答說，「沒有人想要去那裡。」

「那我們該如何找到她呢？」小女孩追問道。

「那倒容易，」這個人回答說，「因為只要邪惡女巫知道你們進入了溫基國，她自己就會來找你們，把你們變成她的奴隸。」

「或許不會吧，」稻草人說，「我們準備去除掉她。」

「噢，那可就不一樣了，」城門守衛說，「在此之前，從來沒有人能除掉她，因此我自然而然就想到她會把你們變成她的奴隸，就像她對待其他人一樣。不過你們可要小心，這個女巫兇狠惡毒，不會這麼輕易地讓你們殺死她的。你們一直往西走，就是太陽下山的地方，肯定可以找到她的。」

他們對他說了聲謝謝、道了聲再見，然後轉向西方，走上柔軟的草地，草地上到處都點綴著雛菊和小黃花。桃樂絲仍舊穿著王宮裡那件美麗的綢衣，可是這時她驚訝地發現，這件衣服不再是綠色的，而是變成了純白色。繫在托托脖子上的綠絲帶也不再是綠色的，而是變成了跟桃樂絲衣服一樣的白色。

很快地，翡翠城就被他們遠遠地拋在了後頭。隨著他們不斷前進，道路也變得越來越崎嶇陡峭，這片土地的西邊，既沒有農田，也沒有房子，土地都沒有開墾過。

到了下午，太陽火辣辣地曬著他們的臉，沒有樹木可以為他們遮蔽陽光，因此，在天黑之前，桃樂絲、托托以及獅子就已經精疲力盡，躺在草地上睡著了，而錫樵夫和稻草人在旁邊守護著。

雖然西方的邪惡女巫只有一隻眼睛，那隻眼睛卻像望遠鏡一樣可以看到任何地方。因此，當她坐在城堡門口，偶然地向四周眺望時，就看見了桃樂絲睡在草地上，她的朋友們全都圍繞在她身旁。雖然還離得非常遙遠，但是邪惡女巫看到他們在自己的地盤就感到很憤怒，因此她吹響了掛在她脖子上的銀笛。

一群惡狼立刻從四面八方奔來。牠們有修長的腿，瞪著兇狠的眼睛，露出尖利的牙齒。

「去那邊，」女巫命令道，「把他們全都撕成碎片。」

「你不把他們變成奴隸嗎？」惡狼頭頭問道。

「不，」她回答，「一個錫樵夫、一個稻草人、一個小女孩，還有一隻獅子。沒有一個可以幹活的，把他們撕成小碎片吧。」

「遵命！」這匹狼說著，用最快的速度跑走，其他狼緊緊跟在後頭。

幸運的是，錫樵夫和稻草人沒有睡覺，他們聽見了惡狼的動靜。

「讓我來對付牠們，」錫樵夫說，「你們躲到我後面去，等牠們來了，就讓我來對付。」

他拿起已經磨得鋒利的斧頭，當惡狼頭頭奔過來時，錫樵夫揮動他的胳膊，砍掉了這匹狼的頭，牠立刻就斷了氣。他剛剛舉起斧頭，就又有一匹狼衝上前來，而牠也在錫樵夫鋒利的斧頭下丟了性命。總共有四十匹惡狼，在揮動四十次斧頭之後，每一匹惡狼全都被砍死了。最後，錫樵夫的面前堆了一大堆惡狼的屍體。

然後，他放下斧頭，坐在稻草人旁邊。稻草人說：「朋友，這一仗打得真漂亮。」

他們一直等到第二天早晨桃樂絲醒來。看見這一大堆毛茸茸的惡狼，這小女孩著實嚇了一跳，不過錫樵夫把事情原原本本地告訴了她。她謝謝錫樵夫救了他們，等坐下來吃完早餐之後，他們又開始了旅程。

就在這天早晨，邪惡女巫來到城堡門口，用她那一隻可以看得很遠的眼睛向外眺望，她看見那些惡狼全都死了，而那些陌生人仍在她的領土上往前走。這令她更加憤怒，於是她又吹響了銀笛。

一大群野烏鴉立刻向她飛了過來，數量多得都已經遮黑了天空。

邪惡女巫對烏鴉王說：「立刻飛到那些陌生人身邊，啄瞎他們的眼睛，把他們撕成碎片。」

一大群野烏鴉朝桃樂絲和她的夥伴們飛去。小女孩看到這群烏鴉，心裡害怕極了。

但是稻草人說：「這次就讓我來對付牠們。你們趴在我身邊，就不會受到傷害了。」

於是他們全都趴在地上，只有稻草人站在那裡，伸出了手臂。當這些烏鴉看見他時都變得驚慌失措，牠們害怕稻草人，於是都不敢再靠近。但是烏鴉王卻叫道：「那只是個稻草人而已。我去啄瞎他的眼睛。」

烏鴉王飛向稻草人，而稻草人一把抓住牠的頭，擰斷了牠的脖子，最後這隻烏鴉斷了氣。接著又有一隻烏鴉向他飛了過來，稻草人同樣擰斷了牠的脖子。總共有四十隻烏鴉，稻草人擰了四十次脖子，到最後，烏鴉們全都死在稻草人的身邊。然後稻草人叫他的同伴們起來，繼續他們的旅程。

當邪惡女巫再次向外眺望，看見自己的烏鴉全都死成了一堆，她大發雷霆，第三次吹響了她的銀笛。

天空中立刻傳來一陣響亮的嗡嗡聲，一群黑蜂向她飛了過來。

「去找那群陌生人，把他們全都螫死！」女巫下令道。於是黑蜂轉過身，迅速飛往桃樂絲和她朋友們趕路的地方。不過錫樵夫已經看見了牠們，而稻草人也已經想好了對付牠們的方法。

「把我身上的稻草全都拿出來，撒在小女孩和小狗以及獅子的身上，」他對錫樵夫說道，「這樣黑蜂就螫不到他們了。」於是錫樵夫照辦，桃樂絲抱著托托，挨在獅子身旁躺了下來，稻草完全把他們給覆蓋住。

黑蜂們趕到時，只看到錫樵夫可以螫，因此牠們全都飛到他的身上，牠們的刺全都被錫片給折斷了，可是卻沒有對錫樵夫造成絲毫傷害。黑蜂的刺一斷，牠們就活不成了，全都散落在錫樵夫的周圍，就像一小堆上等煤塊那麼厚。

　　然後桃樂絲和獅子站了起來，小女孩幫著錫樵夫把稻草全都塞回到稻草人的身子裡，讓他恢復到以前的樣子。接著他們再次踏上了旅程。

　　當邪惡女巫看見黑蜂像一小堆上等煤塊一樣死在那裡時，她跺了跺腳，拉扯著自己的頭髮，氣得咬牙切齒。於是她召集了十二個來自溫基的奴隸，發給他們銳利的長矛，命令他們去殺死那群陌生人。

　　溫基人並不勇敢，但是既然他們受到了命令，就只能去執行。因此他們出發向桃樂絲靠近。這時候獅子發出一聲怒吼，向他們撲了過去。可憐的溫基人害怕極了，拔腿就跑。

　　當他們逃回城堡之後，惡女巫就用鐵條鞭打他們，讓他們回去幹活。在這之後，女巫坐了下來，思考著接下來該如何行動。她不明白自己那些殺人計畫為什麼都會失敗，但她是個法力高強的女巫，而且還是個邪惡女巫，很快地，她又打定了主意。

　　在她的櫥櫃裡放著一頂金帽子，四周鑲嵌著鑽石和寶玉。這頂金帽子有一種魔力，任何戴上它的人都可以召喚三次飛天猴，不管是什麼命令，這些飛天猴都會服從。但是不管是誰都只能召喚這種奇怪的動物三次。這個邪惡女巫已經使用這頂帽子的魔力兩次了。第一次是讓溫基人變成她的奴隸，讓她成為了這片領土的統治者。飛天猴曾經幫助她完成了這個命令。第二次是她跟偉大的奧茲本人作戰，把他驅逐出西方的時候，飛天猴也曾在這件事上助她一臂之力。她只能再利用這頂金帽子的魔力一次，因此在她的其他魔法沒有用盡之前，她並不願動用這頂金帽子。但是如今她的惡狼、烏鴉，還有螫人的黑蜂全都已經敗下陣來，而她的奴隸們也被膽小的獅子嚇退，她知道，只有一個方法可以殺死桃樂絲和她的朋友們。

因此，邪惡女巫從她的衣櫃裡拿出了金冠，戴在頭上。然後她用左腳站立著，慢慢地唸道：

「哎霹，呸霹，卡霹！」

接著她又用右腳站著唸道：

「兮囉，呵囉，嘿囉！」

之後她雙腳站立，大聲地喊道：

「兮兮，蘇兮，兮！」

魔法開始起作用，天色暗了下來，空中傳來一陣低沉的轟隆聲，還有許多翅膀拍動的聲音，以及陣陣喧鬧的叫喊聲和嬉笑聲。陽光從黑暗的天空照射下來，照見了邪惡女巫身旁圍繞著一群猴子，每隻猴子的肩膀上都長著一對寬大有力的翅膀。

其中有一隻最大的猴子，似乎是猴王，牠飛到女巫的面前說：「這已經是您第三次召喚我們，也是最後一次了。您有什麼吩咐？」

「去找那些闖進我領土的陌生人，殺了他們，除了那隻獅子，」邪惡女巫說，「把那隻野獸給我帶回來，我要把牠像馬一樣套上馬具，讓牠幹活。」

「我們會遵從您的命令的。」猴王說。然後，伴隨著一陣嘈雜的叫聲，這些飛天猴向桃樂絲和她朋友們趕路的地方飛了過去。

幾隻飛天猴抓住了錫樵夫，帶著他飛在空中，來到一片堆滿尖銳石頭的地方。他們就從空中把這個可憐的樵夫扔了下去。錫樵夫從那麼高的地方跌落到石頭上，摔得破爛不堪，滿是凹陷，他躺在那裡既不能動彈，也不能呻吟。

又有幾隻猴子抓住了稻草人，用他們長長的爪子把稻草人的衣服和腦袋裡面的稻草全都拉了出來，把他的帽子、鞋子和衣服打成了一個小包，拋在一棵大樹的樹梢頂上。

剩下的猴子們甩出結實的繩子套住獅子，在牠的身上、頭上、腿上繞了好幾圈，使得牠無論如何都沒辦法咬，沒辦法抓，也沒辦法掙扎。然後飛天猴們抬起牠，飛到女巫的城堡中。獅子被關在一個四周圍著高大鐵柵欄的小院子裡，根本無法逃脫。

但是，桃樂絲一點都沒有受到飛天猴的傷害。她手裡抱著托托，站在那裡，眼睜睜地看著同伴們受罪，心裡想著馬上就要輪到自己了。猴王飛到了她面前，伸出牠毛茸茸的手臂，面目可憎的咧嘴大笑著。但是牠看到桃樂絲額頭上那個善良女巫吻過之後留下的印記，便立刻停了下來，示意其他猴子不要去冒犯她。

「我們不能傷害這個小女孩，」牠對其他猴子說道，「因為她受到了善良女巫的保護，善良女巫的法力可比那邪惡女巫強大得多了。我們只能把她帶到邪惡女巫的城堡裡，把她丟在那裡。」

因此，牠們小心翼翼，斯斯文文地抬起桃樂絲，帶著她迅速飛到空中，來到了城堡。飛天猴們把她放在城堡前門的石階上。然後，那猴王對女巫說：

「我們已經儘量完成你的命令了。錫樵夫和稻草人都已經完蛋了，獅子被綁在你的院子裡。只是我們不敢傷害這個小女孩，也不敢傷害抱在她懷裡的小狗。如今，你已經失去了召喚我們的權利，你永遠都不會再見到我們了。」

說完之後，所有的飛天猴伴隨著嘈雜的笑聲和叫聲，飛到了空中，一眨眼工夫就消失在眼前。

當邪惡女巫看見桃樂絲額頭上那個印記的時候，她心裡覺得既驚訝又擔憂，因為她非常清楚，不管是飛天猴還是她自己都不敢傷害這個小女孩。她低下頭看著桃樂絲的腳，發現了那雙銀鞋，她害怕得打起哆嗦，因為她知道這雙銀鞋的魔力有多麼強大。剛開始，這個惡女巫想要逃跑，不過她偶然看見了小女孩的眼睛，發現這雙眼睛背後的心靈是如此純潔，小女孩根本不知道這雙銀鞋賦予她的神奇魔力。因此惡女巫暗地裡笑著，心想：「既然她不知道如何使用自己的魔法，那我仍舊可以讓她變成我的奴隸。」於是，她粗魯而嚴厲地對桃樂絲命令道：

「跟我來，記住我跟你說的每一句話，要不然你的小命可就完了，就像我對待錫樵夫和稻草人那樣。」

桃樂絲跟著女巫，走過了城堡中許多漂亮的房間，最後她們來到了廚房，邪惡女巫命令她把鍋子和水壺洗乾淨、打掃地板，並替火堆添柴火。

桃樂絲乖乖地幹起活來。她下定決心一定要努力幹活；因為她很高興邪惡女巫沒有要殺死她。

桃樂絲辛勤地工作著，邪惡女巫則是想著該去院子裡把那隻膽小的獅子馴服成像馬一樣聽話。她想，如果能讓這頭獅子拉車，無論什麼時候想去哪就能去哪，一定非常有意思。但是當她打開門，獅子就對她怒吼了一聲，兇狠地撲向她，女巫嚇得急急忙忙地跑了出來，關上了門。

「如果我沒辦法馴服你，」女巫透過門閂對裡面的獅子說，「我就讓你挨餓。在你願意替我做事之前，你就別想吃東西了。」

從此以後，她真的沒有給被囚的獅子吃過任何東西，每天中午，她都跑到門前問道：「你願意像馬那樣拉車了嗎？」

而獅子回答說：「不，如果你走進這院子，我就咬死你。」

獅子為什麼不順從女巫呢？原來每天夜裡，當女巫睡著之後，桃樂絲就從櫥櫃裡替牠帶食物過來。吃過東西之後，牠就躺在用稻草鋪成的床上，桃樂絲則躺在牠身旁，把頭枕在牠柔軟蓬鬆的鬃毛上，這時候他們談論著各自的困難，計畫著如何逃脫。但是他們想不出任何可以逃出城堡的方法，因為時時刻刻都有黃色的溫基人看守著城堡，他們是邪惡女巫的奴隸，非常害怕她，不敢違抗她的命令。

白天，小女孩不得不努力幹活，那個邪惡女巫手裡總是拿著一把舊雨傘，恐嚇說要用雨傘打她。事實上，因為桃樂絲額頭上那個印記，邪惡女巫並不敢打她，可是小女孩不知道，經常為了自己和托托而滿心擔憂。

有一次，女巫用她的雨傘打了托托一下，這隻勇敢的小狗向她撲了過去，在她的腿上咬了一口。女巫被咬傷的地方並沒有流血，因為她可惡至極，在好多年以前她的血就已經乾枯了。

桃樂絲的日子變得越來越困苦，她漸漸意識到自己要再回到堪薩斯州，回到艾姆嬸嬸身邊，已經是難上加難了。有時候，她會傷心地哭上好幾個鐘頭，托托坐在她的腳邊，看著她的臉，哀傷地嗚咽著，表明自己為了小主人而傷心。托托一點都不介意自己是在堪薩斯州還是在奧茲國，只要能和桃樂絲在一起就好。但是，牠知道小女孩不快樂，這也讓牠沒辦法快樂起來。

這時候，邪惡女巫極其渴望地想要把小女孩一直穿著的銀鞋占為己有。她的黑蜂、烏鴉和惡狼全都死光了，而金帽子的魔力也已被她用盡，但是，如果她能得到這雙銀鞋，那麼她所失去的一切都會得到彌補，而且還會比以往的魔力更強大。她小心翼翼地監視著桃樂絲，看她是否會脫掉鞋子，想著是不是可以把它們偷出來。但是小女孩非常寶貴她那雙精美的鞋子，除了晚上或是洗澡的時候，她從來都不把鞋子脫下來。可是惡女巫非常怕黑，不敢在夜裡溜進桃樂絲的房間偷鞋子，而且，比起黑暗，她更加怕水，因此在桃樂絲洗澡的時候，她從來都不敢靠近。這個老女巫確實從來都不碰水，也從來都不讓水

121

沾到自己身上。

但是，這個邪惡女巫詭計多端，最後她想到了一個妙招，可以讓她得到自己想要得到的東西。她在廚房地板的中央放了一根鐵棒，然後在上面施了魔法，讓人的眼睛無法看見這根鐵棒。因此，桃樂絲走過時，因為看不見鐵棒而被絆倒了。雖然她沒受什麼傷，但是一隻銀鞋在她摔倒的時候掉了，而在她撿回來之前，就被女巫搶了過去，穿在她那瘦骨嶙峋的腳上。

女巫為自己的詭計大獲成功而沾沾自喜，只要有了這一隻銀鞋，就可以讓她得到一半的魔力，即使將來桃樂絲知道如何使用魔法，她也無法以此來與自己對抗了。

小女孩發現自己丟了一隻美麗的鞋子而生起氣來，對著女巫說道：「把鞋子還給我！」

「不還，」女巫回嘴道，「現在這隻鞋子是我的了，不是你的。」

「你這個可惡的傢伙！」桃樂絲叫喊著，「你沒有權利拿走我的鞋子。」

「我也會像你這樣保存著它，」女巫對著她哈哈大笑道，「總有一天，我還會從你那裡拿走另外一隻鞋的。」

這話讓桃樂絲氣急敗壞，她提起身旁的一桶水，朝女巫潑了過去，把她從頭到腳澆得濕透。

女巫立刻恐懼地大聲尖叫起來，桃樂絲驚訝地看著她，發現女巫的身體開始變小，然後摔倒在地上。

「看你幹的好事！」女巫尖聲叫道，「我馬上就要溶化了！」

「實在是非常抱歉。」桃樂絲說，她看著這個女巫像紅糖一樣在自己面前溶化，著實嚇了一跳。

「你不知道水會要了我的命嗎？」女巫十分絕望地哭著問道。

「當然不知道，」桃樂絲說，「我怎麼會知道呢？」

「好了，用不了幾分鐘我就會完全溶化了，你就可以擁有這座城堡了。我這輩子無惡不作，但是我萬萬沒想到你這樣一個小女孩竟會把我給溶化，結束我的惡行。小心點，我去了！」

說完這番話，女巫就躺在地上，化成了一灘棕色的、溶化的、無形的東西，在整潔寬敞的廚房地板上漫延開來。看著女巫果真化為烏有，桃樂絲又倒了一桶水，沖散了那一灘東西，然後把它們掃出門。她撿起那隻銀鞋，這是老女巫留下的唯一一件東西，然後用布把它洗淨擦乾，穿在自己腳上。現在，她終於獲得自由，她跑了出去，來到院子裡，告訴獅子西方邪惡女巫已經完蛋了的消息，說他們已經不再是這個陌生地方的囚犯了。

第 13 章

救援行動

「如果我們的朋友，稻草人和錫樵夫還
跟我們在一起的話，」獅子說，「我會
更加開心。」

膽小的獅子聽說邪惡女巫被一桶水給溶化了，滿心歡喜，桃樂絲立刻打開了關著牠的牢門，把牠放了出來。他們一起來到城堡，在那裡，桃樂絲做的第一件事就是把所有的溫基人都召集在一起，告訴他們，他們已經不再是奴隸了。

黃色的溫基人發出陣陣歡呼，因為他們已經被邪惡女巫奴役很多年，她經常殘忍地對待他們，如今他們獲得自由了。自此之後，他們就把這一天當成了節日，在盛宴與舞會中紀念這一天。

「如果我們的朋友，稻草人和錫樵夫還跟我們在一起的話，」獅子說，「我會更加開心。」

「你覺得我們沒辦法救出他們了嗎？」小女孩十分不安地問道。

「我們可以試試看。」獅子回答道。

於是，他們叫來了黃色的溫基人，問他們是否願意幫忙拯救他們的朋友。溫基人說他們非常樂意為桃樂絲做些事，因為是她把他們從奴役中解放出來的。於是桃樂絲挑選了好幾個看起來非常聰明的溫基人，然後一起出發了。他們走了一天多，最後來到了一片岩石密佈的平原，錫樵夫就躺在那裡，全身上下扭曲凹陷。他的斧頭落在他的身邊，斧刃已經生鏽了，斧柄也摔成了兩半。

溫基人輕手輕腳地把錫樵夫抬起來，送回黃色城堡。桃樂絲看到老朋友這種糟糕的狀況，不禁流下了眼淚。獅子看了也很傷心。

當他們回到城堡之後，桃樂絲對溫基人說：「你們這裡可有錫匠？」

「噢，有啊，我們這裡有好幾個手藝精湛的錫匠呢。」他們告訴桃樂絲說。

「把他們帶到我這裡來吧。」她說。之後錫匠來了，他們的籃子裝著所有工具。桃樂絲問他們說：「你們能不能把錫樵夫身上的凹陷敲平，讓他恢復原先的樣子？他身上斷裂的地方可以接回去嗎？」

這些錫匠仔細地把錫樵夫檢查了一遍，然後回答說，他們覺得應該可以把他修復，讓他變得跟從前一般完好。於是，他們在城堡中一間寬敞的黃色房子裡工作了整整三天四夜，他們在錫樵夫的腿上、身上和頭上，又是錘打、又是扭動、又是彎曲、又是焊接、又是磨光、又是不斷地敲打，最後終於讓他恢復原樣，所有關節也像從前一樣活動自如。當然，他的身上肯定會多出好幾個補釘，不過錫匠們已經出色地完成了任務，而錫樵夫也不是愛慕虛榮的人，根本不在乎。

最後，錫樵夫來到桃樂絲的房間裡，感謝她對自己的救命之恩，開心地流下喜悅的淚水，桃樂絲用她的圍裙仔細地替錫樵夫擦乾臉上的每一滴眼淚，他的關節才沒有因此而生鏽。與此同時，她自己也因為再次與老朋友重逢而開心得淚流滿面，但是這些眼淚用不著擦掉。至於獅子呢，牠也不停地用尾巴尖擦著眼睛，尾巴上一簇毛都濕透了，牠不得不走出房門，來到院子裡，在太陽下曬乾尾巴。

等桃樂絲把發生的一切全都告訴錫樵夫之後，他說：「如果稻草人能跟我們重新在一起我會非常開心。」

「我們一定要設法找到他。」小女孩說。

於是她又請來了溫基人幫忙。他們走了一天多的路，最後來到一棵大樹前，飛天猴們把稻草人的衣服扔在這棵大樹的樹枝上。

這是一棵參天大樹，樹幹非常光滑，因此沒有人爬得上去。不過錫樵夫立刻說道：「我可以把這棵樹砍倒，我們就能拿到稻草人的衣服了。」

之前，錫匠在修理錫樵夫的時候，另一個溫基人是個金匠，他用純金打了一把斧柄，裝在錫樵夫的斧頭上，替代了原來那根摔斷的斧柄。其他人打磨了斧刃，直到磨去了斧頭上的鏽，讓它像磨光的銀器一樣閃閃發亮。

錫樵夫話一說完，就開始動手砍起樹來，很快地樹就砰地一聲倒下。稻草人的衣服從樹枝上掉了下來，落到地上。

桃樂絲撿起那件衣服，讓溫基人帶回城堡去，他們在那裡用乾淨的稻草塞滿了這件衣服。看，稻草人復活了，就像原來一樣神氣活現的，他一遍遍地感謝著大家對他的救命之恩。

此時，桃樂絲和她的朋友們又重新歡聚在了一起。他們這一群人在黃色的城堡裡快快樂樂地度過了好幾天，在那裡，他們可以得到任何能讓他們過得舒服的東西。

但是有一天，小女孩忽然想到了艾姆嬸嬸，她說：「我們得去找奧茲，讓他實踐他的諾言。」

「是啊，」錫樵夫說，「我終於可以得到我的心了。」

「我可以得到我的腦袋了。」稻草人快活地接著說道。

「我可以得到我的勇氣了。」獅子沉思地說道。

「我也可以回到堪薩斯州了，」桃樂絲拍著手，叫了起來，「明天我們就動身去翡翠城吧！」

他們就這麼決定了。第二天，他們把溫基人都召集起來，跟他們告別。

對於他們的離開，溫基人感到非常不捨，因為他們非常喜歡錫樵夫，懇求他能留下來，管理他們以及這片西方的黃色國土。但是看到他們去意已決，溫基人就分別送給托托和獅子一條金色項圈；送給桃樂絲一只鑲嵌著鑽石的美麗手鐲；送給稻草人一根金頭手杖，免得他走路時被絆倒；送給錫樵夫一個銀質油罐，上面鑲嵌著金子和珍貴的寶石。

每一位旅行者都對這些溫基人說了一番熱情的話，以示答謝，並且跟所有人握了手，最後連手臂都變得酸痛了。

桃樂絲來到女巫的櫥櫃前，用籃子裝滿了食物，準備在路上吃。她在那裡看見了那頂金帽子。她戴在自己的頭上試了試，正好適合她的頭。她完全不知道有關這頂金帽子擁有魔力的事情，但是她發現這頂帽子非常漂亮，就決定戴著它，把自己的無邊遮陽帽放進籃子裡。

在完成旅行的準備之後，他們一行人就動身前往翡翠城了。溫基人向他們歡呼了三聲，送上許多美好的祝福。

第 14 章

長翅膀的猴子

「你為什麼不使用這頂金帽子的魔力，
把飛天猴們召喚過來呢？用不了一個鐘頭，
牠們就能把你們送到奧茲的翡翠城了。」

你們應該記得，在邪惡女巫的城堡和翡翠城之間沒有路相通，甚至連一條小路都沒有。在這四位旅行者尋找邪惡女巫的時候，是邪惡女巫先發現了他們，於是就命令飛天猴把他們給抓過來。如果要穿過大片的小黃花和豔麗雛菊，尋找回去的路，那可比他們被抓時要困難得多了。當然，他們知道必須朝太陽升起的地方一直往東走。於是他們便向著正確的方向動身了。但是到了中午時分，當太陽照在他們頭頂上時，他們無法分辨哪邊是東，哪邊是西，就這樣在廣闊無垠的田野中迷失了方向。不過他們仍舊不停地走著，一直走到了晚上。明月當空，閃耀著明亮的光芒，他們在散發著芳香的黃色花叢中躺了下來，酣睡到天亮。當然，稻草人和錫樵夫是不用睡覺的。

第二天早上，太陽躲到了烏雲後面，不過他們依舊動身趕路，就像知道應該走哪條路似的。

「如果我們一直不斷地走下去，」桃樂絲說，「我想總有一天，我們肯定會走到那個地方的。」

但是日子一天天地過去，在他們面前，除了一片深紅色的田野之外，什麼都看不見。於是稻草人發出了一些怨言。

「我們肯定是迷路了，」他說，「除非我們能重新找到那條路，然後及時趕到翡翠城，要不然我就永遠得不到我的腦袋了。」

「我也得不到我的心了，」錫樵夫說，「我似乎已經沒辦法等到跟奧茲見面的那一天了，你們必須得承認，這趟旅程實在太漫長了。」

「你們看，」膽小的獅子嗚咽地說道，「如果我們這樣走下去而得不到絲毫結果的話，我就再也沒勇氣長途跋涉了。」

這時候，桃樂絲也失去了信心。她坐在草地上，看著自己的夥伴們，他們也坐了下來看著她。托托生平第一次感到那麼疲累，甚至都不想去追逐從牠頭頂上飛過的蝴蝶了。牠吐著舌頭，喘著大口氣，看著桃樂絲，就像是在問她，接下來他們該怎樣辦。

「如果我們叫來那些田鼠，」她提議說，「牠們或許可以告訴我們該如何去翡翠城。」

「牠們肯定知道的，」稻草人叫喊著，「之前我們怎麼就沒想到呢？」

桃樂絲吹響了一隻小哨子，那是田鼠女王送給她的，分別之後她就一直掛在脖子上。不一會兒，他們就聽到了窸窸窣窣的腳步聲，很多灰色的小田鼠向她跑了過來。田鼠女王也在其中，它用急促而尖細的聲音詢問：

「朋友們，有什麼需要幫忙的嗎？」

「我們迷路了，」桃樂絲說，「你能告訴我們翡翠城在哪裡嗎？」

「沒問題，」女王回答說，「可是距離這裡很遠，因為你們一直朝相反的方向走。」這時候，田鼠女王注意到了桃樂絲的金帽子，「你為什麼不使用這頂金帽子的魔力，把飛天猴們召喚過來呢？用不了一個鐘頭，牠們就能把你們送到奧茲的翡翠城了。」

「我都不知道這頂金帽子上面還有魔力，」桃樂絲驚訝地說道，「那咒語是什麼呢？」

「全都寫在金帽子裡面了，」田鼠女王回答說，「但是，如果你們準備叫那些飛天猴來，我們就得先走了，他們滿腦袋都是惡作劇，以為捉弄我們可以得到極大的樂趣。」

「牠們會傷害我嗎？」小女孩不安地問道。

「噢，不會的。牠們必須服從戴著這頂金帽子的人，再見了！」說完，田鼠女王一溜煙地跑開不見了，其他田鼠也都緊跟在後離開了。

桃樂絲看了看金帽子的裡面，發現襯裡上面寫著一些字。她想，這些應該就是咒語了，於是她仔細地把這些說明看了一遍，然後又把金帽子戴在頭上。

「哎霹，吓霹，卡霹！」她一邊用左腳站立著，一邊念念有詞。

稻草人不知道她在幹什麼，就問她說：「你在說什麼呀？」

「兮囉，呵囉，嘿囉！」桃樂絲繼續念著，這一次，她用右腳單獨站立著。

「喂！」錫樵夫冷靜地回答說。

這時候桃樂絲雙腳站立著，唸道：「兮兮，蘇兮，兮！」咒語唸完了，隨後他們聽到一陣嘈雜的叫聲和翅膀拍動的聲音，那群飛天猴朝他們飛了過來。猴王向桃樂絲深深地鞠了個躬，問道：

「您有什麼需要？」

「我們想去翡翠城，」小女孩說，「可是我們迷了路。」

「那我們帶你們去吧。」猴王回答道。話剛說完，兩隻猴子就抬起了桃樂絲，帶著她飛走了。另外幾隻猴子帶了稻草人、錫樵夫和獅子，一隻小猴子抓住托托，跟在牠們後面，儘管這隻小狗一直拼了命地想咬牠。

剛開始，稻草人和錫樵夫嚇得膽戰心驚，因為他們還記得之前這些飛天猴是如何殘忍地對待他們。不過後來他們看出這些飛天猴並沒有想要傷害他們，於是就快活地坐著飛在空中，俯瞰著遠在他們底下的秀麗田園和樹林，好不快活。

桃樂絲坐在兩隻最大的猴子中間，其中一隻就是猴王，覺得非常舒服自在。它們用手搭成椅子的形狀，小心翼翼地不讓自己傷到桃樂絲。

她問道：「你們為什麼要聽從這頂金帽子的魔力呢？」

「這個故事說來話長，」猴王大笑著回答說，「不過我們還有段路要趕，如果你想聽的話，我就把這件事情告訴你，讓你打發時間。」

「我當然想聽。」她回答。

「從前，」猴王開始說道，「我們都是自由自在、無拘無束，幸福地生活在一片大森林中。我們在樹上飛來飛去，吃著堅果和水果，想做什麼就做什麼，不聽命於任何人。我們之中的某些弟兄非常調皮，有時會飛到地上拉扯那些沒有翅膀的動物的尾巴、追逐小鳥、用堅果砸那些行走在森林中的人。但是我們生活得無憂無慮、幸福美滿，充滿著歡聲笑語，享受著每一天每一分鐘。早在奧茲從雲端下來統治這片地方之前，我們就已經這樣生活了很多年。

　　「那時候，遠在北方的土地上住著一位非常漂亮的公主，她也是一位法力無邊的魔法師，她的所有魔法都是用來幫助人類的，從來都沒有傷害過任何好人。她的名字叫做蓋琳特，住在一座用巨大紅寶石砌成的漂亮宮殿裡。每個人都敬愛著她，然而讓她最為傷心的是她找不到一個可以得到她愛情的男人，因為所有的男人都那麼愚蠢醜陋，根本配不上這樣一位美麗又聰明的公主。不過，最終她還是找到了一個男孩，他英俊瀟灑、強壯勇敢、聰明伶俐，這些都超過了他的同齡人。蓋琳特決定等他長大成人之後，就與他結為夫婦。於是她把這個人帶到了紅寶石宮殿中，用盡她所有的法術，把他變得像所有女性心目中的白馬王子那樣強壯、善良、可愛。等到長大成人之後，奎拉拉（這是他的名字）被尊為這片土地上最英俊、聰明的男人，他的男子氣概如此強烈，蓋琳特已經深深地愛上了他，忙著準備結婚所需的每一件東西。

　　「在那個時候，我的祖父是飛天猴中的猴王，住在蓋琳特宮殿附近的森林裡。這個老傢伙喜歡開玩笑，勝過吃上一頓美味佳餚。就在婚禮舉行的前一天，我的祖父帶著牠的隨從們飛了出去，看見奎拉拉在河邊散步。他穿著一件用粉紅色絲綢和紫色天鵝絨做的衣服，顯

136

得十分雍容華貴。我祖父想看看他到底有什麼能耐，於是一聲令下，隨從們就飛了下去，抓住了奎拉拉，帶著他飛到了河水的上空，然後把他丟進河裡。

「『年輕人，游上岸來吧，』我的祖父喊道，『看看河水會不會弄髒你的衣服。』不過奎拉拉那麼聰明，當然不會不知道游泳，而他雖然享盡榮華，卻也知道該怎樣游泳，因此他哈哈大笑著浮上了水面，游到了岸邊。然而，當蓋琳特來到他身邊的時候，卻發現他的絲綢和天鵝絨衣服已經完全被河水弄髒了。

「這位公主大發雷霆，她當然知道這件事情是誰幹的。她把所有飛天猴都召集到她面前，直截了當地說，她要把他們的翅膀全都綁起來，然後像對待奎拉拉那樣懲罰他們，把他們丟進河水裡。但是我的祖父竭力為他們求饒，因為他知道，如果綁著這些飛天猴的翅膀，他們肯定會被河水給淹死的。奎拉拉也替他們說好話。因此蓋琳特最終還是赦免了他們，不過條件就是他們必須順從這頂金帽子主人的三個命令。這頂金帽子是送給奎拉拉的結婚禮物，據說公主因此而花費了半個國家的財富。我的祖父和其他猴子當然是毫不遲疑地答應了這個條件。就這樣，我們要被戴這頂金帽子的人使喚三次，不管這個人是誰都一樣。」

「那這些人都怎麼樣了呢？」桃樂絲問道，她對這個故事表現出了極大的興趣。

「奎拉拉是這頂金帽子的第一位主人，」飛天猴回答說，「他也是第一個對我們提出願望的人。因為他的新娘不想再見到我們，所以在他們結婚之後，他就把我們全都召集到森林之中，讓我們去一個永遠都不會讓公主看見我們的地方。我們當然非常樂意這麼做，因為我們都非常害怕公主。

「我們就做了這麼一件事情，直到後來這頂金帽子落到了西方邪惡女巫的手中，她命令我們把溫基人變成她的奴隸，然後又命令我們把奧茲趕出這片西方國土。現在這頂金帽子是你的了，你有權利讓我們實現你的三個願望。」

當猴王說完這個故事，桃樂絲向下眺望著，發現翡翠城那閃閃發光的綠色城牆已經出現在他們的面前。她為飛天猴們的飛行速度感到驚訝，不過很高興這段旅程終於結束了。這些奇怪的動物小心翼翼地把旅客們放在城門的前面，猴王深深地向桃樂絲鞠了個躬，然後立刻帶著他的隨從們飛走了。

「這趟旅行真是愉快啊！」小女孩說。

「是啊，而且這麼快就解決了我們的難題，」獅子回應說，「你把這頂奇妙的金帽子帶在身邊，還真是幸運呢！」

第 15 章

可怕奥兹的真面目

當然，他們每個人都以為自己將要見到
的魔法師還是之前見過的樣子，但是當
他們看了看大殿，發現裡面空無一人的
時候，他們全都驚訝不已。

這四位旅行者走到翡翠城的大門前，按下門鈴。門鈴響了好幾聲之後，門打開了，仍舊是他們之前見過的那個城門守衛替他們開的門。

「哎呀，你們怎麼回來了？」他驚訝地問道。

「你不是都看見我們了嗎？」稻草人回答說。

「我以為你們已經去找西方邪惡女巫了。」

「我們確實去找過她了。」稻草人說。

「她又放了你們？」城門守衛疑惑地問道。

「她不得不放，因為她溶化了。」稻草人解釋道。

「溶化了！那可真是個好消息，」城門守衛說，「是誰把她溶化的？」

「是桃樂絲。」獅子勇敢地說道。

「這真是太好了！」城門守衛歡呼了起來，他深深地向桃樂絲鞠了躬。

接著，像上次一樣，他帶領著這群人來到他的小屋，從大箱子裡拿出眼鏡給他們戴上，鎖好。然後，他們穿過大門，走進翡翠城。人們聽城門守衛說桃樂絲把西方邪惡女巫給溶化了，紛紛跑過來圍住了這幾位旅行者，這一大堆人跟著他們來到了奧茲的王宮。

　　守在門前的仍舊是那個留著綠鬍子的士兵，不過這一次他毫不猶豫地就把他們帶了進去。依舊是那位漂亮的綠衣女孩招待了他們，把他們帶到各自原先住過的房間，讓他們好好休息，等待偉大的奧茲召見他們。

　　綠鬍子士兵直接把桃樂絲和她的夥伴們殺死邪惡女巫，回到翡翠城的消息告訴了奧茲，但奧茲並沒有回應什麼。他們以為偉大的魔法師會即刻召見他們，但是這位魔法師並沒有這麼做。第二天他們也沒有得到任何消息，第三天、第四天仍舊是杳無音信。這種等待顯得無聊而令人厭倦，最後他們開始責怪起奧茲，埋怨他讓他們遭受了那麼多苦難，經歷了那麼多困苦，如今卻如此冷漠地對待他們。稻草人請綠衣女孩再為奧茲通報一聲，說如果再不讓他們立刻見到他，他們就要召喚飛天猴來幫忙，看看他到底是不是個守信用的人。這個魔法師一聽到這個口信，心裡害怕得不得了，於是下令讓他們第二天早上九點零四分到大殿去見他。他曾經在西方跟飛天猴們打過一次交道，這輩子都不想再見到牠們了。

　　這四位旅行者度過了一個不眠之夜，每個人都想著奧茲答應給他們的禮物。桃樂絲只睡了一下，她夢見自己回到了堪薩斯州，艾姆嬸嬸對她說，看到小侄女平安回家，她真是高興極了。

　　第二天早上剛到九點，綠鬍子士兵就來找他們了，四分鐘之後，他們全都走進了偉大的奧茲的大殿。

　　當然，他們每個人都以為自己將要見到的魔法師還是之前見過的樣子，但是當他們看了看大殿，發現裡面空無一人的時候，他們全都驚訝不已。他們緊挨著彼此，站在門口附近，因為空蕩蕩的大殿裡

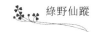

寂靜無聲，這比他們上次見到奧茲時的各種形象都更讓他們害怕。

這時，他們聽到了一個聲音，似乎是從大圓頂附近傳來的，那聲音一本正經地說道：

「我是奧茲，偉大而可怕的奧茲。你們為什麼來找我？」

他們看了看房間裡的每一個角落，還是一個人都沒有，桃樂絲便問：「你在哪裡呀？」

「我無所不在，」那個聲音說，「但是凡人的眼睛是看不到我的。現在我坐到寶座上去，你們可以跟我說話了。」真的，這時候，那個聲音似乎直接從寶座那邊傳了過來。於是他們就向寶座走了過去，站成一排。桃樂絲說：

「奧茲大人，我們是來找你兌現你對我們的承諾的。」

「什麼承諾？」奧茲問。

「你答應過我們，只要殺死了邪惡女巫，你就送我回堪薩斯。」小女孩說。

「你答應過我，要給我腦袋的。」稻草人說。

「你答應過我，要給我一顆心的。」錫樵夫說。

「你答應過我，要給我勇氣的。」膽小的獅子說。

「邪惡女巫真的被你們殺了嗎？」那個聲音問道，桃樂絲察覺到那個聲音有點顫抖。

「是啊，」她回答說，「我用一桶水把她給溶化了。」

「我的天哪，」那個聲音叫道，「真是太突然了！好吧，明天再來找我，我得花點時間好好想一想。」

「你已經想很久了。」錫片樵夫生氣地說道。

「我們一天都不能再等了。」稻草人說。

「你必須信守對我們的承諾！」桃樂絲叫道。

獅子心想嚇嚇這個魔法師也不錯，於是就對他大吼了一聲，那吼聲如此兇猛而可怕，托托驚慌失措地跳開，撞到了一塊放在牆角的屏風。屏風匡噹一聲倒在地上，他們都往那邊看了過去，那一刻他們全都嚇壞了。他們看見屏風後面藏著一個矮小的男人，腦袋光溜溜的沒有頭髮，臉上佈滿了皺紋，看上去跟他們一樣驚訝。錫樵夫舉起了斧頭，朝那個矮小的男人衝了過去，叫道：「你是誰？」

「我是奧茲，偉大而可怕的奧茲，」矮小的男人顫抖地說道，「但是別砍我——求你了！——你們要我做什麼我都答應。」

這幾位朋友看著他，心中滿是驚訝與震驚。

「我以為奧茲是顆巨大的頭顱。」桃樂絲說。

「我以為奧茲是個漂亮的小姐。」稻草人說。

「我以為奧茲是頭可怕的野獸。」錫片樵夫說。

「我以為奧茲是團燃燒的火球。」獅子叫道。

「不，你們都錯了，」矮小的男人溫順地說道，「那些都是我偽裝的。」

「偽裝的！」桃樂絲大聲叫道，「難道你不是偉大的魔法師嗎？」

「噓，親愛的，」他說，「別叫得這麼大聲，會被人偷聽到，到時候我就完蛋了。別人都以為我是個偉大的魔法師。」

「所以你不是？」她問。

「完全沾不上邊，親愛的，我只是個非常普通的人。」

「你不只是個普通人，」稻草人傷心地說道，「你還是個大騙子。」

「沒錯！」矮小的男人一邊說著，一邊揉搓著雙手，似乎這樣可以讓他安定一些，「我是個騙子。」

「但這真是糟透了，」錫樵夫說，「我該如何得到我的心呢？」

「還有我的勇氣？」獅子問。

「還有我的腦袋？」稻草人一邊用袖子擦眼淚，一邊哭著問。

「我親愛的朋友們，」奧茲說，「我求你們就別提這些小事情了。

為我著想一下吧，現在我的事情穿幫了，這個麻煩真是可怕。」

「沒有人知道你是騙子嗎？」桃樂絲問。

「除了你們四個之外就沒人知道了——當然還有我自己，」奧茲回答說，「那麼久以來，我騙過了每一個人，還以為這件事永遠都不會被人發現。我讓你們進我的大殿就已經鑄成了大錯。通常我連自己的臣民都不會接見，因此他們都以為我非常可怕。」

「但是，我不明白，」桃樂絲有些困惑地說道，「你接見我的時候為什麼會變成一顆大腦袋呢？」

「那是我的一個詭計，」奧茲回答道，「請到這邊來，我把所有事情都告訴你們。」

他帶路走進一間位於大殿後面的小房間裡，其他人跟在他後面。他指著其中一個角落，那裡放著一個巨大的腦袋，是用很多厚紙板做的，上面還仔細地畫著一張臉。

「我用一根鐵絲把這個腦袋從天花板上吊下來，」奧茲說，「我就站在屏風後面，拉著一根繩子，讓眼睛和嘴巴活動起來。」

「可那個聲音又是怎麼回事呢？」桃樂絲問。

「噢，我會口技，」矮小的男人說，「我可以隨心所欲地讓我的聲音從任何一個地方發出來，因此你會覺得那個聲音是從腦袋裡發出來的。這裡還有另外一些用來欺騙你們的道具。」他給稻草人看了他裝扮成漂亮小姐時穿的衣服以及戴的面具。錫樵夫發現他裝扮成可怕的野獸時用的道具只不過是把許多皮縫在一起，然後用一些木條把輪廓撐起來。至於那個燃燒的火球，那也是從天花板上吊下來的，其實就是一個氣球，但是在上面澆上汽油之後，它就熊熊地燃燒起來了。

稻草人說：「你真該為自己這種騙人的行為感到羞愧。」

「是的——我確實感到很羞愧，」小老頭傷心地回答，「但是我也只能這麼做。坐下來吧，這裡有很多張椅子。我把我的故事告訴你們。」

於是他們坐了下來，聽他講起故事：

「我出生在奧馬哈——」

「哎呀，那裡離堪薩斯不遠！」桃樂絲叫道。

「是的，但是距離這裡就遠得多了，」他一邊朝她傷心地搖搖頭，一邊說道，「等我長大之後，我就成了一個口技師，接受一位大師的正規訓練。我可以模仿任何鳥類和野獸的叫聲。」說到這裡他學了幾聲貓叫，托托豎起了耳朵，四處張望著，想看看這隻貓在哪。「過了一段時間，」奧茲接著說道，「我就厭倦了口技，學會了駕駛氣球。」

「那是幹什麼的？」桃樂絲問。

「在馬戲團表演節目前，有個人會坐在氣球裡，升到空中，吸引一票人過來，讓他們付錢看馬戲表演。」他解釋說。

「噢，」桃樂絲說，「我明白了。」

「有一天，我坐在氣球裡，升到了空中，可是繩索纏在一起，我就沒辦法下去。氣球飛到了雲層上端，遇到了一股氣流，然後被帶到了好多好多英里之外的地方。我在空中飛了整整一天一夜，到了第二天早晨，我醒過來，發現氣球飛行在一個陌生而美麗的田野上空。

「氣球慢慢地降到地面上，我完全沒有受傷。但是我發現自己被一群陌生人團團圍住了，他們見我從雲層中而來，以為我是個偉大的魔法師。當然，我沒有向他們表明自己的真實身份，因為他們都很怕我，我讓他們幹什麼，他們都會完成。

「我只是為了消遣自己，也是為了讓這些好心人有事可忙，我就命令他們建造了這座城市，以及我的宮殿。他們個個都心甘情願、勤奮地工作。之後，我想，既然這片田野這麼綠意盎然，如此山清水秀，我就叫它翡翠城好了，為了讓這座城市更加符合這個名字的意境，我就讓每個人都戴上綠色眼鏡，這樣他們見到的每一件東西都是綠色的了。」

「但是，這裡的東西不都是綠色的嗎？」桃樂絲問。

「跟其他城市一樣，並非都是綠色的，」奧茲回答，「但是，如果你們戴上了綠色眼鏡，那麼你們所見到的每一樣東西當然都變成綠色的囉。很多年前，翡翠城就已經建成了，因為氣球帶我來這裡時，我還是個年輕人，如今卻已經是個老頭子了。但是，這麼多年來，我的子民們一直都戴著綠色眼鏡，因此他們之中的多數人都相信這真的是一座翡翠城，一個美麗的地方，有許多珠寶和稀有金屬，以及所有可以讓人們幸福的美好事物。我善待著這裡的每個人，而他們也很喜歡我。但是自從這座宮殿建成之後，我就把自己關在裡面，任何人都不接見。

「最讓我感到害怕的就是那些女巫了，因為，我根本就沒有魔力，而且我很快就發現，那些女巫真的可以做出一些令人稱奇的事情。在這片土地上共有四個女巫，她們統治著東南西北四方的人民。幸運的是，南北兩方的女巫都是善良的，我知道她們不會對我造成傷害；但是東西兩方的女巫都非常邪惡，只要讓她們知道我的魔力不及她們，她們肯定就會加害於我。就這樣，我戰戰兢兢地生活了好多年。因此，你可以想像得到，當我聽說你家的房子掉下來壓死了東方邪惡女巫時，我心裡有多高興。當你們來找我時，我心想只要你們能剷除另外一個邪惡女巫，我願意答應你們任何請求。但是，如今你已經把她溶化了，可我卻要慚愧地對你們說我無法兌現自己的諾言。」

「我看你就是個十足的大壞蛋！」桃樂絲說。

「噢，不，親愛的，我其實是個心地善良的好人。但是我必須承認，我是個非常糟糕的魔法師。」

「那你就沒辦法給我腦袋了？」稻草人問說。

「你根本就不需要腦袋，每天你都能學到新的東西。一個嬰兒他雖然有腦袋，但是卻什麼都不懂。只有經驗才能給你帶來知識，你在這個世上活的時間越長，你的經驗肯定就越多。」

「這話也許說得不假，」稻草人說，「但是，除非你給我腦袋，要不然我會非常生氣的。」

這個偽裝的魔法師仔細地看著他。

「好吧，」他嘆了口氣，說道，「我說過，我不是什麼了不起的魔法師，但是，如果明天早晨你過來找我的話，我會把腦子塞進你的頭裡。但是我不能告訴你該如何使用腦袋，你必須得自己找到方法。」

「噢，謝謝你！謝謝你！」稻草人大聲叫道，「不用怕，我會自己學會使用頭腦的。」

「可是我的勇氣呢？」獅子焦急地問道。

「我想你的勇氣已經夠多了，」奧茲回答說，「你缺乏的就是自信。所有生物在面對危險時都會感到害怕，而真正的勇氣就是在害怕的時候，你仍舊迎頭面對危險，而你擁有許多這樣的勇氣。」

「或許我的確是有，但我還是害怕，」獅子說，「除非你能給我可以讓人忘記害怕的勇氣，要不然我會非常生氣的。」

「好吧，明天我就會給你這種勇氣的。」奧茲回答說。

「那我的心呢？」錫樵夫問道。

「噢，這個嘛，」奧茲回答說，「我想你不應該要心的。心讓很多人都過得不開心。如果你知道了這一點，就會覺得自己沒有心是多麼幸運了。」

「那應該只是人們的看法不同而已，」錫樵夫說，「至於我，只要你能給我一顆心，我願意毫無怨言地承擔所有不幸。」

「好吧，」奧茲順從地回答道，「明天你來找我，我會給你一顆心的。我已經假扮魔法師這麼多年了，再多扮一會也無妨。」

「那麼，」桃樂絲說，「我該如何回到堪薩斯州呢？」

「至於這一點，我們應該好好想想，」矮小的男人回答道，「給我兩三天的時間考慮一下，我會儘量找出辦法讓你穿過那片沙漠。在這期間，我會像貴賓般款待你們，你們在我的王宮居住期間，我的僕人們會伺候你們，聽從你們的任何吩咐。不過，作為我這些幫助的回報，我只求你們答應我一件事：保守這個秘密，不能告訴任何人我是個騙子。」

他們答應對這件事情保持沉默，興高采烈地回到了各自的房間。甚至連桃樂絲都希望那個「偉大而可怕的騙子」，這是她對奧茲的稱呼，可以找到一個送她回堪薩斯的辦法，如果他能讓此成真，她願意原諒他所做的一切。

第 16 章

大騙子的魔術

奧茲獨自一個人留在大殿裡，面帶著笑
容，心裡想著，他成功地把稻草人、錫樵
夫和膽小的獅子想要的東西給了他們。

第二天早晨，稻草人對他的朋友們說：「恭喜我吧。我終於要去奧茲那裡拿我的腦袋了。等我回來的時候，我就會跟其他人一樣健全了。」

「我一直都喜歡你原來的樣子。」桃樂絲天真地說道。

「你真善良，連稻草人的樣子都喜歡，」他回答說，「不過，等你聽到我那新腦袋想出的絕妙想法之後，肯定會更加看重我的。」他說完之後，開心地跟所有人告別，走到了大殿，敲了敲門。

「進來。」奧茲說。

稻草人走了進去，矮小的男人正坐在窗子旁邊沉思。

「我來要我的腦袋了。」稻草人有些侷促不安地說。

「噢，是啊。請坐到那邊的椅子上吧，」奧茲回答說，「不過很抱歉，我得先把你的頭拿下來。這樣我才能把腦袋放在正確的位置。」

「沒關係，」稻草人說，「你儘管隨意摘下我的頭吧，只要等你把它裝回去的時候，能比原來的好就行了。」

於是，魔法師摘下了他的腦袋，騰出裡面的稻草。然後他跑進屋裡，拿出許多麥麩，裡面混雜著大量的針，他把這些東西徹底攪勻之後，就把它們倒進稻草人的腦袋裡，再用稻草塞滿空隙，把那些東西固定起來。

當他把稻草人的腦袋重新接回到他身上的時候，他對稻草人說：「從此以後，你就是一個偉大的人物了，因為我給了你一顆嶄新的頭腦。」

稻草人實現了他最大的願望，既開心，又自豪，興奮地感謝奧茲，然後回到朋友的身邊。

桃樂絲好奇地看著他。他的頭頂顯得特別突出。

「你覺得怎麼樣？」她問。

「我真的覺得自己變聰明了，」他認真地回答道，「等我習慣了這個腦袋之後，我就會知道所有事情了。」

「為什麼這些針會戳到你腦袋外面呢？」錫樵夫問道。

「那證明了他的腦袋非常敏捷。」獅子這麼說道。

「好了，我要去奧茲那裡拿我的心了。」錫樵夫說。於是他來到了大殿，敲了敲門。

「進來。」奧茲說。錫樵夫便走了進去，說道：「我來拿我的心了。」

「很好，」矮小男人回答，「但是我得先在你的胸膛上割出一個洞，這樣我才能把你的心放在正確的位置。希望我不會因此而傷害到你。」

「噢，不會，」錫樵夫回答說，「我根本不會有感覺的。」

於是，奧茲拿來一把錫匠的大剪刀，在錫樵夫胸膛的左邊剪了一個方形的小洞。然後，他來到衣櫃面前，拿出了一顆非常漂亮的心，完全是用絲綢織成的，裡面塞滿了木屑 。

　　「這顆心是不是很漂亮？」他問。

　　「是，確實漂亮！」錫樵夫滿懷著興奮回答道，「但這是一顆善良的心嗎？」

　　「噢，非常善良！」奧茲回答說。他把這顆心放進錫樵夫的胸膛，然後，在剛才割開的地方，用一片小錫片把它重新焊接起來。

　　「好了，」他說，「現在你有一顆任何人都會覺得自豪的心了。很抱歉，我不得不在你的胸膛上焊一個補釘，這的確是不可避免的。」

　　「用不著理會這個補釘，」錫樵夫高興地道，「我要大大地感激你，永遠都不會忘記你為我做的好事。」

　　「不要這麼客氣。」奧茲回答說。

　　然後錫樵夫回到朋友們那裡，他們都為他的好運祝福。

　　這時候，獅子也走到了大殿，牠敲了敲門。

　　「進來。」奧茲說。

　　獅子一走進去就開門見山地說：「我來拿我的勇氣了。」

「很好，」矮小的男人回答說，「我會給你拿來的。」

他來到櫥櫃的旁邊，伸手從高處的架子上拿來一個綠色的方形瓶子，然後把裡面的藥水倒在一個雕刻精美的綠色金盤子裡。他把這盤東西拿到膽小的獅子面前，獅子聞了一下，似乎並喜歡這個味道。

「喝下去吧。」

「這是什麼東西？」獅子問道。

奧茲回答說：「這個嘛，如果這東西進到你的身體裡面就會變成勇氣。當然，你應該知道勇氣通常都是在身體裡面的，因此在你把這東西喝下去之前，它還不能被稱為勇氣。我建議你儘快把它喝下去。」

獅子沒有多做猶豫，把這盤子藥水喝個精光。

「現在你覺得怎麼樣？」奧茲問。

「充滿了勇氣！」獅子回答說，然後興高采烈地回到了朋友們的身邊，把自己的好運告訴他們。

奧茲獨自一個人留在大殿裡，面帶著笑容，心裡想著，他成功地把稻草人、錫樵夫和膽小的獅子想要的東西給了他們。「這些人總讓我做一些明知辦不到的事，我又怎麼能不當騙子呢？」要滿足稻草人、錫樵夫和膽小的獅子，讓他們開心，是輕而易舉的事，因為他們以為我無所不能。但是要送桃樂絲回堪薩斯州，那就不能只是空想了，我還不知道該如何辦到呢。」

第 17 章

熱氣球飛上天了

氣球漸漸地膨脹了起來，升到了空中，
到後來那只籃子就只是輕輕地碰到地面而已。

三天過去了，桃樂絲沒有從奧茲那裡聽到任何消息。雖然她的朋友們都非常開心與滿足，可是這種日子對這個小女孩來說，實在是令人憂愁。稻草人告訴他們說，他的腦袋裡滿是奇妙的想法，可是又說不出來是什麼，因為他知道除了自己之外，誰都無法理解這些想法。錫樵夫走路的時候，會覺得自己的心在胸腔內跳動。而且他還告訴桃樂絲說，他發現這顆心要比他還是肉身時擁有的那顆心更加善良，更加溫柔。獅子說他已經不怕這個世界上的任何東西了，並且可以欣然地去迎戰一大群人，或是十來隻兇猛的卡力達。

在這幾個人之中，除了桃樂絲以外，個個都是心滿意足的。因此，桃樂絲就比以往更加渴望回去堪薩斯州了。

到了第四天，奧茲召喚了她，這真是令她喜出望外。當她來到大殿時，奧茲高興地對她說道：

「坐吧，我親愛的孩子，我想我找到讓你離開這個國度的方法了。」

「可以回到堪薩斯州嗎？」她急切地問道。

「這個嘛，我無法肯定是否可以回到堪薩斯州，」奧茲說，「因為我根本不知道這個地方在哪裡。但是首先要做的事情就是穿過這片大沙漠，到時候你就可以輕而易舉地找到回家的路了。」

「我要如何才能穿過這沙漠呢？」她問道。

「噢，我會把我的想法告訴你的，」小老頭說，「你知道，我是乘坐著氣球來到這個地方的。你也是被龍捲風帶到這裡來的，因此，我相信穿過這片沙漠最好的辦法就是從天上飄過去。如今，我已經沒這種魔力製造出一陣龍捲風了，不過我把這件事仔細想了想，我想我可以做出一個氣球來。」

「要怎麼做？」桃樂絲問道。

「氣球是用絲綢做成的，」奧茲說，「上面塗了一層膠水，可以避免裡面的氣體跑出來。這宮殿之中有許多的絲綢，因此做出一個氣球並不難。但是在這整個國家之中卻沒有可以用來填充氣球的氫氣，讓它可以飄在空中。」

「如果氣球飄不起來，那對我們來說就毫無用處了呀。」桃樂絲說。

「是的，」奧茲回答說，「不過還有另外一個方法可以讓它飄起來，那就是用熱氣灌到氣球裡，可是熱氣不如氫氣有效，如果氣體冷卻，氣球就會掉落在沙漠中，我們就會迷失方向。」

「我們！」女孩子大聲叫道，「你要和我一起離開嗎？」

「是啊，當然囉，」奧茲回答說，「我已經厭倦了這種騙子的生活。如果我走出這個宮殿，我的子民們就會馬上發現我不是魔法師，然後他們就會因為我欺騙了他們而感到生氣。我就只能整天待在這些房間裡，真是無聊透頂。我寧願跟你一起回堪薩斯州，重新回到馬戲團裡。」

「我很高興能有你這樣的同伴。」桃樂絲說。

「謝謝你，」他回答說，「那現在我們就開始做氣球吧，你能幫我把這些絲綢縫在一起嗎？」

於是桃樂絲拿出針線，等奧茲把絲綢裁剪成合適大小之後，這個小女孩就把這些布整齊地縫在一起。先是一塊淺綠色的布，然後是深綠色的，接著是翡翠綠的。奧茲有一個奇妙的想法，他想用不同顏色的綢布做出一個五顏六色的氣球。他們花了三天的時間把所有的綢布都縫在一起，完成之後，就變成了一個二十多尺長的大型綠袋子。

接著奧茲就在這袋子裡面塗上一層薄膠，讓它密不透風，完成這一步之後，他就宣佈氣球已經完成。

他說：「不過我們還得找一個籃子來，可以讓我們坐在裡面。」於是他差遣那個綠鬍子的士兵，找來了一個用來放衣服的大籃子。奧茲用許多繩子把這個籃子緊緊地綁在氣球下面。

當一切準備就緒之後，奧茲就頒佈通知，說他準備去拜訪一位住在雲端的大師兄。這個消息迅速地傳遍了全城，每個人都跑來爭相目睹這個神奇的景象。

奧茲下令把氣球拿到宮殿的前面，人們全都好奇地看著它。錫樵夫砍來了一大堆的木柴，這時候正在生火，奧茲把氣球的底部放在火堆上面，使得火堆產生的熱氣全都跑進這個絲綢布袋中。氣球漸漸地膨脹了起來，升到了空中，到後來那只籃子就只是輕輕地碰到地面而已。

然後奧茲就走進籃子裡，用洪亮的聲音對所有的百姓說道：

「現在，我要出門訪問了。在我離開的這段日子裡，就由稻草人掌管這個國家。我命令你們像服從我這樣去服從他。」

這時候，氣球用力地拉扯著把它固定在地上的繩子，因為裡面的氣體是熱的，使得裡面的氣體比外面的輕很多，熱氣使勁地將氣球升到了空中。

「快來，桃樂絲！」魔法師叫道，「趕快上來，要不然氣球就要飛走了。」

「我找不到托托，」桃樂絲回答說，她不想丟下自己的小狗。托托跑到了人群之中，追著一隻小貓亂吠，最後桃樂絲終於找到牠。她一把抓住牠，向氣球跑去。

就在她距離氣球不過幾步路，奧茲伸出手來想要幫助她跨進籃子的時候，「蹦」的一聲！繩子斷了，氣球升到了空中，卻沒有帶走桃樂絲。

「回來！」她大聲叫道，「我也要去！」

「親愛的，我回不去了，」奧茲從籃子裡喊道，「再見！」

「再見！」所有人都叫喊著，每一雙眼睛都注視著那位魔法師乘坐的籃子，看著這只氣球越飛越高，升到了空中。

這是所有人最後一次見到奧茲這位神奇的魔法師，雖然我們都知道，他或許已經平安地到達了奧馬哈，但是這裡的每個人都熱切地思念著他，相互訴說著：「奧茲永遠都是我們的朋友。他在這裡的時

165

候，為我們建造了這座翡翠城，如今他走了，留下這位聰明的稻草人
來領導我們。」

　　翡翠城的百姓失去了這位神奇的魔法師，他們為此傷心了很久，
遲遲無法得到安慰。

第 18 章

出發去南方

「有一條路直通南方，但是據說這條路
上危機四伏。森林裡有野獸，還有一個
奇怪的種族，他們不喜歡陌生人經過他
們的領土。因此，奎德林人從沒有來過
翡翠城。」

桃樂絲再次錯失了回到堪薩斯州的希望，傷心地哭了起來。但是當她把這件事情全盤考慮之後，她反而慶幸自己沒能乘上氣球。她同樣為奧茲的離開感到難過，她的同伴們也是如此。

錫樵夫來到她的身邊，說：「那個人給了我一顆心，如果我沒有為他的離開而感到難過的話，那我實在是太忘恩負義了。奧茲走了，我真想大哭一場，如果你願意好心地幫我擦乾眼淚的話，那樣我就不怕生鏽了。」

「樂意至極。」桃樂絲回答，立刻拿出一條手帕。之後錫樵夫哭了好幾分鐘，桃樂絲仔細地看著流出來的眼淚，用手帕擦乾。等錫樵夫哭完之後，他又非常親切地感謝著桃樂絲，然後用那個鑲嵌著珠寶的油罐，給自己全身上下抹油，以防發生不測。

如今翡翠城由稻草人執政，雖然他不是魔法師，但是百姓們都以他為榮，他們說：「因為在這個世界上，沒有哪個城市是由一個稻草人掌管的。」就他們所知道的而言，這話倒是說得不假。

在奧茲乘坐熱氣球離開的第二天早晨，這四個旅行者聚集在大殿裡，商量著事情。稻草人坐在偉大的王位上，其他幾個則恭敬地站在他面前。

「其實我們也沒那麼不幸，」這位新國王說道，「因為這座宮殿和翡翠城全都是我們的了，我們喜歡做什麼就做什麼。我回想起自己在不久之前，還被束縛在一根竹竿上面，插在農民的稻田裡，可現在，我卻成為了這個美麗城市的領導者，對於自己的命運，我感到非常滿足。」

「我也非常滿意自己這顆新的心，」錫樵夫說，「真的，這是我在這世界上唯一需要的東西了。」

「至於我，雖然我不是最勇敢的，但只要我知道自己比其他野獸更加勇敢，我就心滿意足了。」獅子謙遜地說道。

「如果桃樂絲願意住在翡翠城的話，」稻草人接著說道，「我們就可以幸福地生活在一起了。」

「但是我不想住在這裡，」桃樂絲叫道，「我想回堪薩斯州，跟艾姆嬸嬸和亨利叔叔住在一起。」

「這樣的話，我們該怎麼辦呢？」錫樵夫問。

稻草人決定要好好想一想，他努力地思考著，連頭上的針都戳到了腦袋的外面。最後他說：

「為什麼不把飛天猴們召喚過來，讓牠們把你帶出沙漠呢？」

「我怎麼從來都沒想到呢！」桃樂絲興奮地說道，「就這麼辦。我現在就去拿金帽子。」

當她把金帽子拿到大殿，念完咒語之後，馬上就有一大群飛天猴從打開著的窗子飛了進來，站在她的身旁。

「這是你第二次召喚我們了，」猴王一邊說著，一邊對小女孩鞠了個躬，「您有什麼吩咐呢？」

桃樂絲說：「我想讓你們帶我飛回堪薩斯州。」

171

但是猴王搖了搖頭。

　　「那可辦不到，」他說，「我們只屬於這片國土，不能離開這裡。在堪薩斯州一直都不存在飛天猴，而且我想將來也肯定不會有，因為飛天猴不屬於那個地方。只要是我們能力所及，不管用什麼方法，我們都很樂意為你效勞。但是我們不能穿越沙漠。再見了！」

　　猴王又鞠了個躬，張開翅膀，帶領他的人馬從窗子飛了出去。

　　桃樂絲失望得都快要哭出來了。

　　「飛天猴們幫不了我，」她說，「我白白浪費了一次金帽子的魔力。」

　　「這實在是太糟糕了！」心地善良的錫樵夫說道。

　　稻草人又想了想，他的腦袋可怕地突了起來，桃樂絲擔心它會爆炸。

　　「我們把那個綠鬍子士兵找來，」他說，「問問他有什麼建議。」

　　因此，那個士兵被召喚了過來，他膽怯地走進大殿，奧茲在這裡的時候，從來都沒讓他踏進過這扇門。

　　「這個小女孩想要穿過沙漠，」稻草人對士兵說，「有什麼辦法可以辦到呢？」

　　「我不敢肯定，」士兵回答說，「因為從沒有人走出過這片沙漠，除非是奧茲本人。」

「難道沒有人可以幫我了嗎？」桃樂絲真心誠意地問道。

「或許格琳達可以。」他建議說。

「誰是格琳達？」稻草人詢問道。

「她是南方女巫，是所有女巫之中法力最最高強的，她統治著奎德林。而且，她的城堡就在沙漠旁邊，因此她可能知道走出這片沙漠的辦法。」

「格琳達是個善良女巫，對嗎？」小女孩問道。

「奎德林人都說她心地善良，」士兵說，「她對每個人都非常和善。我還聽說格琳達是個美若天仙的婦人，雖然她的年紀已經很大了，不過她懂得如何永保青春。」

「我要如何去她的城堡呢？」

「有一條路直通南方，」他回答說，「但是據說這條路上危機四伏。森林裡有野獸，還有一個奇怪的種族，他們不喜歡陌生人經過他們的領土。因此，奎德林人從沒有來過翡翠城。」

士兵說完之後就退了下去，稻草人說：「看來，最好的辦法就只能是桃樂絲不顧一切危險，前往南方，尋求格琳達的幫助。因為，當然啦，如果桃樂絲住在這裡，她就永遠無法回到堪薩斯州了。」

「你得再想一想。」錫樵夫說。

「我已經想過了。」稻草人說。

「我跟桃樂絲一起去，」獅子說，「因為我已經厭倦了你的城市，渴望著回到森林，回到我的故鄉。你知道，我是一隻真正的野獸。況且，桃樂絲也需要有人來保護她。」

「那倒沒錯，」錫樵夫同意道，「或許我的斧頭對她有用，所以，我也跟她一起出發去南方。」

「那我們什麼時候出發？」稻草人問。

「你也去嗎？」他們一臉驚訝地問道。

「當然啦。要不是桃樂絲，我就永遠得不到腦袋了。她把我從稻田裡的竹竿上拔了下來，帶我來到翡翠城，因此我的好運都應該歸功於她，在她回到堪薩斯州之前，我永遠都不會離開她的。」

「謝謝你們，」桃樂絲感激地說道，「你們對我太好了，不過我想要盡快動身。」

「我們明天一早就出發，」稻草人回答說，「我們現在就去準備一下，這將是一趟漫長的旅行。」

第 19 章

怪樹的攻擊

帶頭的稻草人終於發現了一棵大樹，枝
繁葉茂，樹底下有足夠的空間可以讓這
群人穿過去。

第二天早晨，桃樂絲吻別了漂亮的綠衣女孩，他們每個人都跟綠鬍子士兵握了握手，士兵一直把他們送到了城門口。當城門守衛再次見到他們，得知他們要離開這座美麗的城市，去招惹新的麻煩時，他驚訝不已。不過他還是立刻摘下了他們的眼鏡，放回綠箱子中，並且給他們送上了美好的祝福。

「你是我們新的統治者，」他對稻草人說道，「因此你必須盡快回到這裡。」

「如果可以的話，我肯定會盡快回來，」稻草人回答說，「但是，首先我必須幫助桃樂絲回到她的故鄉。」

至於桃樂絲，她跟好脾氣的城門守衛做了最後的告別，說道：

「在你們這座美麗的城市中，我受到了友好的款待，所有人都對我很好。我說不出自己有多麼感謝你們。」

「親愛的，那就別說了，」他回答，「我們應該讓你留下來的，不過既然你想回堪薩斯州，我希望你能找到辦法。」他打開外城牆的大門，他們走出城門，開始了新的旅程。

這群人朝南方走去，明媚的陽光照耀著他們。他們個個神采奕奕，一起歡笑，一起閒聊。桃樂絲又一次燃燒起回家的希望，稻草人和錫樵夫很樂意為她服務。至於獅子，牠快活地呼吸著新鮮空氣，為自己重新回到田野之中而興奮地搖晃著尾巴。而托托在他們的身邊奔跑著，追趕著飛蛾和蝴蝶，愉快地叫著。

「我完全無法適應城市生活，」當他們以輕快的步伐向前走時，獅子說，「自從住在那座城裡之後，我都瘦一圈了，現在我渴望有機會可以向別的野獸們展現我有多勇敢。」

這時候，他們轉過身來，最後看了一眼翡翠城。他們只能望見綠色城牆後面那許許多多的塔樓和教堂尖頂，以及高出所有建築的奧茲宮殿的塔尖和圓屋頂。

「其實奧茲也不算是個壞魔法師。」錫樵夫說，他感覺到自己的心在胸膛裡怦怦跳動。

「他知道該如何給我腦袋，而且還是一個非常聰明的腦袋。」稻草人說。

「如果奧茲的勇氣和他給我的一樣大，」獅子接著說道，「他就是一個勇敢的人了。」

桃樂絲什麼也沒說，雖然奧茲沒能兌現他所許下的承諾，但是他已經盡力了，因此她原諒了奧茲。正如奧茲所說的那樣，即使他是個說謊的魔法師，他仍舊是一個好人。

旅程的第一天，他們穿過了從翡翠城四周延伸出來的綠色田野和鮮豔花叢。當晚，他們就睡在草地上，繁星閃耀，他們睡得相當安穩。

第二天早晨，他們繼續趕路，來到了一片茂密的森林，完全沒有路可以繞過去，因為這片樹林似乎是從左右兩邊延伸開來，一望無際。他們擔心會迷路，不敢改變行進的方向。因此他們決定在這裡找個最容易進入森林的地方。

帶頭的稻草人終於發現了一棵大樹，枝繁葉茂，樹底下有足夠的空間可以讓這群人穿過去。於是他向那棵樹走了過去，但是正當他走到最前面的樹枝下時，它們都彎曲下來纏住他，把他舉到空中，倒栽蔥似的丟回到其他旅行者中間。

這樣根本傷害不到稻草人，但是當桃樂絲扶他起來的時候，他感覺到頭暈目眩，這令他驚訝不已。

「這邊樹叢中有另外一個空隙。」獅子叫道。

「讓我先去試試看，」稻草人說，「就算把我丟出來，我也不會受傷的。」他一邊說著，一邊走向另外一棵樹，但是樹枝們立刻抓住了他，又把他丟了回來。

「真奇怪啊，」桃樂絲喊道，「我們該怎麼辦？」

「這些樹似乎故意跟我們作對，阻擋我們的路。」獅子說道。

「我想應該讓我去試試看。」錫樵夫說著，舉起他的斧頭，走向第一棵粗暴對待過稻草人的樹。當一根大樹枝彎下來抓他時，錫樵夫兇狠地將它砍成了兩段。此時，那棵樹像是感到了疼痛，搖動著所有樹枝。錫樵夫從樹底下安全地走了過去。

「來吧，」他對同伴們叫喊道，「快點！」

他們全都跑向前去，毫髮無傷地從樹下穿了過去，只有托托，它被一根小樹枝抓住了，不停地吠著。不過錫樵夫迅速砍下了那根樹枝，救出了這隻小狗。

　　森林中的其他樹木都沒有擋住他們的去路，因此他們確定只有第一排的樹木才會彎下樹枝，或許它們就是這片森林的員警，擁有這種神奇的本領，防止陌生人的進入。

　　四個旅行者輕鬆自在地穿行在樹林中，一直走到樹林的邊界。這時候，他們驚訝地發現前面有一道高牆，像是用白瓷堆砌而成的，牆面非常光滑，就像盤子的表面一樣，而且比他們的頭還要高出許多。

　　桃樂絲問：「我們現在該怎麼辦？」

　　「我來搭一個梯子，」錫樵夫說，「我們肯定要從這牆上爬過去。」

第 20 章

精緻的白瓷城

「那樣一點都不會讓我覺得開心，」
陶瓷公主回答說，「我們在自己的國家過
得非常愉快、滿足，只要自己開心，想說
什麼就說什麼、想去哪裡就去哪裡。」

正當錫樵夫用從樹林中砍來的木材做木梯的時候，桃樂絲已經因為長途跋涉而疲倦不堪，躺在地上睡著了。她已經疲倦不堪。獅子也蜷縮著身子睡著，托托則躺在牠的身旁。

稻草人看著錫樵夫工作，對他說：

「我不知道為什麼這裡會有一道牆，建這個東西有什麼用呢？」

「讓你的腦袋休息休息吧，別再想這道牆的事了，」錫樵夫回答，「等我們爬過去之後，就會知道對面有什麼東西了。」

過了一會，梯子完成了，雖然看上去有些笨拙，但是錫樵夫相信它很牢固，肯定可以派上用場。稻草人喚醒了桃樂絲、獅子和托托，告訴他們梯子已經準備就緒。稻草人第一個爬上梯子，但是他的動作如此笨拙，使得桃樂絲只好緊緊地跟在他後面，以防他掉下來。當稻草人把頭探過牆頂的時候，他喊道：「天哪！」

「快爬上去呀！」桃樂絲大聲叫道。

於是稻草人又往前爬過去，坐在牆頂上。桃樂絲把頭探過牆頂，也像稻草人一樣叫了起來：「天哪！」

接著托托也爬了上去，牠立刻就吠了起來，不過桃樂絲讓牠安靜下來。

再來換獅子爬上了梯子，錫樵夫最後上來，當他們倆從牆頂望過去的時候，都叫了一聲「天哪」。此刻他們全都並排坐在城牆上向下望，看到了一片奇特的景象。

在他們面前出現了一片廣闊的城市，那地面平滑、光亮、潔白，就像大盤子的底部。四周散佈著許多房子，全都是用陶瓷築成的，上面漆著鮮明的色彩。這些房子都非常小，其中最大一座也只有桃樂絲的腰部這麼高。那裡還有許多漂亮的小馬廄，四周圍繞著瓷製的籬笆，裡面站著一群牛、羊、馬、豬和小雞，全都是用陶瓷做成的。

但是，最令人感到驚奇的是那些住在這個奇異國度裡的百姓。擠奶女工和牧羊女孩身穿著色彩明亮的背心，金黃色點點佈滿了衣服；公主們身穿銀色、金色和紫色的華麗長袍；牧羊人穿著粉色、黃色和藍色條紋的短褲，他們的鞋子上有一顆金色鈕扣；王子們頭上戴著鑲嵌寶石的皇冠，身上穿著貂皮長袍和錦緞上衣；滑稽的小丑們穿著皺巴巴的長袍，兩邊的臉頰上畫著紅色的圓點，頭上戴著尖頂的高帽子。最奇怪的是，這些人全都是用陶瓷做成的，甚至連他們的衣服也是。他們的個子都非常矮小，最高的還不到桃樂絲的膝蓋。

剛開始，沒有人注意到這幾個旅行者，除了一隻紫色的、腦袋特別大的小瓷狗，牠跑到了城牆邊上朝著他們吠了起來，聲音非常細小。之後牠又跑了回去。

「我們該怎麼下去呢？」桃樂絲問道。

他們發現梯子非常笨重，根本無法把它搬上來，於是稻草人從牆上倒下去，其他人跳到他身上，如此一來，堅硬的地面就不會傷到他們的腳了。當然，他們都儘量不往稻草人的頭上跳，要不然他頭上的針會戳到他們的腳。當所有人都安全跳下來之後，他們扶起稻草人，他的身體已經被踩扁了，他們拍打著稻草人，讓他恢復原樣。

「想要走到另外一邊，我們必須穿過這個奇怪的地方，」桃樂絲說，「如果不向著南方，而改走其他路，那我們就太不明智了。」

他們開始穿過這個陶瓷之城。他們遇到的第一個人就是一個陶瓷的擠奶女工，擠著一頭瓷牛的奶。當他們慢慢走近時，那頭瓷牛突然蹬了一腳，踢翻了凳子和奶桶，甚至連擠奶女工也沒能倖免，匡噹一聲摔倒在陶瓷地面上。

桃樂絲驚訝地看到那頭瓷牛斷了一條腿，牛奶桶也摔成了許多碎片，而可憐的擠奶女工的左肘上也摔出了一道裂痕。

「喂！」擠奶女工生氣地叫喊著，「看看你們都做了些什麼！我的牛斷了一條腿，我必須帶牠去修理，把這條腿黏回去。你們為什麼要跑過來驚嚇我的牛？」

「真是對不起，」桃樂絲回答說，「請原諒我們。」

但是這位漂亮的擠奶女工仍舊非常生氣，根本就不理他們。她生著悶氣撿起斷腿，牽著牛走了，那頭可憐的牛只能一瘸一瘸地用三隻腳走路。擠奶女工一邊走著，一邊轉過頭來，對這些愚蠢的陌生人投以責備的目光，並將受傷的手臂緊靠在自己身邊。

對於這次不幸，桃樂絲感到非常懊惱。

「我們在這裡必須要小心謹慎，」心地善良的錫樵夫說，「要不然我們可能會傷害到這些可愛的小人，令他們永遠都無法痊癒。」

剛走了幾步，桃樂絲就遇見一位衣著非常漂亮的年輕公主，公主看見這些陌生人時停頓了片刻後就逃跑了。

桃樂絲想要多看看這位公主，於是追了上去，但是這位陶瓷公主喊道：

「別追我！別追我！」

她那細小的聲音中流露出恐懼，桃樂絲停下了腳步，問道：「為什麼？」

公主也停下腳步，跟桃樂絲隔著一段安全距離，回答道：「因為我跑起來的時候可能會跌倒，這樣就會摔破的。」

「可是你不能修補回去嗎？」小女孩問道。

「噢，可以。但是你知道，修補之後，這個人就永遠不會那麼漂亮了。」公主回答說。

「應該吧。」桃樂絲說。

「這裡有一位喬克先生，他是一個小丑，」陶瓷公主繼續說道，「他總是想用頭站在地上，所以經常摔倒，他身上已經修補一百多個地方了，變得一點都不好看。他過來了，你可以親自看看他的樣子。」

果然，一個滑稽的小丑正朝她們走了過來。儘管他穿著紅色、黃色和綠色的漂亮衣服，桃樂絲仍舊可以看出他身上滿是裂縫，每走一步，就可以清楚地看到他修補過很多地方。

小丑的雙手插在衣袋裡，鼓起腮幫子，粗魯莽撞地向他們點點頭，唱道：

> 「漂亮的女孩，為什麼盯著可憐的老喬克？
> 你如此呆板拘謹，就像吞下了一張撲克！」

「先生，別唱了！」公主說，「你沒看見這幾位陌生朋友嗎？你應該恭敬地對待他們！」

「噢，希望這樣算有禮貌。」小丑說著，立刻用頭倒立在地上。

「請別介意這位喬克先生，」公主對桃樂絲說，「他的腦袋傷得很重，所以變愚蠢了。」

「噢，我一點都不介意，」桃樂絲說，「不過你長得這麼漂亮，」她接著說道，「我非常喜歡你，你願意讓我帶你去堪薩斯州，把你放在艾姆嬸嬸的壁爐架上面嗎？我可以把你放在籃子裡帶走。」

「那樣一點都不會讓我覺得開心，」陶瓷公主回答說，「我們在自己的國家過得非常愉快、滿足，只要自己開心，想說什麼就說什麼、想去哪裡就去哪裡。但是不管什麼時候，只要我們一被人帶走，我們的關節就會立刻僵硬，只能筆直地站著，供人賞玩。當然，人們希望我們可以站在壁爐臺上、櫥櫃裡，或是客廳的桌子上，但是我們在自己的國家過得更加快樂。」

「不管怎麼樣，我都不想讓你不快樂！」桃樂絲說，「那我這就跟你告別了。」

「再見。」公主回答說。

他們小心翼翼地走過這個陶瓷之國。所有的小動物和小人都躲開他們，擔心這幾個陌生人把自己弄碎。一個鐘頭之後，這些旅行者就來到了這個國度的另一邊，遇到了另一道瓷牆。

這道牆沒有之前那道來得高，只要站在獅子的背上，他們就可以爬上牆頭。然後獅子併攏四肢，就跳上了瓷牆。但是在他起跳的時候，尾巴掃到了一座陶瓷教堂，把它打得粉碎。

「這真是太糟糕了，」桃樂絲說，「不過我想我們還算走運的，除了弄斷一頭牛的腿，打碎一座教堂之外，沒有對這些小人造成更多的傷害。他們全都那麼脆弱！」

「是啊，」稻草人說，「我真感謝自己是稻草做的，不會這麼輕易受傷。原來在這個世界上，還有比稻草人更脆弱的東西。」

第 21 章

獅子成為萬獸之王

「這片森林真是賞心悅目，」
獅子一邊說，一邊興奮地東張西望，
「我從沒見過比這裡更漂亮的地方。」

翻過瓷牆之後，這幾位旅行者發現自己來到了一個令人不快的地方，到處都是沼澤與濕地，長滿了長長的雜草。因為雜草濃密，擋住了他們的視線，所以沒走幾步路就會掉進泥濘的水潭裡。不過，他們小心翼翼地選擇行走路線，最後平安地走到了硬土地上。然而這個地方似乎比先前更加荒蕪，他們疲憊不堪地走了很長一段時間，穿過了低矮的灌木林，來到了另一片森林，那裡的樹木比他們以前見過的都要來得高大、古老。

「這片森林真是賞心悅目，」獅子一邊說，一邊興奮地東張西望，「我從沒見過比這裡更漂亮的地方。」

「好像陰森森的。」稻草人說。

「一點也不，」獅子回答說，「我真想永遠住在這裡。看看你們腳下這些乾草有多柔軟，這些老樹上的苔蘚有多豐厚、多碧綠。這裡絕對是任何一頭野獸最渴望的家。」

「或許現在就已經有野獸住在這片森林裡了吧。」桃樂絲說。

「我想有吧，」獅子回答，「不過我還沒有在這附近看見過。」

他們行走在這片森林之中，直到天色太黑、無法繼續前進，他們才停下了腳步。桃樂絲、托托和獅子躺下來睡覺，與此同時，錫樵夫和稻草人像平常一樣守護著他們。

等天亮之後，他們繼續上路。他們還沒走多遠，就聽見一陣低沉的聲音，好像有許多野獸在怒吼。托托小聲地嗚咽著，不過其他人都沒有感到害怕，繼續沿著小徑往前走，最後來到了樹林中的一片空地上，裡面聚集著好幾百隻各種各樣的野獸。有老虎、大象、熊、狼和狐狸，以及自然界中的所有獸類。桃樂絲立刻就被嚇壞了。不過獅子解釋說這是動物們在舉行會議，從牠們的怒吼與咆哮聲中，牠判斷出牠們遇到了大麻煩。

正在獅子說話的時候，好幾隻野獸看見了牠，一瞬間，這一大群野獸就像是著了魔似的，鴉雀無聲。有一頭最大的老虎走向獅子，鞠了個躬，說：

「歡迎，萬獸之王！您來得正是時候，請您幫我們打敗敵人，還這森林中的野獸們一個和平吧。」

「你們遇上什麼麻煩了？」獅子鎮靜地問道。

「最近在這片森林中來了一隻極其兇猛的野獸，我們都受到了牠的威脅，」老虎回答說，「牠是一隻極其可怕的怪物，長得像一隻大蜘蛛，體形跟大象一樣魁梧，腿跟樹幹一樣修長。牠長著八條這麼長的腿，當這個怪物爬行在這片森林中時，牠用一隻腳抓住動物，然後塞進嘴裡，吃下去，就像一隻蜘蛛吃蒼蠅一樣。只要這頭兇猛的怪物存在於世，我們就會永遠不得安寧。您來到這裡的時候，我們正在召開會議，商量該如何保衛自己。」

獅子沉思了片刻。

「這片森林裡，還有其他獅子嗎？」他問。

「沒有了，從前是有幾隻，可是這個怪物把牠們全都吃掉了。況且，牠們之中沒有　隻像您這麼魁梧、這麼勇敢。」

「如果我解決了你們的敵人，你們會不會服從我，像服從森林之王那樣地服從我？」獅子問道。

「我們非常樂意服從您。」老虎回答說，其他的所有野獸也都發出震耳欲聾的吼聲：「我們願意！」

「那隻大蜘蛛現在在哪裡？」獅子說。

「在那邊的櫟樹林中，」老虎一邊說，一邊用前腳指著方向。

「替我小心照顧我的朋友們，」獅子說，「我立刻就去跟那個怪物會一會。」

牠跟同伴們告了別，驕傲地向前走，迎戰那頭怪物。

當獅子找到那隻大蜘蛛時，牠正躺著睡覺，那樣子看上去醜惡至極，使得獅子厭惡地掩著自己的鼻子。牠的腳長得跟老虎所說的一樣長，身上覆蓋著粗糙的黑色毛髮。牠長著一張大嘴，一排鋒利的牙齒足有一尺長；但是連著牠的頭和矮胖身子的脖子卻和黃蜂的腰一樣纖細。這給了獅子一個主意，讓他想出了一個攻擊這頭怪物的好辦法，他知道在牠睡著時攻擊牠，會比牠醒來時容易很多。因此獅子猛地跳了起來，直接撲到那個怪物的背上，然後舉起一隻沉重且長著利爪的腳掌打了下去，將那蜘蛛的頭從牠身上敲了下來。獅子看著牠那些長腳不再抖動，知道牠已經徹底完蛋之後，才跳了下來。

獅子回到空地，森林中的野獸們正在那裡等候著牠。獅子驕傲地說：

「你們再也不用害怕那個敵人了。」

於是野獸們尊獅子為萬獸之王，膜拜著牠。獅子答應牠們，等桃樂絲平安踏上回堪薩斯州的路之後就會回來統治牠們。

第 22 章

奎德林國

「帶我們飛過這座山，去奎德林。」
小女孩回答說。

四位旅行者平安地走出了這片森林，當他們從陰森的樹林中出來之後，看見了一座陡峭的山橫在他們的面前，從山腳到山頂，全都堆著大塊大塊的岩石。

「要爬過這座山真是困難，」稻草人說，「儘管如此，我們還是得爬過去。」

於是他在前面帶路，其他人緊跟在後。在他們剛剛接近第一塊岩石時，就聽見一個粗厲的聲音喊道：「滾回去！」

「你是誰？」稻草人問說。

這時，一顆腦袋從岩石後面探了出來，用同樣的聲音說道：「這座山是我們的，任何人都不許翻越這座山。」

「可是我們必須爬過去，」稻草人說，「我們要去奎德林。」

「但是你們不能去！」那聲音回答道，然後從岩石後面走出一個人來，這幾位旅行者從來都沒有見過這麼奇怪的人。

他的身子非常矮小，卻十分結實，粗壯而長滿皺紋的脖子上支撐著一個大腦袋，而且頭頂是平的，但是他沒有手臂。看到這個情景，稻草人根本不擔心這樣的東西可以阻止他們爬過山頂。於是他說：「很抱歉，我們無法如你的願，不管你喜不喜歡，我們都必須爬過你這座山。」說著，稻草人就大膽地往前走了過去。

就在這個時候，這個人的腦袋就像閃電似的射了出來，脖子向前伸長，直到平平的腦袋把稻草人撞個正著，稻草人摔倒在地上，滾啊滾，滾到了山腳下。那顆腦袋像伸出來時那般迅速地縮了回去，並且發出刺耳的笑聲：「這可不像你想像的那麼容易！」

這時候，其他的岩石後面同時傳出一陣喧鬧的笑聲，桃樂絲看到山坡上有好幾百個沒有手臂的大頭人，每塊岩石後面都站著一個。

由於稻草人的不幸而引發的嘲笑聲讓獅子感到非常憤怒，牠怒吼了一聲，衝上山去，那回聲像雷聲一樣在山間回蕩。

又有一顆腦袋迅速地射了出來，大獅子就像是被炮彈打中似的滾下了山。

桃樂絲跑過去扶起稻草人，獅子也跑到她的身邊，他摔得滿身是傷，渾身疼痛，說道：「跟這些腦袋可以攻擊的人鬥也是白鬥，沒有人可以抵擋得住他們的攻擊。」

「那我們該怎麼辦呢？」桃樂絲問道。

「把飛天猴們召喚過來，」錫樵夫建議道，「你還有權利再命令牠們一次。」

「是啊。」她回答，然後戴上金帽子，念起咒語。飛天猴們像往常一樣迅速，不一會兒就全都站在了她的面前。

「您有什麼命令？」猴王深深地鞠了個躬，問道。

「帶我們飛過這座山，去奎德林。」小女孩回答說。

「沒問題。」猴王說，然後飛天猴們立刻抓住這四位旅行者和托托，帶著他們飛上了天。當他們飛過山頭的時候，這些大頭人懊惱地叫喊著，腦袋高高地射到空中，但是他們怎麼都沒辦法射到飛天猴們。飛天猴們帶著桃樂絲和她的同伴們平安地越過了這座山，降落在美麗的奎德林。

「這是你最後一次召喚我們了，」猴王對桃樂絲說，「那麼再見了，祝你好運。」

「再見，非常感謝你們的幫助。」女孩子回答道。飛天猴們飛到空中，一眨眼就消失了。

奎德林這個地方似乎非常富裕、幸福。這裡有一片片成熟的稻田，平坦的道路橫亙其中，潺潺流動的溪流上面架著堅固的橋樑。籬笆、房子和橋樑全都漆著鮮豔的紅色，就像溫基國漆成黃色，芒奇金國漆成藍色一樣。奎德林人長得矮小精壯，看起來胖乎乎的，脾氣很好。他們全都穿著紅色的衣服，在綠油油的青草和黃澄澄的穀物相襯之下，顯得格外鮮明。

飛天猴們把他們放在一間農舍附近，這四位旅行者走上前去，敲了敲門。開門的是農夫的妻子，當桃樂絲向她要點東西填飽肚子時，這個婦人給了他們一頓美味的午飯，有三種糕點，四種小餅乾，還給托托喝了一碗牛奶。

「這裡距離格琳達的宮殿還有多遠？」小女孩問。

「不是很遠，」農夫的妻子回答說，「一直往南走，用不了多少時間，你們就能到那裡了。」

　　他們向這位好心的婦人道謝之後，又重新出發，沿著田野，走過美麗的小橋，最後他們看見一座非常雄偉的城堡出現在眼前。城門前站著三個年輕女子，穿著裝飾著金邊的紅色漂亮制服。當桃樂絲走近時，其中一個問道：

　　「你為什麼來到南方國度？」

　　「我來拜訪統治這裡的善良女巫，」她回答說，「你可以帶我去見她嗎？」

　　「告訴我你叫什麼名字，我會通報格琳達，看她是否願意接見。」於是他們報上了各自的名字，然後這位女士兵就走進了城堡。幾分鐘之後，她回來了，說桃樂絲和她的同伴們可以立刻去拜見格琳達。

第 23 章

桃樂絲如願以償

「你的心地這麼善良，」她說，「我想
我一定會告訴你如何回到堪薩斯州的。」
然後她接著說，「但是如果我這麼做了，
你必須把這頂金帽子送給我。」

但是在他們見到格琳達之前，先被帶到了城堡的一個房間裡。桃樂絲在那裡洗了把臉，整理了一下頭髮。獅子抖了抖鬃毛上的灰塵。稻草人拍了拍身子，讓自己變得圓鼓鼓的。錫樵夫擦了擦自己的錫片，在關節上添了些油。

等他們全都準備完畢之後，女士兵就帶著他們走進一個大房間裡，格琳達正坐在紅寶石王位上。

在他們的眼中，這位女巫顯得既漂亮又年輕，她的頭髮是深紅色的，鬆軟地垂在肩膀上。她穿著潔白的衣服，一雙藍色的眼睛和藹地注視著這個小女孩。

「我的孩子，我能為你做些什麼呢？」她問道。

桃樂絲把自己的故事全都告訴了女巫，從龍捲風如何把她帶到奧茲國，她如何遇見自己的同伴們，以及他們遇到的一件件奇妙的冒險故事。

「現在我最大的願望就是回到堪薩斯州，」她接著說道，「因為艾姆嬸嬸肯定會以為我遇到了什麼不測，並為此辦理喪事。除非今年的收成比去年好，要不然，我想亨利叔叔肯定負擔不了這筆費用。」

格琳達俯身向前，親吻著這個可愛小女孩仰起的臉頰。

「你的心地這麼善良，」她說，「我想我一定會告訴你如何回到堪薩斯州的。」然後她接著說，「但是如果我這麼做了，你必須把這頂金帽子送給我。」

「我願意！」桃樂絲叫了起來，「其實這頂帽子對我來說已經沒有用處了，不過你擁有它之後可以命令飛天猴三次。」

「我想我正好需要牠們替我服務三次。」格琳達微笑地回答道。

於是桃樂絲把金帽子給了她，然後女巫對稻草人說：「等桃樂絲離開我們之後，你打算做什麼？」

「我會回到翡翠城，」他回答說，「因為奧茲任命我統治那個國家，百姓們也很喜歡我。唯一讓我感到擔憂的就是要如何越過那座由大頭人佔據的山峰。」

「我會用這頂金帽子的魔力，命令飛天猴們帶你到翡翠城的大門前，」格琳達說，「如果那裡的百姓失去了一位像你這樣神奇的領袖就太可惜了。」

「我真有那麼神奇嗎？」稻草人問道。

「你非比尋常。」格琳達回答說。

然後她轉向錫樵夫，問道：「等桃樂絲離開這個國家之後，你會怎麼樣呢？」

錫樵夫靠在他的斧頭上，沉思了一會，然後說：

「溫基人對我非常親切，邪惡女巫死了之後，他們就想讓我去領導他們。我也喜歡溫基人，如果我能夠回到西方，我想我會永遠領導他們的。」

「那我對飛天猴的第二個命令就是讓他們把你安全地帶到溫基國。」格琳達說，「你的腦袋看起來可能沒有稻草人那麼大，但是只要你把自己擦亮了，你就會比他聰明了，我想你肯定會英明地領導溫基人的。」

然後，女巫又看著那隻龐大、多毛的獅子，問道：

「等桃樂絲回到家鄉之後，你會怎麼樣？」

「在大頭人佔領的山坡的另一邊，」他回答說，「有一片非常古老的森林，住在那裡的所有野獸都尊我為大王。如果我能回到那片森林，我會在那裡非常幸福地度過我的一生。」

「那我對飛天猴們的第三個命令就是把你帶回森林。」格琳達說，「在用完這頂金帽子的魔力之後，我會把它還給猴王，從此之後，他和他的隨從們就永遠自由了。」

這時候，稻草人、錫樵夫和獅子都真誠地感謝善良女巫的仁慈。桃樂絲喊道：

「你的心就像你的容顏那麼漂亮善良！可是你還沒告訴我要如何回到堪薩斯州呢。」

「你腳上那雙銀鞋可以帶你穿過沙漠，」格琳達回答說，「如果你知道它們的魔力，在你來到這個國度的第一天，你就可以回到艾姆嬸嬸的身邊了。」

「可是這樣我就不會有這神奇的腦袋了！」稻草人說，「我可能要在農民的稻田裡度過我的一生。」

「我也不會有我這顆可愛的心了，」錫樵夫說，「我可能會生鏽地站在森林中，直到世界末日。」

「而我就會永遠膽小地生活了，」獅子說，「在所有的森林中，沒有一隻野獸會對我說一句好話。」

「你們說的都沒錯，」桃樂絲說，「我很高興能對好朋友們產生點作用。但是現在，他們每個人都實現了自己最大的願望，領導著一個國家，幸福地生活著，我想我應該回堪薩斯州了。」

「這雙銀鞋具有神奇的魔力。」善良的女巫說道，「其中一個最神奇的魔力就是可以在三步之內，帶你去這個世界上的任何地方，每一步都只要一眨眼的工夫。你只需要碰三次後腳跟，然後就能命令這雙鞋子帶你去任何你想去的地方了。」

「如果這是真的，」小女孩興高采烈地說道，「我立刻就讓它們帶我回到堪薩斯州。」

她伸出雙手，抱住獅子的脖子，親了牠一下，溫柔地拍了拍牠那碩大的腦袋，然後她又親吻了一下錫樵夫，他流著眼淚，這對他的關節來說太危險了。不過，她沒有親吻稻草人那張畫出來的臉，而是擁抱著他那塞著稻草的柔軟身子。跟自己親愛的朋友們告別，讓桃樂絲傷心地哭了起來。

格琳達從紅寶石王位上走了下來，親吻這個小女孩，跟她告別。桃樂絲感謝她友善地接見了自己以及朋友們。

這時候，桃樂絲鄭重其事地抱起托托，最後說了一聲再見，然後連續敲了三次鞋跟，說：

「帶我回家，回到艾姆嬸嬸身邊！」

一瞬間，她就被捲到了空中，速度如此之快，她所能看到或感受到的就只有大風吹過耳畔的呼嘯聲。

這雙銀鞋只不過走了三步，桃樂絲就突然停了下來，她在草地上打了好幾個滾之後，才知道自己降落在什麼地方。

最後，她終於坐了起來，看了看自己的周圍。

「天哪！」她叫喊了起來。

因為她已經坐在了堪薩斯州的大草原上，在她面前的是一座新的農舍，在龍捲風刮走那座舊農舍之後，亨利叔叔蓋了一座新的。亨利叔叔正在農場穀倉周圍的空地上擠著牛奶。托托已經從她的懷抱中跳了出去，愉快地吠著，跑向了那個穀倉。

桃樂絲站了起來，發現自己的腳上只穿了一雙襪子。因為當她在空中飛行時，那雙銀鞋就掉了，永遠遺失在沙漠之中。

第 2 4 章

重返家園

「我去奧茲國了，還有托托也是，啊，
艾姆嬸嬸，我又在家裡了，真高興呀！」

艾姆嬸嬸剛好從房子裡走出來，要給高麗菜澆水，她抬起頭來，看見桃樂絲正朝她跑來。

「我親愛的孩子！」艾姆嬸嬸一邊叫著，一邊把小女孩抱在懷裡，親吻著她的臉蛋，「你究竟去哪裡了！」

「我去奧茲國了，還有托托也是，啊，艾姆嬸嬸，我又在家裡了，真高興呀！」

The Wonderful
Wizard of
Oz

Chapter 1

The Cyclone

A strange thing then happened.

The house whirled around two
or three times and rose slowly
through the air. Dorothy felt as
if she were going up in a balloon.

Dorothy lived in the midst of the great Kansas prairies, with Uncle Henry, who was a farmer, and Aunt Em, who was the farmer's wife. Their house was small, for the lumber to build it had to be carried by wagon many miles. There were four walls, a floor and a roof, which made one room; and this room contained a rusty-looking cooking stove, a cupboard for the dishes, a table, three or four chairs, and the beds. Uncle Henry and Aunt Em had a big bed in one corner, and Dorothy a little bed in another corner. There was no upstairs at all, and no cellar – except a small hole dug in the ground, called a cyclone cellar, where the family could go in case one of those great whirlwinds arose, mighty enough to crush any building in its path. It was reached by a trap door in the middle of the floor, from which a ladder led down into the small, dark hole.

When Dorothy stood in the doorway and looked around, she could see nothing but the great gray prairie on every side. Not a tree nor a house broke the broad sweep of flat country that reached to the edge of the sky in all directions. The sun had baked the plowed land into a gray mass, with little cracks running through it. Even the grass was not green, for the sun had burned the tops of the long blades until they were the same gray color to be seen everywhere. Once the house had been painted, but the sun blistered the paint and the rains washed it away, and now the house was as dull and gray as everything else.

When Aunt Em came there to live, she was a young, pretty wife. The sun and wind had changed her, too. They had taken the sparkle from her eyes and left them a sober gray; they had taken the red from

her cheeks and lips, and they were gray also. She was thin and gaunt, and never smiled now. When Dorothy, who was an orphan, first came to her, Aunt Em had been so startled by the child's laughter that she would scream and press her hand upon her heart whenever Dorothy's merry voice reached her ears; and she still looked at the little girl with wonder that she could find anything to laugh at.

Uncle Henry never laughed. He worked hard from morning till night and did not know what joy was. He was gray also, from his long beard to his rough boots, and he looked stern and solemn, and rarely spoke.

It was Toto that made Dorothy laugh, and saved her from growing as gray as her other surroundings. Toto was not gray; he was a little black dog, with long silky hair and small black eyes that twinkled merrily on either side of his funny, wee nose. Toto played all day long, and Dorothy played with him, and loved him dearly.

Today, however, they were not playing. Uncle Henry sat upon the doorstep and looked anxiously at the sky, which was even grayer than usual. Dorothy stood in the door with Toto in her arms, and looked at the sky too. Aunt Em was washing the dishes.

From the far north they heard a low wail of the wind, and Uncle Henry and Dorothy could see where the long grass bowed in waves before the coming storm. There now came a sharp whistling in the air from the south, and as they turned their eyes that way they saw ripples in the grass coming from that direction also.

Suddenly Uncle Henry stood up.

"There's a cyclone coming, Em," he called to his wife. "I'll go look after the stock." Then he ran toward the sheds where the cows and horses were kept.

Aunt Em dropped her work and came to the door. One glance told her of the danger close at hand.

"Quick, Dorothy!" she screamed. "Run for the cellar!"

Toto jumped out of Dorothy's arms and hid under the bed, and the girl started to get him. Aunt Em, badly frightened, threw open the trap door in the floor and climbed down the ladder into the small, dark hole. Dorothy caught Toto at last and started to follow her aunt. When she was halfway across the room there came a great shriek from the wind, and the house shook so hard that she lost her footing and sat down suddenly upon the floor.

A strange thing then happened.

The house whirled around two or three times and rose slowly through the air. Dorothy felt as if she were going up in a balloon.

The north and south winds met where the house stood, and made it the exact center of the cyclone. In the middle of a cyclone the air is generally still, but the great pressure of the wind on every side of the house raised it up higher and higher, until it was at the very top of the cyclone; and there it remained and was carried miles and miles away as easily as you could carry a feather.

It was very dark, and the wind howled horribly around her, but Dorothy found she was riding quite easily. After the first few whirls around, and one other time when the house tipped badly, she felt as if she were being rocked gently, like a baby in a cradle.

Toto did not like it. He ran about the room, now here, now there, barking loudly; but Dorothy sat quite still on the floor and waited to see what would happen.

Once, Toto got too near the open trap door, and fell in; and at first the little girl thought she had lost him. But soon she saw one of his ears sticking up through the hole, for the strong pressure of the air was keeping him up so that he could not fall. She crept to the hole, caught Toto by the ear, and dragged him into the room again, afterward closing the trap door so that no more accidents could happen.

Hour after hour passed, and slowly Dorothy got over her fright; but she felt quite lonely, and the wind shrieked so loudly all about her that she nearly became deaf. At first she had wondered if she would be dashed to pieces when the house fell again; but as the hours passed and nothing terrible happened, she stopped worrying and resolved to wait calmly and see what the future would bring. At last she crawled over the swaying floor to her bed, and lay down upon it; and Toto followed and lay down beside her.

In spite of the swaying of the house and the wailing of the wind, Dorothy soon closed her eyes and fell fast asleep.

Chapter 2

The Council
with the Munchkins

While she stood looking eagerly
at the strange and beautiful
sights, she noticed coming
towards her a group of the
queerest people she had ever seen.

She was awakened by a shock, so sudden and severe that if Dorothy had not been lying on the soft bed she might have been hurt. As it was, the jar made her catch her breath and wonder what had happened; and Toto put his cold little nose into her face and whined dismally. Dorothy sat up and noticed that the house was not moving; nor was it dark, for the bright sunshine came in at the window, flooding the little room. She sprang from her bed and with Toto at her heels ran and opened the door.

The little girl gave a cry of amazement and looked about her, her eyes growing bigger and bigger at the wonderful sights she saw.

The cyclone had set the house down very gently – for a cyclone – in the midst of a country of marvelous beauty. There were lovely patches of greensward all about, with stately trees bearing rich and luscious fruits. Banks of gorgeous flowers were on every hand, and birds with rare and brilliant plumage sang and fluttered in the trees and bushes. A little way off was a small brook, rushing and sparkling along between green banks, and murmuring in a voice very grateful to a little girl who had lived so long on the dry, gray prairies.

While she stood looking eagerly at the strange and beautiful sights, she noticed coming towards her a group of the queerest people she had ever seen. They were not as big as the grown folk she had always been used to; but neither were they very small. In fact, they seemed about as tall as Dorothy, who was a well-grown child for her age, although they were, so far as looks go, many years older.

Three were men and one a woman, and all were oddly dressed. They wore round hats that rose to a small point a foot above their heads, with little bells around the brims that tinkled sweetly as they moved. The hats of the men were blue; the little woman's hat was white, and she wore a white gown that hung in pleats from her shoulders. Over it were sprinkled little stars that glistened in the sun like diamonds. The men were dressed in blue, of the same shade as their hats, and wore well-polished boots with a deep roll of blue at the tops. The men, Dorothy thought, were about as old as Uncle Henry, for two of them had beards. But the little woman was doubtless much older. Her face was covered with wrinkles, her hair was nearly white, and she walked rather stiffly.

When these people drew near the house where Dorothy was standing in the doorway, they paused and whispered among themselves, as if afraid to come farther. But the little old woman walked up to Dorothy, made a low bow and said, in a sweet voice:

"You are welcome, most noble Sorceress, to the land of the Munchkins. We are so grateful to you for having killed the Wicked Witch of the East, and for setting our people free from bondage."

Dorothy listened to this speech with wonder. What could the little woman possibly mean by calling her a sorceress, and saying she had killed the Wicked Witch of the East? Dorothy was an innocent, harmless little girl, who had been carried by a cyclone many miles from home; and she had never killed anything in all her life.

But the little woman evidently expected her to answer; so Dorothy said, with hesitation, "You are very kind, but there must be some mistake. I have not killed anything."

"Your house did, anyway," replied the little old woman, with a laugh, "and that is the same thing. See!" she continued, pointing to the corner of the house. "There are her two toes, still sticking out from under a block of wood."

Dorothy looked, and gave a little cry of fright. There, indeed, just under the corner of the great beam the house rested on, two feet were sticking out, shod in silver shoes with pointed toes.

"Oh, dear! Oh, dear!" cried Dorothy, clasping her hands together in dismay. "The house must have fallen on her. Whatever shall we do?"

"There is nothing to be done," said the little woman calmly.

"But who was she?" asked Dorothy.

"She was the Wicked Witch of the East, as I said," answered the little woman. "She has held all the Munchkins in bondage for many years, making them slave for her night and day. Now they are all set free, and are grateful to you for the favor."

"Who are the Munchkins?" inquired Dorothy.

"They are the people who live in this land of the East where the Wicked Witch ruled."

"Are you a Munchkin?" asked Dorothy.

"No, but I am their friend, although I live in the land of the North. When they saw the Witch of the East was dead the Munchkins sent a swift messenger to me, and I came at once. I am the Witch of the North."

"Oh, gracious!" cried Dorothy. "Are you a real witch?"

"Yes, indeed," answered the little woman. "But I am a good witch, and the people love me. I am not as powerful as the Wicked Witch was who ruled here, or I should have set the people free myself."

"But I thought all witches were wicked," said the girl, who was half frightened at facing a real witch.

"Oh, no, that is a great mistake. There were only four witches in all the Land of Oz, and two of them, those who live in the North and the South, are good witches. I know this is true, for I am one of them myself, and cannot be mistaken. Those who dwelt in the East and the West were, indeed, wicked witches; but now that you have killed one of them, there is but one Wicked Witch in all the Land of Oz – the one who lives in the West."

"But," said Dorothy, after a moment's thought, "Aunt Em has told me that the witches were all dead – years and years ago."

"Who is Aunt Em?" inquired the little old woman.

"She is my aunt who lives in Kansas, where I came from."

The Witch of the North seemed to think for a time, with her head bowed and her eyes upon the ground. Then she looked up and said, "I do not know where Kansas is, for I have never heard that country mentioned before. But tell me, is it a civilized country?"

"Oh, yes," replied Dorothy.

"Then that accounts for it. In the civilized countries I believe there are no witches left, nor wizards, nor sorceresses, nor magicians. But, you see, the Land of Oz has never been civilized, for we are cut off from all the rest of the world. Therefore we still have witches and wizards amongst us."

"Who are the wizards?" asked Dorothy.

"Oz himself is the Great Wizard," answered the Witch, sinking her voice to a whisper. "He is more powerful than all the rest of us together. He lives in the City of Emeralds."

Dorothy was going to ask another question, but just then the Munchkins, who had been standing silently by, gave a loud shout and pointed to the corner of the house where the Wicked Witch had been lying.

"What is it?" asked the little old woman, and looked, and began to laugh. The feet of the dead Witch had disappeared entirely, and nothing was left but the silver shoes.

"She was so old," explained the Witch of the North, "that she dried up quickly in the sun. That is the end of her. But the silver shoes are yours, and you shall have them to wear." She reached down and picked up the shoes, and after shaking the dust out of them, handed them to Dorothy.

"The Witch of the East was proud of those silver shoes," said one of the Munchkins, "and there is some charm connected with them; but what it is we never knew."

Dorothy carried the shoes into the house and placed them on the table. Then she came out again to the Munchkins and said:

"I am anxious to get back to my aunt and uncle, for I am sure they will worry about me. Can you help me find my way?"

The Munchkins and the Witch first looked at one another, and then at Dorothy, and then shook their heads.

"At the East, not far from here," said one, "there is a great desert, and none could live to cross it."

"It is the same at the South," said another, "for I have been there and seen it. The South is the country of the Quadlings."

"I am told," said the third man, "that it is the same at the West. And that country, where the Winkies live, is ruled by the Wicked Witch of the West, who would make you her slave if you passed her way."

"The North is my home," said the old lady, "and at its edge is the same great desert that surrounds this Land of Oz. I'm afraid, my dear, you will have to live with us."

Dorothy began to sob at this, for she felt lonely among all these strange people. Her tears seemed to grieve the kind-hearted Munchkins, for they immediately took out their handkerchiefs and began to weep also. As for the little old woman, she took off her cap and balanced the point on the end of her nose, while she counted "One, two, three" in a solemn voice. At once the cap changed to a slate, on which was written in big, white chalk marks:

"LET DOROTHY GO TO THE CITY OF EMERALDS"

The little old woman took the slate from her nose, and having read the words on it, asked, "Is your name Dorothy, my dear?"

"Yes," answered the child, looking up and drying her tears.

"Then you must go to the City of Emeralds. Perhaps Oz will help you."

"Where is this city?" asked Dorothy.

"It is exactly in the center of the country, and is ruled by Oz, the Great Wizard I told you of."

"Is he a good man?" inquired the girl anxiously.

"He is a good Wizard. Whether he is a man or not I cannot tell, for I have never seen him."

"How can I get there?" asked Dorothy.

"You must walk. It is a long journey, through a country that is sometimes pleasant and sometimes dark and terrible. However, I will use all the magic arts I know of to keep you from harm."

"Won't you go with me?" pleaded the girl, who had begun to look upon the little old woman as her only friend.

"No, I cannot do that," she replied, "but I will give you my kiss, and no one will dare injure a person who has been kissed by the Witch of the North."

She came close to Dorothy and kissed her gently on the forehead. Where her lips touched the girl, they left a round, shining mark, as Dorothy found out soon after.

"The road to the City of Emeralds is paved with yellow brick," said the Witch, "so you cannot miss it. When you get to Oz do not be afraid of him, but tell your story and ask him to help you. Good-bye, my dear."

The three Munchkins bowed low to her and wished her a pleasant journey, after which they walked away through the trees. The Witch gave Dorothy a friendly little nod, whirled around on her left heel three times, and straightway disappeared, much to the surprise of little Toto, who barked after her loudly enough when she had gone, because he had been afraid even to growl while she stood by.

But Dorothy, knowing her to be a witch, had expected her to disappear in just that way, and was not surprised in the least.

Chapter 3

How Dorothy
Saved the Scarecrow

While Dorothy was looking
earnestly into the queer, painted
face of the Scarecrow, she was
surprised to see one of the eyes
slowly wink at her.

When Dorothy was left alone she began to feel hungry. So she went to the cupboard and cut herself some bread, which she spread with butter. She gave some to Toto, and taking a pail from the shelf she carried it down to the little brook and filled it with clear, sparkling water. Toto ran over to the trees and began to bark at the birds sitting there. Dorothy went to get him, and saw such delicious fruit hanging from the branches that she gathered some of it, finding it just what she wanted to help out her breakfast.

Then she went back to the house, and having helped herself and Toto to a good drink of the cool, clear water, she set about making ready for the journey to the City of Emeralds.

Dorothy had only one other dress, but that happened to be clean and was hanging on a peg beside her bed. It was gingham, with checks of white and blue; and although the blue was somewhat faded with many washings, it was still a pretty frock. The girl washed herself carefully, dressed herself in the clean gingham, and tied her pink sunbonnet on her head. She took a little basket and filled it with bread from the cupboard, laying a white cloth over the top. Then she looked down at her feet and noticed how old and worn her shoes were.

"They surely will never do for a long journey, Toto," she said. And Toto looked up into her face with his little black eyes and wagged his tail to show he knew what she meant.

At that moment Dorothy saw lying on the table the silver shoes that had belonged to the Witch of the East.

"I wonder if they will fit me," she said to Toto. "They would be just the thing to take a long walk in, for they could not wear out."

She took off her old leather shoes and tried on the silver ones, which fitted her as well as if they had been made for her.

Finally she picked up her basket.

"Come along, Toto," she said. "We will go to the Emerald City and ask the Great Oz how to get back to Kansas again."

She closed the door, locked it, and put the key carefully in the pocket of her dress. And so, with Toto trotting along soberly behind her, she started on her journey.

There were several roads nearby, but it did not take her long to find the one paved with yellow bricks. Within a short time she was walking briskly toward the Emerald City, her silver shoes tinkling merrily on the hard, yellow road-bed. The sun shone bright and the birds sang sweetly, and Dorothy did not feel nearly so bad as you might think a little girl would who had been suddenly whisked away from her own country and set down in the midst of a strange land.

She was surprised, as she walked along, to see how pretty the country was about her. There were neat fences at the sides of the road, painted a dainty blue color, and beyond them were fields of grain and vegetables in abundance. Evidently the Munchkins were good farmers and able to raise large crops. Once in a while she would pass a house, and the people came out to look at her and bow low as she went by; for everyone knew she had been the means of destroying the Wicked Witch and setting them free from bondage. The houses of the Munchkins were odd-looking dwellings, for each was round, with a big dome for a roof. All were painted blue, for in this country of the East blue was the favorite color.

Towards evening, when Dorothy was tired with her long walk and began to wonder where she should pass the night, she came to a house rather larger than the rest. On the green lawn before it many men and women were dancing. Five little fiddlers played as loudly as possible, and the people were laughing and singing, while a big table near by was loaded with delicious fruits and nuts, pies and cakes, and many other good things to eat.

The people greeted Dorothy kindly, and invited her to supper and to pass the night with them; for this was the home of one of the richest Munchkins in the land, and his friends were gathered with him to celebrate their freedom from the bondage of the Wicked Witch.

Dorothy ate a hearty supper and was waited upon by the rich Munchkin himself, whose name was Boq. Then she sat upon a settee and watched the people dance.

When Boq saw her silver shoes he said, "You must be a great sorceress."

"Why?" asked the girl.

"Because you wear silver shoes and have killed the Wicked

Witch. Besides, you have white in your frock, and only witches and sorceresses wear white."

"My dress is blue and white checked," said Dorothy, smoothing out the wrinkles in it.

"It is kind of you to wear that," said Boq. "Blue is the color of the Munchkins, and white is the witch color. So we know you are a friendly witch."

Dorothy did not know what to say to this, for all the people seemed to think her a witch, and she knew very well she was only an ordinary little girl who had come by the chance of a cyclone into a strange land.

When she had tired watching the dancing, Boq led her into the house, where he gave her a room with a pretty bed in it. The sheets were made of blue cloth, and Dorothy slept soundly in them till morning, with Toto curled up on the blue rug beside her.

She ate a hearty breakfast, and watched a wee Munchkin baby, who played with Toto and pulled his tail and crowed and laughed in a way that greatly amused Dorothy. Toto was a fine curiosity to all the people, for they had never seen a dog before.

"How far is it to the Emerald City?" the girl asked.

"I do not know," answered Boq gravely, "for I have never been there. It is better for people to keep away from Oz, unless they have business with him. But it is a long way to the Emerald City, and it will take you many days. The country here is rich and pleasant, but you must pass through rough and dangerous places before you reach the end of your journey."

This worried Dorothy a little, but she knew that only the Great Oz could help her get to Kansas again, so she bravely resolved not to turn back.

She bade her friends good-bye, and again started along the road of yellow brick. When she had gone several miles she thought she would stop to rest, and so climbed to the top of the fence beside the road and sat down. There was a great cornfield beyond the fence, and not far away she saw a Scarecrow, placed high on a pole to keep the birds from the ripe corn.

Dorothy leaned her chin upon her hand and gazed thoughtfully at the Scarecrow. Its head was a small sack stuffed with straw, with eyes, nose, and mouth painted on it to represent a face. An old, pointed blue hat, that had belonged to some Munchkin, was perched on his head, and the rest of the figure was a blue suit of clothes, worn and faded, which had also been stuffed with straw. On the feet were some old boots with blue tops, such as every man wore in this country, and the figure was raised above the stalks of corn by means of the pole stuck up its back.

While Dorothy was looking earnestly into the queer, painted face of the Scarecrow, she was surprised to see one of the eyes slowly wink at her. She thought she must have been mistaken at first, for none of the scarecrows in Kansas ever wink; but presently the figure nodded its head to her in a friendly way. Then she climbed down from the fence and walked up to it, while Toto ran around the pole and barked.

"Good day," said the Scarecrow, in a rather husky voice.

"Did you speak?" asked the girl, in wonder.

"Certainly," answered the Scarecrow. "How do you do?"

"I'm pretty well, thank you," replied Dorothy politely. "How do you do?"

"I'm not feeling well," said the Scarecrow, with a smile, "for it is very tedious being perched up here night and day to scare away crows."

"Can't you get down?" asked Dorothy.

"No, for this pole is stuck up my back. If you will please take away the pole I shall be greatly obliged to you."

Dorothy reached up both arms and lifted the figure off the pole, for, being stuffed with straw, it was quite light.

"Thank you very much," said the Scarecrow, when he had been set down on the ground. "I feel like a new man."

Dorothy was puzzled at this, for it sounded queer to hear a stuffed man speak, and to see him bow and walk along beside her.

"Who are you?" asked the Scarecrow when he had stretched himself and yawned. "And where are you going?"

"My name is Dorothy," said the girl, "and I am going to the Emerald City, to ask the Great Oz to send me back to Kansas."

"Where is the Emerald City?" he inquired. "And who is Oz?"

"Why, don't you know?" she returned, in surprise.

"No, indeed. I don't know anything. You see, I am stuffed, so I have no brains at all," he answered sadly.

"Oh," said Dorothy, "I'm awfully sorry for you."

"Do you think," he asked, "if I go to the Emerald City with you, that Oz would give me some brains?"

"I cannot tell," she returned, "but you may come with me, if you like. If Oz will not give you any brains you will be no worse off than you are now."

"That is true," said the Scarecrow. "You see," he continued confidentially, "I don't mind my legs and arms and body being stuffed, because I cannot get hurt. If anyone treads on my toes or sticks a pin into me, it doesn't matter, for I can't feel it. But I do not want people to call me a fool, and if my head stays stuffed with straw instead of with brains, as yours is, how am I ever to know anything?"

"I understand how you feel," said the little girl, who was truly sorry for him. "If you will come with me I'll ask Oz to do all he can for you."

"Thank you," he answered gratefully.

They walked back to the road. Dorothy helped him over the fence, and they started along the path of yellow brick for the Emerald City.

Toto did not like this addition to the party at first. He smelled around the stuffed man as if he suspected there might be a nest of rats in the straw, and he often growled in an unfriendly way at the Scarecrow.

"Don't mind Toto," said Dorothy to her new friend. "He never bites."

"Oh, I'm not afraid," replied the Scarecrow. "He can't hurt the straw. Do let me carry that basket for you. I shall not mind it, for I can't get tired. I'll tell you a secret," he continued, as he walked along. "There is only one thing in the world I am afraid of."

"What is that?" asked Dorothy; "the Munchkin farmer who made you?"

"No," answered the Scarecrow; "it's a lighted match."

Chapter 4

The Road
Through the Forest

"If this road goes in, it must
come out," said the Scarecrow,
"and as the Emerald City is at
the other end of the road, we
must go wherever it leads us."

After a few hours the road began to be rough, and the walking grew so difficult that the Scarecrow often stumbled over the yellow bricks, which were here very uneven. Sometimes, indeed, they were broken or missing altogether, leaving holes that Toto jumped across and Dorothy walked around. As for the Scarecrow, having no brains, he walked straight ahead, and so stepped into the holes and fell at full length on the hard bricks. It never hurt him, however, and Dorothy would pick him up and set him upon his feet again, while he joined her in laughing merrily at his own mishap.

The farms were not nearly so well cared for here as they were farther back. There were fewer houses and fewer fruit trees, and the farther they went the more dismal and lonesome the country became.

At noon they sat down by the roadside, near a little brook, and Dorothy opened her basket and got out some bread. She offered a piece to the Scarecrow, but he refused.

"I am never hungry," he said, "and it is a lucky thing I am not, for my mouth is only painted, and if I should cut a hole in it so I could eat, the straw I am stuffed with would come out, and that would spoil the shape of my head."

Dorothy saw at once that this was true, so she only nodded and went on eating her bread.

"Tell me something about yourself and the country you came from," said the Scarecrow, when she had finished her dinner. So she told him all about Kansas, and how gray everything was there, and how the cyclone had carried her to this queer Land of Oz.

The Scarecrow listened carefully, and said, "I cannot understand why you should wish to leave this beautiful country and go back to the dry, gray place you call Kansas."

"That is because you have no brains" answered the girl. "No matter how dreary and gray our homes are, we people of flesh and blood would rather live there than in any other country, be it ever so beautiful. There is no place like home."

The Scarecrow sighed.

"Of course I cannot understand it," he said. "If your heads were stuffed with straw, like mine, you would probably all live in the beautiful places, and then Kansas would have no people at all. It is fortunate for Kansas that you have brains."

"Won't you tell me a story, while we are resting?" asked the child.

The Scarecrow looked at her reproachfully, and answered: "My life has been so short that I really know nothing whatever. I was only made the day before yesterday. What happened in the world before that time is all unknown to me. Luckily, when the farmer made my head, one of the first things he did was to paint my ears, so that I heard what was going on. There was another Munchkin with him, and the first thing I heard was the farmer saying, 'How do you like those ears?'

" 'They aren't straight,' answered the other.

" 'Never mind,' said the farmer. 'They are ears just the same,' which was true enough.

" 'Now I'll make the eyes,' said the farmer. So he painted my right eye, and as soon as it was finished I found myself looking at him and at everything around me with a great deal of curiosity, for this was my first glimpse of the world.

" 'That's a rather pretty eye,' remarked the Munchkin who was watching the farmer. 'Blue paint is just the color for eyes.'

" 'I think I'll make the other a little bigger,' said the farmer. And when the second eye was done I could see much better than before. Then he made my nose and my mouth. But I did not speak, because at that time I didn't know what a mouth was for. I had the fun of watching them make my body and my arms and legs; and when they fastened on my head, at last, I felt very proud, for I thought I was just as good a man as anyone.

" 'This fellow will scare the crows fast enough,' said the farmer. 'He looks just like a man.'

" 'Why, he is a man,' said the other, and I quite agreed with him. The farmer carried me under his arm to the cornfield, and set me up on a tall stick, where you found me. He and his friend soon after walked away and left me alone.

"I did not like to be deserted this way. So I tried to walk after them. But my feet would not touch the ground, and I was forced to stay on that pole. It was a lonely life to lead, for I had nothing to think of, having been made such a little while before. Many crows and other birds flew into the cornfield, but as soon as they saw me they flew away again, thinking I was a Munchkin; and this pleased me and made me feel that I was quite an important person. By and by an old crow flew near me, and after looking at me carefully he perched upon my shoulder and said:

" 'I wonder if that farmer thought to fool me in this clumsy manner. Any crow of sense could see that you are only stuffed with straw.' Then he hopped down at my feet and ate all the corn he wanted. The other birds, seeing he was not harmed by me, came to eat the corn too, so in a short time there was a great flock of them about me.

"I felt sad at this, for it showed I was not such a good Scarecrow after all; but the old crow comforted me, saying, 'If you only had brains in your head you would be as good a man as any of them, and a better man than some of them. Brains are the only things worth having in this world, no matter whether one is a crow or a man.'

"After the crows had gone I thought this over, and decided I would try hard to get some brains. By good luck you came along and pulled me off the stake, and from what you say I am sure the Great Oz will give me brains as soon as we get to the Emerald City."

"I hope so," said Dorothy earnestly, "since you seem anxious to have them."

"Oh, yes; I am anxious," returned the Scarecrow. "It is such an un-

247

comfortable feeling to know one is a fool."

"Well," said the girl, "let us go." And she handed the basket to the Scarecrow.

There were no fences at all by the roadside now, and the land was rough and untilled. Toward evening they came to a great forest, where the trees grew so big and close together that their branches met over the road of yellow brick. It was almost dark under the trees, for the branches shut out the daylight; but the travelers did not stop, and went on into the forest.

"If this road goes in, it must come out," said the Scarecrow, "and as the Emerald City is at the other end of the road, we must go wherever it leads us."

"Anyone would know that," said Dorothy.

"Certainly; that is why I know it," returned the Scarecrow. "If it required brains to figure it out, I never should have said it."

After an hour or so the light faded away, and they found themselves stumbling along in the darkness. Dorothy could not see at all, but Toto could, for some dogs see very well in the dark; and the Scarecrow declared he could see as well as by day. So she took hold of his arm and managed to get along fairly well.

"If you see any house, or any place where we can pass the night," she said, "you must tell me; for it is very uncomfortable walking in the dark."

Soon after the Scarecrow stopped.

"I see a little cottage at the right of us," he said, "built of logs and branches. Shall we go there?"

"Yes, indeed," answered the child. "I am all tired out."

So the Scarecrow led her through the trees until they reached the cottage, and Dorothy entered and found a bed of dried leaves in one corner. She lay down at once, and with Toto beside her soon fell into a sound sleep. The Scarecrow, who was never tired, stood up in another corner and waited patiently until morning came.

Chapter 5

The Rescue
of the Tin Woodman

His head and arms and legs were jointed upon his body, but he stood perfectly motionless, as if he could not stir at all.

When Dorothy awoke the sun was shining through the trees and Toto had long been out chasing birds around him and squirrels. She sat up and looked around her. There was the Scarecrow, still standing patiently in his corner, waiting for her.

"We must go and search for water," she said to him.

"Why do you want water?" he asked.

"To wash my face clean after the dust of the road, and to drink, so the dry bread will not stick in my throat."

"It must be inconvenient to be made of flesh," said the Scarecrow thoughtfully, "for you must sleep, and eat and drink. However, you have brains, and it is worth a lot of bother to be able to think properly."

They left the cottage and walked through the trees until they found a little spring of clear water, where Dorothy drank and bathed and ate her breakfast. She saw there was not much bread left in the basket, and the girl was thankful the Scarecrow did not have to eat anything, for there was scarcely enough for herself and Toto for the day.

When she had finished her meal, and was about to go back to the road of yellow brick, she was startled to hear a deep groan near by.

"What was that?" she asked timidly.

"I cannot imagine," replied the Scarecrow; "but we can go and see."

Just then another groan reached their ears, and the sound seemed to come from behind them. They turned and walked through the forest a few steps, when Dorothy discovered something shining in a ray of sunshine that fell between the trees. She ran to the place and then stopped short, with a little cry of surprise.

One of the big trees had been partly chopped through, and standing beside it, with an uplifted axe in his hands, was a man made entirely of tin. His head and arms and legs were jointed upon his body, but he stood perfectly motionless, as if he could not stir at all.

Dorothy looked at him in amazement, and so did the Scarecrow, while Toto barked sharply and made a snap at the tin legs, which hurt his teeth.

"Did you groan?" asked Dorothy.

"Yes," answered the tin man, "I did. I've been groaning for more than a year, and no one has ever heard me before or come to help me."

"What can I do for you?" she inquired softly, for she was moved by the sad voice in which the man spoke.

"Get an oil-can and oil my joints," he answered. "They are rusted so badly that I cannot move them at all; if I am well oiled I shall soon be all right again. You will find an oil-can on a shelf in my cottage."

Dorothy at once ran back to the cottage and found the oil-can, and then she returned and asked anxiously, "Where are your joints?"

"Oil my neck, first," replied the Tin Woodman. So she oiled it, and as it was quite badly rusted the Scarecrow took hold of the tin head and moved it gently from side to side until it worked freely, and then the man could turn it himself.

"Now oil the joints in my arms," he said. And Dorothy oiled them and the Scarecrow bent them carefully until they were quite free from rust and as good as new.

The Tin Woodman gave a sigh of satisfaction and lowered his axe, which he leaned against the tree.

"This is a great comfort," he said. "I have been holding that axe in the air ever since I rusted, and I'm glad to be able to put it down at last. Now, if you will oil the joints of my legs, I shall be all right once more."

So they oiled his legs until he could move them freely; and he thanked them again and again for his release, for he seemed a very polite creature, and very grateful.

"I might have stood there always if you had not come along," he said; "so you have certainly saved my life. How did you happen to be here?"

"We are on our way to the Emerald City to see the Great Oz," she answered, "and we stopped at your cottage to pass the night."

"Why do you wish to see Oz?" he asked.

"I want him to send me back to Kansas, and the Scarecrow wants him to put a few brains into his head," she replied.

The Tin Woodman appeared to think deeply for a moment. Then he said:

"Do you suppose Oz could give me a heart?"

"Why, I guess so," Dorothy answered. "It would be as easy as to give the Scarecrow brains."

"True," the Tin Woodman returned. "So, if you will allow me to join your party, I will also go to the Emerald City and ask Oz to help me."

"Come along," said the Scarecrow heartily, and Dorothy added that she would be pleased to have his company. So the Tin Woodman shouldered his axe and they all passed through the forest until they came to the road that was paved with yellow brick.

The Tin Woodman had asked Dorothy to put the oil-can in her basket. "For," he said, "if I should get caught in the rain, and rust again, I would need the oil-can badly."

It was a bit of good luck to have their new comrade join the party, for soon after they had begun their journey again they came to a place where the trees and branches grew so thick over the road that the travelers could not pass. But the Tin Woodman set to work with his axe and chopped so well that soon he cleared a passage for the entire party.

Dorothy was thinking so earnestly as they walked along that she did not notice when the Scarecrow stumbled into a hole and rolled over to the side of the road. Indeed he was obliged to call to her to help him up again.

"Why didn't you walk around the hole?" asked the Tin Woodman.

"I don't know enough," replied the Scarecrow cheerfully. "My head is stuffed with straw, you know, and that is why I am going to Oz to ask him for some brains."

"Oh, I see," said the Tin Woodman. "But, after all, brains are not the best things in the world."

"Have you any?" inquired the Scarecrow.

"No, my head is quite empty," answered the Woodman. "But once I had brains, and a heart also; so, having tried them both, I should much rather have a heart."

"And why is that?" asked the Scarecrow.

"I will tell you my story, and then you will know."

So, while they were walking through the forest, the Tin Woodman told the following story:

"I was born the son of a woodman who chopped down trees in the forest and sold the wood for a living. When I grew up, I too became a woodchopper, and after my father died I took care of my old mother as long as she lived. Then I made up my mind that instead of living alone I would marry, so that I might not become lonely.

"There was one of the Munchkin girls who was so beautiful that I soon grew to love her with all my heart. She, on her part, promised to marry me as soon as I could earn enough money to build a better house for her; so I set to work harder than ever. But the girl lived with an old woman who did not want her to marry anyone, for she was so lazy, she wished the girl to remain with her and do the cooking and the housework. So the old woman went to the Wicked Witch of the East, and promised her two sheep and a cow if she would prevent the marriage. Thereupon the Wicked Witch enchanted my axe, and when I was chopping away at my best one day, for I was anxious to get the new house and my wife as soon as possible, the axe slipped all at once and cut off my left leg.

"This at first seemed a great misfortune, for I knew a one-legged man could not do very well as a wood-chopper. So I went to a tinsmith and had him make me a new leg out of tin. The leg worked very well, once I was used to it. But my action angered the Wicked Witch of the East, for she had promised the old woman I should not marry the pretty Munchkin girl. When I began chopping again, my axe slipped and cut off my right leg. Again I went to the tinsmith, and again he made me a leg out of tin. After this the enchanted axe cut off my arms, one after the other; but, nothing daunted, I had them replaced with tin ones. The Wicked Witch then made the axe slip and cut off my head, and at first I thought that was the end of me. But the tinsmith happened to come along, and he made me a new head out of tin.

"I thought I had beaten the Wicked Witch then, and I worked harder than ever; but I little knew how cruel my enemy could be. She thought of a new way to kill my love for the beautiful Munchkin maiden, and made my axe slip again, so that it cut right through my body, splitting me into two halves. Once more the tinsmith came to my help and made me a body of tin, fastening my tin arms and legs and head to it, by means of joints, so that I could move around as well as ever. But, alas! I had now no heart, so that I lost all my love for the Munchkin girl, and did not care whether I married her or not. I suppose she is still living with the old woman, waiting for me to come after her.

"My body shone so brightly in the sun that I felt very proud of it and it did not matter now if my axe slipped, for it could not cut me. There was only one danger – that my joints would rust; but I kept an oil-can in my cottage and took care to oil myself whenever I needed it. However, there came a day when I forgot to do this, and, being caught in a rainstorm, before I thought of the danger, my joints had rusted, and I was left to stand in the woods until you came to help me. It was a terrible thing to undergo, but during the year I stood there, I had time to think that the greatest loss I had known was the loss of my heart. While I was in love I was the happiest man on earth; but no one can love who has not a heart, and so I am resolved to ask Oz to give me one. If he does, I will go back to the Munchkin maiden and marry her."

Both Dorothy and the Scarecrow had been greatly interested in the story of the Tin Woodman, and now they knew why he was so anxious to get a new heart.

"All the same," said the Scarecrow, "I shall ask for brains instead of a heart; for a fool would not know what to do with a heart if he had one."

"I shall take the heart," returned the Tin Woodman; "for brains do not make one happy, and happiness is the best thing in the world."

Dorothy did not say anything, for she was puzzled to know which of her two friends was right, and she decided if she could only get back to Kansas and Aunt Em, it did not matter so much whether the Woodman had no brains and the Scarecrow no heart, or each got what he wanted.

What worried her most was that the bread was nearly gone, and another meal for herself and Toto would empty the basket. To be sure neither the Woodman nor the Scarecrow ever ate anything, but she was not made of tin nor straw, and could not live unless she was fed.

Chapter 6

The Cowardly Lion

Little Toto, now that he had an enemy to face, ran barking toward the Lion, and the great beast had opened his mouth to bite the dog.

All this time Dorothy and her companions had been walking through the thick woods. The road was still paved with yellow brick, but these were much covered by dried branches and dead leaves from the trees, and the walking was not at all good.

There were few birds in this part of the forest, for birds love the open country where there is plenty of sunshine. But now and then there came a deep growl from some wild animal hidden among the trees. These sounds made the little girl's heart beat fast, for she did not know what made them; but Toto knew, and he walked close to Dorothy's side, and did not even bark in return.

"How long will it be," the child asked of the Tin Woodman, "before we are out of the forest?"

"I cannot tell," was the answer, "for I have never been to the Emerald City. But my father went there once, when I was a boy, and he said it was a long journey through a dangerous country, although nearer to the city where Oz dwells the country is beautiful. But I am not afraid so long as I have my oil-can, and nothing can hurt the Scarecrow, while you bear upon your forehead the mark of the Good Witch's kiss, and that will protect you from harm."

"But Toto!" said the girl anxiously. "What will protect him?"

"We must protect him ourselves if he is in danger," replied the Tin Woodman.

Just as he spoke there came from the forest a terrible roar, and the next moment a great Lion bounded into the road. With one blow of his paw he sent the Scarecrow spinning over and over to the edge of the road, and then he struck at the Tin Woodman with his sharp claws. But, to the Lion's surprise, he could make no impression on the tin, although the Woodman fell over in the road and lay still.

Little Toto, now that he had an enemy to face, ran barking toward the Lion, and the great beast had opened his mouth to bite the dog, when Dorothy, fearing Toto would be killed, and heedless to danger, rushed forward and slapped the Lion upon his nose as hard as she could, while she cried out:

"Don't you dare to bite Toto! You ought to be ashamed of yourself, a big beast like you, to bite a poor little dog!"

"I didn't bite him," said the Lion, as he rubbed his nose with his paw where Dorothy had hit it.

"No, but you tried to," she retorted. "You are nothing but a big coward."

"I know it," said the Lion, hanging his head in shame. "I've always known it. But how can I help it?"

"I don't know, I'm sure. To think of your striking a stuffed man, like the poor Scarecrow!"

"Is he stuffed?" asked the Lion in surprise, as he watched her pick up the Scarecrow and set him upon his feet, while she patted him into shape again.

"Of course he's stuffed," replied Dorothy, who was still angry.

"That's why he went over so easily," remarked the Lion. "It astonished me to see him whirl around so. Is the other one stuffed also?"

"No," said Dorothy, "he's made of tin." And she helped the Woodman up again.

"That's why he nearly blunted my claws," said the Lion. "When they scratched against the tin it made a cold shiver run down my back. What is that little animal you are so tender with?"

"He is my dog, Toto," answered Dorothy.

"Is he made of tin, or stuffed?" asked the Lion.

"Neither. He's a – a – a meat dog," said the girl.

"Oh! He's a curious animal and seems remarkably small, now that I look at him. No one would think of biting such a little thing, except a coward like me," continued the Lion sadly.

"What makes you a coward?" asked Dorothy, looking at the great beast in wonder, for he was as big as a small horse.

"It's a mystery," replied the Lion. "I suppose I was born that way. All the other animals in the forest naturally expect me to be brave, for the Lion is everywhere thought to be the King of Beasts. I learned that if I roared very loudly every living thing was frightened and got out of my way. Whenever I've met a man I've been awfully scared; but I just roared at him, and he has always run away as fast as he could go. If the elephants and the tigers and the bears had ever tried to fight me, I should have run myself – I'm such a coward; but just as soon as they hear me roar they all try to get away from me, and of course I let them go."

"But that isn't right. The King of Beasts shouldn't be a coward," said the Scarecrow.

"I know it," returned the Lion, wiping a tear from his eye with the tip of his tail. "It is my great sorrow, and makes my life very unhappy. But whenever there is danger, my heart begins to beat fast."

"Perhaps you have heart disease," said the Tin Woodman.

"It may be," said the Lion.

"If you have," continued the Tin Woodman, "you ought to be glad, for it proves you have a heart. For my part, I have no heart; so I cannot have heart disease."

"Perhaps," said the Lion thoughtfully, "if I had no heart I should not be a coward."

"Have you brains?" asked the Scarecrow.

"I suppose so. I've never looked to see," replied the Lion.

"I am going to the Great Oz to ask him to give me some," remarked the Scarecrow, "for my head is stuffed with straw."

"And I am going to ask him to give me a heart," said the Woodman.

"And I am going to ask him to send Toto and me back to Kansas," added Dorothy.

"Do you think Oz could give me courage?" asked the Cowardly Lion.

"Just as easily as he could give me brains," said the Scarecrow.

"Or give me a heart," said the Tin Woodman.

"Or send me back to Kansas," said Dorothy.

"Then, if you don't mind, I'll go with you," said the Lion, "for my life is simply unbearable without a bit of courage."

"You will be very welcome," answered Dorothy, "for you will help to keep away the other wild beasts. It seems to me they must be more cowardly than you are if they allow you to scare them so easily."

"They really are," said the Lion, "but that doesn't make me any braver, and as long as I know myself to be a coward I shall be unhappy."

So once more the little company set off upon the journey, the Lion walking with stately strides at Dorothy's side. Toto did not approve of this new comrade at first, for he could not forget how nearly he had been crushed between the Lion's great jaws. But after a time he became more at ease, and presently Toto and the Cowardly Lion had grown to be good friends.

During the rest of that day there was no other adventure to mar the peace of their journey. Once, indeed, the Tin Woodman stepped upon a beetle that was crawling along the road, and killed the poor little thing. This made the Tin Woodman very unhappy, for he was always careful not to hurt any living creature; and as he walked along he wept several tears of sorrow and regret. These tears ran slowly down his face and over the hinges of his jaw, and there they rusted. When Dorothy presently asked him a question the Tin Woodman could not open his mouth, for his jaws were tightly rusted together. He became greatly frightened at this and made many motions to Dorothy to relieve him, but she could not understand. The Lion was also puzzled to know what was wrong. But the Scarecrow seized the oil-can from Dorothy's basket and oiled the Woodman's jaws, so that after a few moments he could talk as well as before.

"This will serve me a lesson," said he, "to look where I step. For if I should kill another bug or beetle I should surely cry again, and crying rusts my jaws so that I cannot speak."

Thereafter he walked very carefully, with his eyes on the road, and when he saw a tiny ant toiling by he would step over it, so as not to harm it. The Tin Woodman knew very well he had no heart, and therefore he took great care never to be cruel or unkind to anything.

"You people with hearts," he said, "have something to guide you, and need never do wrong; but I have no heart, and so I must be very careful. When Oz gives me a heart of course I needn't mind so much."

Chapter 7

*The Journey
to the Great Oz*

"We are lost, for they will surely tear us to pieces with their sharp claws. But stand close behind me, and I will fight them as long as I am alive."

They were obliged to camp out that night under a large tree in the forest, for there were no houses near. The tree made a good, thick covering to protect them from the dew, and the Tin Woodman chopped a great pile of wood with his axe and Dorothy built a splendid fire that warmed her and made her feel less lonely. She and Toto ate the last of their bread, and now she did not know what they would do for breakfast.

"If you wish," said the Lion, "I will go into the forest and kill a deer for you. You can roast it by the fire, since your tastes are so peculiar that you prefer cooked food, and then you will have a very good breakfast."

"Don't! Please don't," begged the Tin Woodman. "I should certainly weep if you killed a poor deer, and then my jaws would rust again."

But the Lion went away into the forest and found his own supper, and no one ever knew what it was, for he didn't mention it. And the Scarecrow found a tree full of nuts and filled Dorothy's basket with them, so that she would not be hungry for a long time. She thought this was very kind and thoughtful of the Scarecrow, but she laughed heartily at the awkward way in which the poor creature picked up the nuts. His padded hands were so clumsy and the nuts were so small that he dropped almost as many as he put in the basket. But the Scarecrow did not mind how long it took him to fill the basket, for it enabled him to keep away from the fire, as he feared a spark might get into his straw and burn him up. So he kept a good distance away from the flames, and only came near to cover Dorothy with dry leaves when she lay down to sleep. These kept her very snug and warm, and she slept soundly until morning.

When it was daylight, the girl bathed her face in a little rippling brook, and soon after they all started toward the Emerald City.

This was to be an eventful day for the travelers. They had hardly been walking an hour when they saw before them a great ditch that crossed the road and divided the forest as far as they could see on either side. It was a very wide ditch, and when they crept up to the edge and looked into it they could see it was also very deep, and there were many big, jagged rocks at the bottom. The sides were so steep that none of them could climb down, and for a moment it seemed that their journey must end.

"What shall we do?" asked Dorothy despairingly.

"I haven't the faintest idea," said the Tin Woodman, and the Lion shook his shaggy mane and looked thoughtful.

But the Scarecrow said, "We cannot fly, that is certain. Neither can we climb down into this great ditch. Therefore, if we cannot jump over it, we must stop where we are."

"I think I could jump over it," said the Cowardly Lion, after measuring the distance carefully in his mind.

"Then we are all right," answered the Scarecrow, "for you can carry us all over on your back, one at a time."

"Well, I'll try it," said the Lion. "Who will go first?"

"I will," declared the Scarecrow, "for, if you found that you could not jump over the gulf, Dorothy would be killed, or the Tin Woodman badly dented on the rocks below. But if I am on your back it will not matter so much, for the fall would not hurt me at all."

"I am terribly afraid of falling, myself," said the Cowardly Lion, "but I suppose there is nothing to do but try it. So get on my back and we will make the attempt."

The Scarecrow sat upon the Lion's back, and the big beast walked to the edge of the gulf and crouched down.

"Why don't you run and jump?" asked the Scarecrow.

"Because that isn't the way we Lions do these things," he replied. Then giving a great spring, he shot through the air and landed safely on the other side. They were all greatly pleased to see how easily he did it, and after the Scarecrow had got down from his back the Lion sprang across the ditch again.

Dorothy thought she would go next; so she took Toto in her arms and climbed on the Lion's back, holding tightly to his mane with one hand. The next moment it seemed as if she were flying through the air; and then, before she had time to think about it, she was safe on the other side. The Lion went back a third time and got the Tin Woodman, and then they all sat down for a few moments to give the beast a chance to rest, for his great leaps had made his breath short, and he panted like a big dog that has been running too long.

They found the forest very thick on this side, and it looked dark and gloomy. After the Lion had rested they started along the road of yellow brick, silently wondering, each in his own mind, if ever they would come to the end of the woods and reach the bright sunshine again. To add to their discomfort, they soon heard strange noises in the depths of the forest, and the Lion whispered to them that it was in this part of the country that the Kalidahs lived.

"What are the Kalidahs?" asked the girl.

"They are monstrous beasts with bodies like bears and heads like tigers," replied the Lion, "and with claws so long and sharp that they could tear me in two as easily as I could kill Toto. I'm terribly afraid of the Kalidahs."

"I'm not surprised that you are," returned Dorothy. "They must be dreadful beasts."

The Lion was about to reply when suddenly they came to another gulf across the road. But this one was so broad and deep that the Lion knew at once he could not leap across it.

So they sat down to consider what they should do, and after serious thought the Scarecrow said:

"Here is a great tree, standing close to the ditch. If the Tin Woodman can chop it down, so that it will fall to the other side, we can walk across it easily."

"That is a first-rate idea," said the Lion. "One would almost suspect you had brains in your head, instead of straw."

The Woodman set to work at once, and so sharp was his axe that the tree was soon chopped nearly through. Then the Lion put his strong front legs against the tree and pushed with all his might, and slowly the big tree tipped and fell with a crash across the ditch, with its top branches on the other side.

They had just started to cross this queer bridge when a sharp growl made them all look up, and to their horror they saw running towards them two great beasts with bodies like bears and heads like tigers.

"They are the Kalidahs!" said the Cowardly Lion, beginning to tremble.

"Quick!" cried the Scarecrow. "Let us cross over."

So Dorothy went first, holding Toto in her arms, the Tin Woodman followed, and the Scarecrow came next. The Lion, although he was certainly afraid, turned to face the Kalidahs, and then he gave so loud and terrible a roar that Dorothy screamed and the Scarecrow fell over backward, while even the fierce beasts stopped short and looked at him in surprise.

But, seeing they were bigger than the Lion, and remembering that there were two of them and only one of him, the Kalidahs again rushed forward, and the Lion crossed over the tree and turned to see what they would do next. Without stopping an instant the fierce beasts also began to cross the tree. And the Lion said to Dorothy:

"We are lost, for they will surely tear us to pieces with their sharp claws. But stand close behind me, and I will fight them as long as I am alive."

"Wait a minute!" called the Scarecrow. He had been thinking what was best to be done, and now he asked the Woodman to chop away the end of the tree that rested on their side of the ditch. The Tin Woodman began to use his axe at once, and, just as the two Kalidahs were nearly across, the tree fell with a crash into the gulf, carrying the ugly, snarling brutes with it, and both were dashed to pieces on the sharp rocks at the bottom.

"Well," said the Cowardly Lion, drawing a long breath of relief, "I see we are going to live a little while longer, and I am glad of it, for it must be a very uncomfortable thing not to be alive. Those creatures frightened me so badly that my heart is beating yet."

"Ah," said the Tin Woodman sadly, "I wish I had a heart to beat."

This adventure made the travelers more anxious than ever to get out of the forest, and they walked so fast that Dorothy became tired, and had to ride on the Lion's back. To their great joy the trees became thinner the farther they advanced, and in the afternoon they suddenly came upon a broad river, flowing swiftly just before them. On the other side of the water they could see the road of yellow brick running through a beautiful country, with green meadows dotted with bright flowers and all the road bordered with trees hanging full of delicious fruits. They were greatly pleased to see this delightful country before them.

"How shall we cross the river?" asked Dorothy.

"That is easily done," replied the Scarecrow. "The Tin Woodman must build us a raft, so we can float to the other side."

So the Woodman took his axe and began to chop down small trees to make a raft, and while he was busy at this the Scarecrow found on the riverbank a tree full of fine fruit. This pleased Dorothy, who had eaten nothing but nuts all day, and she made a hearty meal of the ripe fruit.

But it takes time to make a raft, even when one is as industrious and untiring as the Tin Woodman, and when night came the work was not done. So they found a cozy place under the trees where they slept well until the morning; and Dorothy dreamed of the Emerald City, and of the good Wizard Oz, who would soon send her back to her own home again.

Chapter 8
The Deadly Poppy Field

There were big yellow and white
and blue and purple blossoms,
besides great clusters of scarlet
poppies, which were so brilliant
in color they almost dazzled
Dorothy's eyes.

Our little party of travelers awakened the next morning refreshed and full of hope, and Dorothy breakfasted like a princess off peaches and plums from the trees beside the river. Behind them was the dark forest they had passed safely through, although they had suffered many discouragements; but before them was a lovely, sunny country that seemed to beckon them on to the Emerald City.

To be sure, the broad river now cut them off from this beautiful land. But the raft was nearly done, and after the Tin Woodman had cut a few more logs and fastened them together with wooden pins, they were ready to start. Dorothy sat down in the middle of the raft and held Toto in her arms. When the Cowardly Lion stepped upon the raft it tipped badly, for he was big and heavy; but the Scarecrow and the Tin Woodman stood upon the other end to steady it, and they had long poles in their hands to push the raft through the water.

They got along quite well at first, but when they reached the middle of the river the swift current swept the raft downstream, farther and farther away from the road of yellow brick. And the water grew so deep that the long poles would not touch the bottom.

"This is bad," said the Tin Woodman, "for if we cannot get to the land we shall be carried into the country of the Wicked Witch of the West, and she will enchant us and make us her slaves."

"And then I should get no brains," said the Scarecrow.

"And I should get no courage," said the Cowardly Lion.

"And I should get no heart," said the Tin Woodman.

"And I should never get back to Kansas," said Dorothy.

"We must certainly get to the Emerald City if we can," the Scarecrow continued, and he pushed so hard on his long pole that it stuck fast in the mud at the bottom of the river. Then, before he could pull it out again, or let go, the raft was swept away, and the poor Scarecrow left clinging to the pole in the middle of the river.

"Good-bye!" he called after them, and they were very sorry to leave him. Indeed, the Tin Woodman began to cry, but fortunately remembered that he might rust, and so dried his tears on Dorothy's apron.

Of course this was a bad thing for the Scarecrow.

"I am now worse off than when I first met Dorothy," he thought. "Then, I was stuck on a pole in a cornfield, where I could pretend to scare the crows, at any rate. But surely there is no use for a Scarecrow stuck on a pole in the middle of a river. I am afraid I shall never have any brains, after all!"

Down the stream the raft floated, and the poor Scarecrow was left far behind. Then the Lion said:

"Something must be done to save us. I think I can swim to the shore and pull the raft after me, if you will only hold fast to the tip of my tail."

So he sprang into the water, and the Tin Woodman caught fast hold of his tail. When the Lion began to swim with all his might toward the shore. It was hard work, although he was so big; but by and by they were drawn out of the current, and then Dorothy took the Tin Woodman's long pole and helped push the raft to the land.

They were all tired out when they reached the shore at last and stepped off upon the pretty green grass, and they also knew that the stream had carried them a long way past the road of yellow brick that led to the Emerald City.

"What shall we do now?" asked the Tin Woodman, as the Lion lay down on the grass to let the sun dry him.

"We must get back to the road, in some way," said Dorothy.

"The best plan will be to walk along the riverbank until we come to the road again," remarked the Lion.

So, when they were rested, Dorothy picked up her basket and they started along the grassy bank, back to the road from which the river had carried them. It was a lovely country, with plenty of flowers and fruit trees and sunshine to cheer them, and had they not felt so sorry for the poor Scarecrow, they could have been very happy.

They walked along as fast as they could, Dorothy only stopping once to pick a beautiful flower; and after a time the Tin Woodman cried out: "Look!"

Then they all looked at the river and saw the Scarecrow perched upon his pole in the middle of the water, looking very lonely and sad.

"What can we do to save him?" asked Dorothy.

The Lion and the Woodman both shook their heads, for they did not know. So they sat down upon the bank and gazed wistfully at the Scarecrow until a Stork flew by, who, upon seeing them, stopped to rest at the water's edge.

"Who are you and where are you going?" asked the Stork.

"I am Dorothy," answered the girl, "and these are my friends, the Tin Woodman and the Cowardly Lion; and we are going to the Emerald City."

"This isn't the road," said the Stork, as she twisted her long neck and looked sharply at the queer party.

"I know it," returned Dorothy, "but we have lost the Scarecrow, and are wondering how we shall get him again."

"Where is he?" asked the Stork.

"Over there in the river," answered the little girl.

"If he wasn't so big and heavy I would get him for you," remarked the Stork.

"He isn't heavy a bit," said Dorothy eagerly, "for he is stuffed with straw; and if you will bring him back to us, we shall thank you ever and ever so much."

"Well, I'll try," said the Stork, "but if I find he is too heavy to carry I shall have to drop him in the river again."

So the big bird flew into the air and over the water till she came to where the Scarecrow was perched upon his pole. Then the Stork with her great claws grabbed the Scarecrow by the arm and carried him up into the air and back to the bank, where Dorothy and the Lion and the Tin Woodman and Toto were sitting.

When the Scarecrow found himself among his friends again, he was so happy that he hugged them all, even the Lion and Toto; and as they walked along he sang "Tol-de-ri-de-oh!" at every step, he felt so gay.

"I was afraid I should have to stay in the river forever," he said, "but the kind Stork saved me, and if I ever get any brains I shall find the Stork again and do her some kindness in return."

"That's all right," said the Stork, who was flying along beside them. "I always like to help anyone in trouble. But I must go now, for my babies are waiting in the nest for me. I hope you will find the Emerald City and that Oz will help you."

"Thank you," replied Dorothy, and then the kind Stork flew into the air and was soon out of sight.

They walked along listening to the singing of the brightly colored birds and looking at the lovely flowers which now became so thick that the ground was carpeted with them. There were big yellow and white and blue and purple blossoms, besides great clusters of scarlet poppies, which were so brilliant in color they almost dazzled Dorothy's eyes.

"Aren't they beautiful?" the girl asked, as she breathed in the spicy scent of the flowers.

"I suppose so," answered the Scarecrow. "When I have brains, I shall probably like them better."

"If I only had a heart, I should love them," added the Tin Woodman.

"I always did like flowers," said the Lion. "They seem so helpless and frail. But there are none in the forest so bright as these."

They now came upon more and more of the big scarlet poppies, and fewer and fewer of the other flowers; and soon they found themselves in the midst of a great meadow of poppies. Now it is well known that when there are many of these flowers together their odor is so powerful that anyone who breathes it falls asleep, and if the sleeper is not carried away from the scent of the flowers, he sleeps on and on forever. But Dorothy did not know this, nor could she get away from the bright red flowers that were everywhere about; so presently her eyes grew heavy and she felt she must sit down to rest and to sleep.

But the Tin Woodman would not let her do this.

"We must hurry and get back to the road of yellow brick before dark," he said; and the Scarecrow agreed with him. So they kept walking until Dorothy could stand no longer. Her eyes closed in spite of herself and she forgot where she was and fell among the poppies, fast asleep.

"What shall we do?" asked the Tin Woodman.

"If we leave her here she will die," said the Lion. "The smell of the flowers is killing us all. I myself can scarcely keep my eyes open, and the dog is asleep already."

It was true; Toto had fallen down beside his little mistress. But the Scarecrow and the Tin Woodman, not being made of flesh, were not troubled by the scent of the flowers.

"Run fast," said the Scarecrow to the Lion, "and get out of this deadly flower bed as soon as you can. We will bring the little girl with us, but if you should fall asleep you are too big to be carried."

So the Lion aroused himself and bounded forward as fast as he could go. In a moment he was out of sight.

"Let us make a chair with our hands and carry her," said the Scarecrow. So they picked up Toto and put the dog in Dorothy's lap, and then they made a chair with their hands for the seat and their arms for the arms and carried the sleeping girl between them through the flowers.

On and on they walked, and it seemed that the great carpet of deadly flowers that surrounded them would never end. They followed the bend of the river, and at last came upon their friend the Lion, lying fast asleep among the poppies. The flowers had been too strong for the huge beast and he had given up at last, and fallen only a short distance from the end of the poppy bed, where the sweet grass spread in beautiful green fields before them.

"We can do nothing for him," said the Tin Woodman, sadly; "for he is much too heavy to lift. We must leave him here to sleep on forever, and perhaps he will dream that he has found courage at last."

"I'm sorry," said the Scarecrow. "The Lion was a very good comrade for one so cowardly. But let us go on."

They carried the sleeping girl to a pretty spot beside the river, far enough from the poppy field to prevent her breathing any more of the poison of the flowers, and here they laid her gently on the soft grass and waited for the fresh breeze to waken her.

Chapter 9

The Queen
of the Field Mice

"Only a mouse!" cried the little animal, indignantly. "Why, I am a Queen – the Queen of all the Field Mice!"

"We cannot be far from the road of yellow brick, now," remarked the Scarecrow, as he stood beside the girl, "for we have come nearly as far as the river carried us away."

The Tin Woodman was about to reply when he heard a low growl, and turning his head (which worked beautifully on hinges) he saw a strange beast come bounding over the grass toward them. It was, indeed, a great yellow Wildcat, and the Woodman thought it must be chasing something, for its ears were lying close to its head and its mouth was wide open, showing two rows of ugly teeth, while its red eyes glowed like balls of fire. As it came nearer the Tin Woodman saw that running before the beast was a little gray field mouse, and although he had no heart he knew it was wrong for the Wildcat to try to kill such a pretty, harmless creature.

So the Woodman raised his axe, and as the Wildcat ran by he gave it a quick blow that cut the beast's head clean off from its body, and it rolled over at his feet in two pieces.

The field mouse, now that it was freed from its enemy, stopped short; and coming slowly up to the Woodman it said, in a squeaky little voice:

"Oh, thank you! Thank you ever so much for saving my life."

"Don't speak of it, I beg of you," replied the Woodman. "I have no heart, you know, so I am careful to help all those who may need a friend, even if it happens to be only a mouse."

"Only a mouse!" cried the little animal, indignantly. "Why, I am a Queen – the Queen of all the Field Mice!"

"Oh, indeed," said the Woodman, making a bow.

"Therefore you have done a great deed, as well as a brave one, in saving my life," added the Queen.

At that moment several mice were seen running up as fast as their little legs could carry them, and when they saw their Queen they exclaimed:

"Oh, your Majesty, we thought you would be killed! How did you manage to escape the great Wildcat?" They all bowed so low to the little Queen that they almost stood upon their heads.

"This funny tin man," she answered, "killed the Wildcat and saved my life. So hereafter you must all serve him, and obey his slightest wish."

"We will!" cried all the mice, in a shrill chorus. And then they scampered in all directions, for Toto had awakened from his sleep, and seeing all these mice around him he gave one bark of delight and jumped right into the middle of the group. Toto had always loved to chase mice when he lived in Kansas, and he saw no harm in it.

But the Tin Woodman caught the dog in his arms and held him tight, while he called to the mice, "Come back! Come back! Toto shall not hurt you."

At this the Queen of the Mice stuck her head out from underneath a clump of grass and asked, in a timid voice, "Are you sure he will not bite us?"

"I will not let him," said the Woodman; "so do not be afraid."

One by one the mice came creeping back, and Toto did not bark again, although he tried to get out of the Woodman's arms, and would have bitten him had he not known very well he was made of tin. Finally one of the biggest mice spoke.

"Is there anything we can do," it asked, "to repay you for saving the life of our Queen?"

"Nothing that I know of," answered the Woodman; but the Scarecrow, who had been trying to think, but could not because his head was stuffed with straw, said, quickly, "Oh, yes; you can save our friend, the Cowardly Lion, who is asleep in the poppy bed."

"A Lion!" cried the little Queen. "Why, he would eat us all up."

"Oh, no," declared the Scarecrow; "this Lion is a coward."

"Really?" asked the Mouse.

"He says so himself," answered the Scarecrow, "and he would never hurt anyone who is our friend. If you will help us to save him I promise that he shall treat you all with kindness."

"Very well," said the Queen, "we trust you. But what shall we do?"

"Are there many of these mice which call you Queen and are willing to obey you?"

"Oh, yes; there are thousands," she replied.

"Then send for them all to come here as soon as possible, and let each one bring a long piece of string."

The Queen turned to the mice that attended her and told them to go at once and get all her people. As soon as they heard her orders they ran away in every direction as fast as possible.

"Now," said the Scarecrow to the Tin Woodman, "you must go to those trees by the riverside and make a truck that will carry the Lion."

So the Woodman went at once to the trees and began to work; and he soon made a truck out of the limbs of trees, from which he chopped away all the leaves and branches. He fastened it together with wooden pegs and made the four wheels out of short pieces of a big tree trunk. So fast and so well did he work that by the time the mice began to arrive the truck was all ready for them.

They came from all directions, and there were thousands of them: big mice and little mice and middle-sized mice; and each one brought a piece of string in his mouth. It was about this time that Dorothy woke from her long sleep and opened her eyes. She was greatly astonished to find herself lying upon the grass, with thousands of mice standing around and looking at her timidly. But the Scarecrow told her about everything, and turning to the dignified little Mouse, he said: "Permit me to introduce to you her Majesty, the Queen."

Dorothy nodded gravely and the Queen made a curtsy, after which she became quite friendly with the little girl.

The Scarecrow and the Woodman now began to fasten the mice to the truck, using the strings they had brought. One end of a string was tied around the neck of each mouse and the other end to the truck. Of course the truck was a thousand times bigger than any of the mice who were to draw it; but when all the mice had been harnessed, they were able to pull it quite easily. Even the Scarecrow and the Tin Woodman could sit on it, and were drawn swiftly by their queer little horses to the place where the Lion lay asleep.

After a great deal of hard work, for the Lion was heavy, they managed to get him up on the truck. Then the Queen hurriedly gave her people the order to start, for she feared if the mice stayed among the poppies too long they also would fall asleep.

At first the little creatures, many though they were, could hardly stir the heavily loaded truck; but the Woodman and the Scarecrow both pushed from behind, and they got along better. Soon they rolled the Lion out of the poppy bed to the green fields, where he could breathe the sweet, fresh air again, instead of the poisonous scent of the flowers.

Dorothy came to meet them and thanked the little mice warmly for saving her companion from death. She had grown so fond of the big Lion she was glad he had been rescued.

Then the mice were unharnessed from the truck and scampered away through the grass to their homes. The Queen of the Mice was the last to leave.

"If you ever need us again," she said, "come out into the field and call, and we shall hear you and come to your assistance. Good-bye!"

"Good-bye!" they all answered, and away the Queen ran, while Dorothy held Toto tightly lest he should run after her and frighten her.

After this they sat down beside the Lion until he should awaken; and the Scarecrow brought Dorothy some fruit from a tree near by, which she ate for her dinner.

Chapter 10

The Guardian
of the Gates

In front of them, and at the
end of the road of yellow brick,
was a big gate, all studded with
emeralds that glittered so in the
sun that even the painted eyes of
the Scarecrow were dazzled by
their brilliancy.

It was some time before the Cowardly Lion awakened, for he had lain among the poppies a long while, breathing in their deadly fragrance; but when he did open his eyes and roll off the truck he was very glad to find himself still alive.

"I ran as fast as I could," he said, sitting down and yawning, "but the flowers were too strong for me. How did you get me out?"

Then they told him of the field mice, and how they had generously saved him from death; and the Cowardly Lion laughed, and said:

"I have always thought myself very big and terrible; yet such little things as flowers came near to killing me, and such small animals as mice have saved my life. How strange it all is! But, comrades, what shall we do now?"

"We must journey on until we find the road of yellow brick again," said Dorothy, "and then we can keep on to the Emerald City."

So, the Lion being fully refreshed, and feeling quite himself again, they all started upon the journey, greatly enjoying the walk through the soft, fresh grass; and it was not long before they reached the road of yellow brick and turned again toward the Emerald City where the great Oz dwelt.

The road was smooth and well paved, now, and the country about was beautiful, so that the travelers rejoiced in leaving the forest far behind, and with it the many dangers they had met in its gloomy shades. Once more they could see fences built beside the road; but these were painted green, and when they came to a small house, in which a farmer evidently lived, that also was painted green. They passed by several of these houses during the afternoon, and sometimes people came to the doors and looked at them as if they would like to ask questions; but no one came near them nor spoke to them because of the great Lion, of which they were very much afraid. The people were all dressed in clothing of a lovely emerald-green color and wore peaked hats like those of the Munchkins.

"This must be the Land of Oz," said Dorothy, "and we are surely getting near the Emerald City."

"Yes," answered the Scarecrow. "Everything is green here, while in the country of the Munchkins blue was the favorite color. But the people do not seem to be as friendly as the Munchkins, and I'm afraid we shall be unable to find a place to pass the night."

"I should like something to eat besides fruit," said the girl, "and I'm sure Toto is nearly starved. Let us stop at the next house and talk to the people."

So, when they came to a good-sized farmhouse, Dorothy walked boldly up to the door and knocked.

A woman opened it just far enough to look out, and said, "What do you want, child, and why is that great Lion with you?"

"We wish to pass the night with you, if you will allow us," answered Dorothy; "and the Lion is my friend and comrade, and would not hurt you for the world."

"Is he tame?" asked the woman, opening the door a little wider.

"Oh, yes," said the girl, "and he is a great coward, too. He will be more afraid of you than you are of him."

"Well," said the woman, after thinking it over and taking another peep at the Lion, "if that is the case you may come in, and I will give you some supper and a place to sleep."

So they all entered the house, where there were, besides the woman, two children and a man. The man had hurt his leg, and was lying on the couch in a corner. They seemed greatly surprised to see so strange a company, and while the woman was busy laying the table the man asked:

"Where are you all going?"

"To the Emerald City," said Dorothy, "to see the Great Oz."

"Oh, indeed!" exclaimed the man. "Are you sure that Oz will see you?"

"Why not?" she replied.

"Why, it is said that he never lets anyone come into his presence. I have been to the Emerald City many times, and it is a beautiful and wonderful place; but I have never been permitted to see the Great Oz, nor do I know of any living person who has seen him."

"Does he never go out?" asked the Scarecrow.

"Never. He sits day after day in the great throne room of his Palace, and even those who wait upon him do not see him face to face."

"What is he like?" asked the girl.

"That is hard to tell," said the man thoughtfully. "You see, Oz is a Great Wizard, and can take on any form he wishes. So that some say he looks like a bird; and some say he looks like an elephant; and some say he looks like a cat. To others he appears as a beautiful fairy, or a brownie, or in any other form that pleases him. But who the real Oz is, when he is in his own form, no living person can tell."

"That is very strange," said Dorothy, "but we must try, in some way, to see him, or we shall have made our journey for nothing."

"Why do you wish to see the terrible Oz?" asked the man.

"I want him to give me some brains," said the Scarecrow eagerly.

"Oh, Oz could do that easily enough," declared the man. "He has more brains than he needs."

"And I want him to give me a heart," said the Tin Woodman.

"That will not trouble him," continued the man, "for Oz has a large collection of hearts, of all sizes and shapes."

"And I want him to give me courage," said the Cowardly Lion.

"Oz keeps a great pot of courage in his throne room," said the man, "which he has covered with a golden plate, to keep it from running over. He will be glad to give you some."

"And I want him to send me back to Kansas," said Dorothy.

"Where is Kansas?" asked the man, with surprise.

"I don't know," replied Dorothy sorrowfully, "but it is my home, and I'm sure it's somewhere."

"Very likely. Well, Oz can do anything; so I suppose he will find Kansas for you. But first you must get to see him, and that will be a hard task; for the Great Wizard does not like to see anyone, and he usually has his own way. But what do you want?" he continued, speaking to Toto. Toto only wagged his tail; for, strange to say, he could not speak.

The woman now called to them that supper was ready, so they gathered around the table and Dorothy ate some delicious porridge and a dish of scrambled eggs and a plate of nice white bread, and enjoyed her meal. The Lion ate some of the porridge, but did not care for it, saying it was made from oats and oats were food for horses, not for lions. The Scarecrow and the Tin Woodman ate nothing at all. Toto ate a little of everything, and was glad to get a good supper again.

The woman now gave Dorothy a bed to sleep in, and Toto lay down beside her, while the Lion guarded the door of her room so she might not be disturbed. The Scarecrow and the Tin Woodman stood up in a corner and kept quiet all night, although of course they could not sleep.

The next morning, as soon as the sun was up, they started on their way, and soon saw a beautiful green glow in the sky just before them.

"That must be the Emerald City," said Dorothy.

As they walked on, the green glow became brighter and brighter, and it seemed that at last they were nearing the end of their travels. Yet it was afternoon before they came to the great wall that surrounded the City. It was high and thick and of a bright green color.

In front of them, and at the end of the road of yellow brick, was a big gate, all studded with emeralds that glittered so in the sun that even the painted eyes of the Scarecrow were dazzled by their brilliancy.

There was a bell beside the gate, and Dorothy pushed the button and heard a silvery tinkle sound within. Then the big gate swung slowly open, and they all passed through and found themselves in a high arched room, the walls of which glistened with countless emeralds.

Before them stood a little man about the same size as the Munchkins. He was clothed all in green, from his head to his feet, and even his skin was of a greenish tint. At his side was a large green box.

When he saw Dorothy and her companions the man asked, "What do you wish in the Emerald City?"

"We came here to see the Great Oz," said Dorothy.

The man was so surprised at this answer that he sat down to think it over.

"It has been many years since anyone asked me to see Oz," he said, shaking his head in perplexity. "He is powerful and terrible, and if you come on an idle or foolish errand to bother the wise reflections of the Great Wizard, he might be angry and destroy you all in an instant."

"But it is not a foolish errand, nor an idle one," replied the Scarecrow; "it is important. And we have been told that Oz is a good Wizard."

"So he is," said the green man, "and he rules the Emerald City wisely and well. But to those who are not honest, or who approach him from curiosity, he is most terrible, and few have ever dared ask to see his face. I am the Guardian of the Gates, and since you demand to see the Great Oz I must take you to his palace. But first you must put on the spectacles."

"Why?" asked Dorothy.

"Because if you did not wear spectacles the brightness and glory of the Emerald City would blind you. Even those who live in the City must wear spectacles night and day. They are all locked on, for Oz so ordered it when the City was first built, and I have the only key that will unlock them."

He opened the big box, and Dorothy saw that it was filled with spectacles of every size and shape. All of them had green glasses in them. The Guardian of the Gates found a pair that would just fit Dorothy and put them over her eyes. There were two golden bands fastened to them that passed around the back of her head, where they were locked together by a little key that was at the end of a chain the Guardian of the Gates wore around his neck. When they were on, Dorothy could not take them off had she wished, but of course she did not wish to be blinded by the glare of the Emerald City, so she said nothing.

Then the green man fitted spectacles for the Scarecrow and the Tin Woodman and the Lion, and even on little Toto; and all were locked fast with the key.

Then the Guardian of the Gates put on his own glasses and told them he was ready to show them to the palace. Taking a big golden key from a peg on the wall, he opened another gate, and they all followed him through the portal into the streets of the Emerald City.

Chapter 11

The Wonderful Emerald City of Oz

"If you wish me to use my magic power to send you home again you must do something for me first. Help me and I will help you."

Even with eyes protected by the green spectacles, Dorothy and her friends were at first dazzled by the brilliancy of the wonderful City. The streets were lined with beautiful houses all built of green marble and studded everywhere with sparkling emeralds. They walked over a pavement of the same green marble, and where the blocks were joined together were rows of emeralds, set closely, and glittering in the brightness of the sun. The window panes were of green glass; even the sky above the City had a green tint, and the rays of the sun were green.

There were many people – men, women, and children – walking about, and these were all dressed in green clothes and had greenish skins. They looked at Dorothy and her strangely assorted company with wondering eyes, and the children all ran away and hid behind their mothers when they saw the Lion; but no one spoke to them. Many shops stood in the street, and Dorothy saw that everything in them was green. Green candy and green pop corn were offered for sale, as well as green shoes, green hats, and green clothes of all sorts. At one place a man was selling green lemonade, and when the children bought it Dorothy could see that they paid for it with green pennies.

There seemed to be no horses nor animals of any kind; the men carried things around in little green carts, which they pushed before them. Everyone seemed happy and contented and prosperous.

The Guardian of the Gates led them through the streets until they came to a big building, exactly in the middle of the City, which was the Palace of Oz, the Great Wizard. There was a soldier before the door, dressed in a green uniform and wearing a long green beard.

"Here are strangers," said the Guardian of the Gates to him, "and they demand to see the Great Oz."

"Step inside," answered the soldier, "and I will carry your message to him."

So they passed through the Palace Gates and were led into a big room with a green carpet and lovely green furniture set with emeralds. The soldier made them all wipe their feet upon a green mat before entering this room, and when they were seated he said politely:

"Please make yourselves comfortable while I go to the door of the Throne Room and tell Oz you are here."

They had to wait a long time before the soldier returned. When, at last, he came back, Dorothy asked:

"Have you seen Oz?"

"Oh, no," returned the soldier; "I have never seen him. But I spoke to him as he sat behind his screen and gave him your message. He said he will grant you an audience, if you so desire; but each one of you must enter his presence alone, and he will admit but one each day. Therefore, as you must remain in the Palace for several days, I will have you shown to rooms where you may rest in comfort after your journey."

"Thank you," replied the girl; "that is very kind of Oz."

The soldier now blew upon a green whistle, and at once a young girl, dressed in a pretty green silk gown, entered the room. She had lovely green hair and green eyes, and she bowed low before Dorothy as she said, "Follow me and I will show you your room."

So Dorothy said good-bye to all her friends except Toto, and taking the dog in her arms followed the green girl through seven passages and up three flights of stairs until they came to a room at the front of the Palace. It was the sweetest little room in the world, with a soft comfortable bed that had sheets of green silk and a green velvet counterpane. There was a tiny fountain in the middle of the room, that shot a spray of green perfume into the air, to fall back into a beautifully carved green marble basin. Beautiful green flowers stood in the windows, and there was a shelf with a row of little green books. When Dorothy had time to open these books she found them full of queer green pictures that made her laugh, they were so funny.

In a wardrobe were many green dresses, made of silk and satin and velvet; and all of them fitted Dorothy exactly.

"Make yourself perfectly at home," said the green girl, "and if you wish for anything ring the bell. Oz will send for you tomorrow morning."

She left Dorothy alone and went back to the others. These she also led to rooms, and each one of them found himself lodged in a very pleasant part of the Palace. Of course this politeness was wasted on the Scarecrow; for when he found himself alone in his room he stood stupidly in one spot, just within the doorway, to wait till morning. It would not rest him to lie down, and he could not close his eyes; so he remained all night staring at a little spider which was weaving its web in a corner of the room, just as if it were not one of the most wonderful rooms in the world. The Tin Woodman lay down on his bed from force of habit, for he remembered when he was made of flesh; but not being able to sleep, he passed the night moving his joints up and down to make sure they kept in good working order. The Lion would have preferred a bed of dried leaves in the forest, and did not like being shut up in a room; but he had too much sense to let this worry him, so he sprang upon the bed and rolled himself up like a cat and purred himself asleep in a minute.

The next morning, after breakfast, the green maiden came to fetch Dorothy, and she dressed her in one of the prettiest gowns, made of green brocaded satin. Dorothy put on a green silk apron and tied a green ribbon around Toto's neck, and they started for the Throne Room of the Great Oz.

First they came to a great hall in which were many ladies and gentlemen of the court, all dressed in rich costumes. These people had nothing to do but talk to each other, but they always came to wait outside the Throne Room every morning, although they were never permitted to see Oz. As Dorothy entered they looked at her curiously, and one of them whispered:

"Are you really going to look upon the face of Oz the Terrible?"

"Of course," answered the girl, "if he will see me."

"Oh, he will see you," said the soldier who had taken her message to the Wizard, "although he does not like to have people ask to see him. Indeed, at first he was angry and said I should send you back where you came from. Then he asked me what you looked like, and when I mentioned your silver shoes he was very much interested. At last I told him about the mark upon your forehead, and he decided he would admit you to his presence."

Just then a bell rang, and the green girl said to Dorothy, "That is the signal. You must go into the Throne Room alone."

She opened a little door and Dorothy walked boldly through and found herself in a wonderful place. It was a big, round room with a high arched roof, and the walls and ceiling and floor were covered with large emeralds set closely together. In the center of the roof was a great light, as bright as the sun, which made the emeralds sparkle in a wonderful manner.

But what interested Dorothy most was the big throne of green marble that stood in the middle of the room. It was shaped like a chair and sparkled with gems, as did everything else. In the center of the chair was an enormous Head, without a body to support it or any arms or legs whatever. There was no hair upon this head, but it had eyes and a nose and mouth, and was much bigger than the head of the biggest giant.

As Dorothy gazed upon this in wonder and fear, the eyes turned slowly and looked at her sharply and steadily. Then the mouth moved, and Dorothy heard a voice say:

"I am Oz, the Great and Terrible. Who are you, and why do you seek me?"

It was not such an awful voice as she had expected to come from the big Head; so she took courage and answered:

"I am Dorothy, the Small and Meek. I have come to you for help."

The eyes looked at her thoughtfully for a full minute. Then said the voice:

"Where did you get the silver shoes?"

"I got them from the Wicked Witch of the East, when my house fell on her and killed her," she replied.

"Where did you get the mark upon your forehead?" continued the voice.

"That is where the Good Witch of the North kissed me when she bade me good-bye and sent me to you," said the girl.

Again the eyes looked at her sharply, and they saw she was telling the truth. Then Oz asked, "What do you wish me to do?"

"Send me back to Kansas, where my Aunt Em and Uncle Henry are," she answered earnestly. "I don't like your country, although it is so beautiful. And I am sure Aunt Em will be dreadfully worried over my being away so long."

The eyes winked three times, and then they turned up to the ceiling and down to the floor and rolled around so queerly that they seemed to see every part of the room. And at last they looked at Dorothy again.

"Why should I do this for you?" asked Oz.

"Because you are strong and I am weak; because you are a Great Wizard and I am only a helpless little girl."

"But you were strong enough to kill the Wicked Witch of the East," said Oz.

"That just happened," returned Dorothy simply; "I could not help it."

"Well," said the Head, "I will give you my answer. You have no right to expect me to send you back to Kansas unless you do something for me in return. In this country everyone must pay for everything he gets. If you wish me to use my magic power to send you home again you must do something for me first. Help me and I will help you."

"What must I do?" asked the girl.

"Kill the Wicked Witch of the West," answered Oz.

"But I cannot!" exclaimed Dorothy, greatly surprised.

"You killed the Witch of the East and you wear the silver shoes, which bear a powerful charm. There is now but one Wicked Witch left in all this land, and when you can tell me she is dead I will send you back to Kansas – but not before."

The little girl began to weep, she was so much disappointed; and the eyes winked again and looked upon her anxiously, as if the Great Oz felt that she could help him if she would.

"I never killed anything, willingly," she sobbed. "Even if I wanted to, how could I kill the Wicked Witch? If you, who are Great and Terrible, cannot kill her yourself, how do you expect me to do it?"

"I do not know," said the Head; "but that is my answer, and until the Wicked Witch dies you will not see your uncle and aunt again. Remember that the Witch is Wicked – tremendously Wicked – and ought to be killed. Now go, and do not ask to see me again until you have done your task."

Sorrowfully Dorothy left the Throne Room and went back where the Lion and the Scarecrow and the Tin Woodman were waiting to hear what Oz had said to her. "There is no hope for me," she said sadly, "for Oz will not send me home until I have killed the Wicked Witch of the West; and that I can never do."

Her friends were sorry, but could do nothing to help her; so Dorothy went to her own room and lay down on the bed and cried herself to sleep.

The next morning the soldier with the green whiskers came to the Scarecrow and said:

"Come with me, for Oz has sent for you."

So the Scarecrow followed him and was admitted into the great Throne Room, where he saw, sitting in the emerald throne, a most lovely Lady. She was dressed in green silk gauze and wore upon her flowing green locks a crown of jewels. Growing from her shoulders were wings, gorgeous in color and so light that they fluttered if the slightest breath of air reached them.

When the Scarecrow had bowed, as prettily as his straw stuffing would let him, before this beautiful creature, she looked upon him sweetly, and said:

"I am Oz, the Great and Terrible. Who are you, and why do you seek me?"

Now the Scarecrow, who had expected to see the great Head Dorothy had told him of, was much astonished; but he answered her bravely.

"I am only a Scarecrow, stuffed with straw. Therefore I have no brains, and I come to you praying that you will put brains in my head instead of straw, so that I may become as much a man as any other in your dominions."

"Why should I do this for you?" asked the Lady.

"Because you are wise and powerful, and no one else can help me," answered the Scarecrow.

"I never grant favors without some return," said Oz; "but this much I will promise. If you will kill for me the Wicked Witch of the West, I will bestow upon you a great many brains, and such good brains that you will be the wisest man in all the Land of Oz."

"I thought you asked Dorothy to kill the Witch," said the Scarecrow, in surprise.

"So I did. I don't care who kills her. But until she is dead I will not grant your wish. Now go, and do not seek me again until you have earned the brains you so greatly desire."

The Scarecrow went sorrowfully back to his friends and told them what Oz had said; and Dorothy was surprised to find that the great Wizard was not a Head, as she had seen him, but a lovely Lady.

"All the same," said the Scarecrow, "she needs a heart as much as the Tin Woodman."

On the next morning the soldier with the green whiskers came to the Tin Woodman and said:

"Oz has sent for you. Follow me."

So the Tin Woodman followed him and came to the great Throne Room. He did not know whether he would find Oz a lovely Lady or a Head, but he hoped it would be the lovely Lady. "For," he said to himself, "if it is the Head, I am sure I shall not be given a heart, since a head has no heart of its own and therefore cannot feel for me. But if it is the lovely Lady I shall beg hard for a heart, for all ladies are themselves said to be kindly hearted."

But when the Woodman entered the great Throne Room he saw neither the Head nor the Lady, for Oz had taken the shape of a most terrible Beast. It was nearly as big as an elephant, and the green throne seemed hardly strong enough to hold its weight. The Beast had a head like that of a rhinoceros, only there were five eyes in its face. There were five long arms growing out of its body, and it also had five long, slim legs. Thick, woolly hair covered every part of it, and a more dreadful-looking monster could not be imagined. It was fortunate the Tin Woodman had no heart at that moment, for it would have beat loud and fast from terror. But being only tin, the Woodman was not at all afraid, although he was much disappointed.

"I am Oz, the Great and Terrible," spoke the Beast, in a voice that was one great roar. "Who are you, and why do you seek me?"

"I am a Woodman, and made of tin. Therefore I have no heart, and cannot love. I pray you to give me a heart that I may be as other men are."

"Why should I do this?" demanded the Beast.

"Because I ask it, and you alone can grant my request," answered the Woodman.

Oz gave a low growl at this, but said, gruffly: "If you indeed desire a heart, you must earn it."

"How?" asked the Woodman.

"Help Dorothy to kill the Wicked Witch of the West," replied the Beast. "When the Witch is dead, come to me, and I will then give you the biggest and kindest and most loving heart in all the Land of Oz."

So the Tin Woodman was forced to return sorrowfully to his friends and tell them of the terrible Beast he had seen. They all wondered greatly at the many forms the great Wizard could take upon himself, and the Lion said:

"If he is a Beast when I go to see him, I shall roar my loudest, and so frighten him that he will grant all I ask. And if he is the lovely Lady, I shall pretend to spring upon her, and so compel her to do my bidding. And if he is the great Head, he will be at my mercy; for I will roll this head all about the room until he promises to give us what we desire. So be of good cheer, my friends, for all will yet be well."

The next morning the soldier with the green whiskers led the Lion to the great Throne Room and bade him enter the presence of Oz.

The Lion at once passed through the door, and glancing around saw, to his surprise, that before the throne was a Ball of Fire, so fierce and glowing he could scarcely bear to gaze upon it. His first thought was that Oz had by accident caught on fire and was burning up; but when he tried to go nearer, the heat was so intense that it singed his whiskers, and he crept back tremblingly to a spot nearer the door.

Then a low, quiet voice came from the Ball of Fire, and these were the words it spoke:

"I am Oz, the Great and Terrible. Who are you, and why do you seek me?"

And the Lion answered, "I am a Cowardly Lion, afraid of everything. I came to you to beg that you give me courage, so that in reality I may become the King of Beasts, as men call me."

"Why should I give you courage?" demanded Oz.

"Because of all Wizards you are the greatest, and alone have power to grant my request," answered the Lion.

The Ball of Fire burned fiercely for a time, and the voice said, "Bring me proof that the Wicked Witch is dead, and that moment I will give you courage. But as long as the Witch lives, you must remain a coward."

The Lion was angry at this speech, but could say nothing in reply, and while he stood silently gazing at the Ball of Fire it became so furiously hot that he turned tail and rushed from the room. He was glad to find his friends waiting for him, and told them of his terrible interview with the Wizard.

"What shall we do now?" asked Dorothy sadly.

"There is only one thing we can do," returned the Lion, "and that is to go to the land of the Winkies, seek out the Wicked Witch, and destroy her."

"But suppose we cannot?" said the girl.

"Then I shall never have courage," declared the Lion.

"And I shall never have brains," added the Scarecrow.

"And I shall never have a heart," spoke the Tin of Woodman.

"And I shall never see Aunt Em and Uncle Henry," said Dorothy, beginning to cry.

"Be careful!" cried the green girl. "The tears will fall on your green silk gown and spot it."

So Dorothy dried her eyes and said, "I suppose we must try it; but I am sure I do not want to kill anybody, even to see Aunt Em again."

"I will go with you; but I'm too much of a coward to kill the Witch," said the Lion.

"I will go too," declared the Scarecrow; "but I shall not be of much help to you, I am such a fool."

"I haven't the heart to harm even a Witch," replied the Tin Woodman; "but if you go I certainly shall go with you."

Therefore it was decided to start upon their journey the next morning, and the Woodman sharpened his axe on a green grindstone and had all his joints properly oiled. The Scarecrow stuffed himself with fresh straw and Dorothy put new paint on his eyes that he might see better. The green girl, who was very kind to them, filled Dorothy's basket with good things to eat, and fastened a little bell around Toto's neck with a green ribbon.

They went to bed quite early and slept soundly until daylight, when they were awakened by the crowing of a green cock that lived in the back yard of the palace, and the cackling of a hen that had laid a green egg.

Chapter 12

The Search
for the Wicked Witch

Now the Wicked Witch of the West had but one eye, yet that was as powerful as a telescope, and could see everywhere. So, as she sat in the door of her castle, she happened to look around and saw Dorothy lying asleep, with her friends all about her.

The soldier with the green whiskers led them through the streets of the Emerald City until they reached the room where the Guardian of the Gates lived. This officer unlocked their spectacles to put them back in his great box, and then he politely opened the gate for our friends.

"Which road leads to the Wicked Witch of the West?" asked Dorothy.

"There is no road," answered the Guardian of the Gates. "No one ever wishes to go that way."

"How, then, are we to find her?" inquired the girl.

"That will be easy," replied the man, "for when she knows you are in the country of the Winkies she will find you, and make you all her slaves."

"Perhaps not," said the Scarecrow, "for we mean to destroy her."

"Oh, that is different," said the Guardian of the Gates. "No one has ever destroyed her before, so I naturally thought she would make slaves of you, as she has of the rest. But take care; for she is wicked and fierce, and may not allow you to destroy her. Keep to the West, where the sun sets, and you cannot fail to find her."

They thanked him and bade him good-bye, and turned toward the West, walking over fields of soft grass dotted here and there with daisies and buttercups. Dorothy still wore the pretty silk dress she had put on in the palace, but now, to her surprise, she found it was no longer green, but pure white. The ribbon around Toto's neck had also lost its green color and was as white as Dorothy's dress.

The Emerald City was soon left far behind. As they advanced the ground became rougher and hillier, for there were no farms nor houses in this country of the West, and the ground was untilled.

In the afternoon the sun shone hot in their faces, for there were no trees to offer them shade; so that before night Dorothy and Toto and the Lion were tired, and lay down upon the grass and fell asleep, with the Woodman and the Scarecrow keeping watch.

Now the Wicked Witch of the West had but one eye, yet that was as powerful as a telescope, and could see everywhere. So, as she sat in the door of her castle, she happened to look around and saw Dorothy lying asleep, with her friends all about her. They were a long distance off, but the Wicked Witch was angry to find them in her country; so she blew upon a silver whistle that hung around her neck.

At once there came running to her from all directions a pack of great wolves. They had long legs and fierce eyes and sharp teeth.

"Go to those people," said the Witch, "and tear them to pieces."

"Are you not going to make them your slaves?" asked the leader of the wolves.

"No," she answered, "one is of tin, and one of straw; one is a girl and another a Lion. None of them is fit to work, so you may tear them into small pieces."

"Very well," said the wolf, and he dashed away at full speed, followed by the others.

It was lucky the Scarecrow and the Woodman were wide awake and heard the wolves coming.

"This is my fight," said the Woodman, "so get behind me and I will meet them as they come."

He seized his axe, which he had made very sharp, and as the leader of the wolves came on the Tin Woodman swung his arm and chopped the wolf's head from its body, so that it immediately died. As soon as he could raise his axe, another wolf came up, and he also fell under the sharp edge of the Tin Woodman's weapon. There were forty wolves, and forty times a wolf was killed, so that at last they all lay dead in a heap before the Woodman.

Then he put down his axe and sat beside the Scarecrow, who said, "It was a good fight, friend."

They waited until Dorothy awoke the next morning. The little girl was quite frightened when she saw the great pile of shaggy wolves, but the Tin Woodman told her all. She thanked him for saving them and sat down to breakfast, after which they started again upon their journey.

Now this same morning the Wicked Witch came to the door of her castle and looked out with her one eye that could see far off. She saw all her wolves lying dead, and the strangers still traveling through her country. This made her angrier than before, and she blew her silver whistle twice.

Straightway a great flock of wild crows came flying toward her, enough to darken the sky.

And the Wicked Witch said to the King Crow, "Fly at once to the strangers; peck out their eyes and tear them to pieces."

The wild crows flew in one great flock toward Dorothy and her companions. When the little girl saw them coming she was afraid.

But the Scarecrow said, "This is my battle, so lie down beside me and you will not be harmed."

So they all lay upon the ground except the Scarecrow, and he stood up and stretched out his arms. And when the crows saw him they were frightened, as these birds always are by scarecrows, and did not dare to come any nearer. But the King Crow said:

"It is only a stuffed man. I will peck his eyes out."

The King Crow flew at the Scarecrow, who caught it by the head and twisted its neck until it died. And then another crow flew at him, and the Scarecrow twisted its neck also. There were forty crows, and forty times the Scarecrow twisted a neck, until at last all were lying dead beside him. Then he called to his companions to rise, and again they went upon their journey.

When the Wicked Witch looked out again and saw all her crows lying in a heap, she got into a terrible rage, and blew three times upon her silver whistle.

Forthwith there was heard a great buzzing in the air, and a swarm of black bees came flying toward her.

"Go to the strangers and sting them to death!" commanded the Witch, and the bees turned and flew rapidly until they came to where Dorothy and her friends were walking. But the Woodman had seen them coming, and the Scarecrow had decided what to do.

"Take out my straw and scatter it over the little girl and the dog and the Lion," he said to the Woodman, "and the bees cannot sting them." This the Woodman did, and as Dorothy lay close beside the Lion and held Toto in her arms, the straw covered them entirely.

The bees came and found no one but the Woodman to sting, so they flew at him and broke off all their stings against the tin, without hurting the Woodman at all. And as bees cannot live when their stings are broken that was the end of the black bees, and they lay scattered thick about the Woodman, like little heaps of fine coal.

Then Dorothy and the Lion got up, and the girl helped the Tin Woodman put the straw back into the Scarecrow again, until he was as good as ever. So they started upon their journey once more.

The Wicked Witch was so angry when she saw her black bees in little heaps like fine coal that she stamped her foot and tore her hair and gnashed her teeth. And then she called a dozen of her slaves, who were the Winkies, and gave them sharp spears, telling them to go to the strangers and destroy them.

The Winkies were not a brave people, but they had to do as they were told. So they marched away until they came near to Dorothy. Then the Lion gave a great roar and sprang toward them, and the poor Winkies were so frightened that they ran back as fast as they could.

When they returned to the castle the Wicked Witch beat them well with a strap, and sent them back to their work, after which she sat down to think what she should do next. She could not understand how all her plans to destroy these strangers had failed; but she was a powerful Witch, as well as a wicked one, and she soon made up her mind how to act.

There was, in her cupboard, a Golden Cap, with a circle of diamonds and rubies running round it. This Golden Cap had a charm. Whoever owned it could call three times upon the Winged Monkeys, who would obey any order they were given. But no person could command these strange creatures more than three times. Twice already the Wicked Witch had used the charm of the Cap. Once was when she had made the Winkies her slaves, and set herself to rule over their country. The Winged Monkeys had helped her do this. The second time was when she had fought against the Great Oz himself, and driven him out of the land of the West. The Winged Monkeys had also helped her in doing this. Only once more could she use this Golden Cap, for which reason she did not like to do so until all her other powers were exhausted. But now that her fierce wolves and her wild crows and her stinging bees were gone, and her slaves had been scared away by the Cowardly Lion, she saw there was only one way left to destroy Dorothy and her friends.

So the Wicked Witch took the Golden Cap from her cupboard and placed it upon her head. Then she stood upon her left foot and said slowly:

"Ep-pe, pep-pe, kak-ke!"

Next she stood upon her right foot and said:

"Hil-lo, hol-lo, hel-lo!"

After this she stood upon both feet and cried in a loud voice:

"Ziz-zy, zuz-zy, zik!"

Now the charm began to work. The sky was darkened, and a low rumbling sound was heard in the air. There was a rushing of many wings, a great chattering and laughing, and the sun came out of the dark sky to show the Wicked Witch surrounded by a crowd of monkeys, each with a pair of immense and powerful wings on his shoulder.

One, much bigger than the others, seemed to be their leader. He flew close to the Witch and said, "You have called us for the third and last time. What do you command?"

"Go to the strangers who are within my land and destroy them all except the Lion," said the Wicked Witch. "Bring that beast to me, for I have a mind to harness him like a horse, and make him work."

"Your commands shall be obeyed," said the leader. Then, with a great deal of chattering and noise, the Winged Monkeys flew away to the place where Dorothy and her friends were walking.

Some of the Monkeys seized the Tin Woodman and carried him through the air until they were over a country thickly covered with sharp rocks. Here they dropped the poor Woodman, who fell a great distance to the rocks, where he lay so battered and dented that he could neither move nor groan.

Others of the Monkeys caught the Scarecrow, and with their long fingers pulled all of the straw out of his clothes and head. They made his hat and boots and clothes into a small bundle and threw it into the top branches of a tall tree.

The remaining Monkeys threw pieces of stout rope around the Lion and wound many coils about his body and head and legs, until he was unable to bite or scratch or struggle in any way. Then they lifted him up and flew away with him to the Witch's castle, where he was placed in a small yard with a high iron fence around it, so that he could not escape.

But Dorothy they did not harm at all. She stood, with Toto in her arms, watching the sad fate of her comrades and thinking it would soon be her turn. The leader of the Winged Monkeys flew up to her, his long, hairy arms stretched out and his ugly face grinning terribly; but he saw the mark of the Good Witch's kiss upon her forehead and stopped short, motioning the others not to touch her.

"We dare not harm this little girl," he said to them, "for she is protected by the Power of Good, and that is greater than the Power of Evil. All we can do is to carry her to the castle of the Wicked Witch and leave her there."

So, carefully and gently, they lifted Dorothy in their arms and carried her swiftly through the air until they came to the castle, where they set her down upon the front doorstep. Then the leader said to the Witch:

"We have obeyed you as far as we were able. The Tin Woodman and the Scarecrow are destroyed, and the Lion is tied up in your yard. The little girl we dare not harm, nor the dog she carries in her arms. Your power over our band is now ended, and you will never see us again."

Then all the Winged Monkeys, with much laughing and chattering and noise, flew into the air and were soon out of sight.

The Wicked Witch was both surprised and worried when she saw the mark on Dorothy's forehead, for she knew well that neither the Winged Monkeys nor she, herself, dare hurt the girl in any way. She looked down at Dorothy's feet, and seeing the Silver Shoes, began to tremble with fear, for she knew what a powerful charm belonged to them. At first the Witch was tempted to run away from Dorothy; but she happened to look into the child's eyes and saw how simple the soul behind them was, and that the little girl did not know of the wonderful power the Silver Shoes gave her. So the Wicked Witch laughed to herself, and thought, "I can still make her my slave, for she does not know how to use her power." Then she said to Dorothy, harshly and severely:

"Come with me; and see that you mind everything I tell you, for if you do not I will make an end of you, as I did of the Tin Woodman and the Scarecrow."

Dorothy followed her through many of the beautiful rooms in her castle until they came to the kitchen, where the Witch bade her clean the pots and kettles and sweep the floor and keep the fire fed with wood.

Dorothy went to work meekly, with her mind made up to work as hard as she could; for she was glad the Wicked Witch had decided not to kill her.

With Dorothy hard at work, the Witch thought she would go into the courtyard and harness the Cowardly Lion like a horse; it would amuse her, she was sure, to make him draw her chariot whenever she wished to go to drive. But as she opened the gate the Lion gave a loud roar and bounded at her so fiercely that the Witch was afraid, and ran out and shut the gate again.

"If I cannot harness you," said the Witch to the Lion, speaking through the bars of the gate, "I can starve you. You shall have nothing to eat until you do as I wish."

So after that she took no food to the imprisoned Lion; but every day she came to the gate at noon and asked, "Are you ready to be harnessed like a horse?"

And the Lion would answer, "No. If you come in this yard, I will bite you."

The reason the Lion did not have to do as the Witch wished was that every night, while the woman was asleep, Dorothy carried him food from the cupboard. After he had eaten he would lie down on his bed of straw, and Dorothy would lie beside him and put her head on his soft, shaggy mane, while they talked of their troubles and tried to plan some way to escape. But they could find no way to get out of the castle, for it was constantly guarded by the yellow Winkies, who were the slaves of the Wicked Witch and too afraid of her not to do as she told them.

The girl had to work hard during the day, and often the Witch threatened to beat her with the same old umbrella she always carried in her hand. But, in truth, she did not dare to strike Dorothy, because of the mark upon her forehead. The child did not know this, and was full of fear for herself and Toto. Once the Witch struck Toto a blow with her umbrella and the brave little dog flew at her and bit her leg in return. The Witch did not bleed where she was bitten, for she was so wicked that the blood in her had dried up many years before.

Dorothy's life became very sad as she grew to understand that it would be harder than ever to get back to Kansas and Aunt Em again. Sometimes she would cry bitterly for hours, with Toto sitting at her feet and looking into her face, whining dismally to show how sorry he was for his little mistress. Toto did not really care whether he was in Kansas or the Land of Oz so long as Dorothy was with him; but he knew the little girl was unhappy, and that made him unhappy too.

Now the Wicked Witch had a great longing to have for her own the Silver Shoes which the girl always wore. Her bees and her crows and her wolves were lying in heaps and drying up, and she had used up all the power of the Golden Cap; but if she could only get hold of the Silver Shoes, they would give her more power than all the other things she had lost. She watched Dorothy carefully, to see if she ever took off her shoes, thinking she might steal them. But the child was so proud of her pretty shoes that she never took them off except at night and when she took her bath. The Witch was too much afraid of the dark to dare go in Dorothy's room at night to take the shoes, and her dread of water was greater than her fear of the dark, so she never came near when Dorothy was bathing. Indeed, the old Witch never touched water, nor ever let water touch her in any way.

But the wicked creature was very cunning, and she finally thought of a trick that would give her what she wanted. She placed a bar of iron in the middle of the kitchen floor, and then by her magic arts made the iron invisible to human eyes. So that when Dorothy walked across the floor she stumbled over the bar, not being able to see it, and fell at full length. She was not much hurt, but in her fall one of the Silver Shoes came off; and before she could reach it, the Witch had snatched it away and put it on her own skinny foot.

The wicked woman was greatly pleased with the success of her trick, for as long as she had one of the shoes she owned half the power of their charm, and Dorothy could not use it against her, even had she known how to do so.

The little girl, seeing she had lost one of her pretty shoes, grew angry, and said to the Witch, "Give me back my shoe!"

"I will not," retorted the Witch, "for it is now my shoe, and not yours."

"You are a wicked creature!" cried Dorothy. "You have no right to take my shoe from me."

"I shall keep it, just the same," said the Witch, laughing at her, "and someday I shall get the other one from you, too."

This made Dorothy so very angry that she picked up the bucket of water that stood near and dashed it over the Witch, wetting her from head to foot.

Instantly the wicked woman gave a loud cry of fear, and then, as Dorothy looked at her in wonder, the Witch began to shrink and fall away.

"See what you have done!" she screamed. "In a minute I shall melt away."

"I'm very sorry, indeed," said Dorothy, who was truly frightened to see the Witch actually melting away like brown sugar before her very eyes.

"Didn't you know water would be the end of me?" asked the Witch, in a wailing, desperate voice.

"Of course not," answered Dorothy. "How should I?"

"Well, in a few minutes I shall be all melted, and you will have the castle to yourself. I have been wicked in my day, but I never thought a little girl like you would ever be able to melt me and end my wicked deeds. Look out – here I go!"

With these words the Witch fell down in a brown, melted, shapeless mass and began to spread over the clean boards of the kitchen floor. Seeing that she had really melted away to nothing, Dorothy drew another bucket of water and threw it over the mess. She then swept it all out the door. After picking out the silver shoe, which was all that was left of the old woman, she cleaned and dried it with a cloth, and put it on her foot again. Then, being at last free to do as she chose, she ran out to the courtyard to tell the Lion that the Wicked Witch of the West had come to an end, and that they were no longer prisoners in a strange land.

Chapter 13

The Rescue

"If our friends, the Scarecrow and the Tin Woodman, were only with us," said the Lion, "I should be quite happy."

The Cowardly Lion was much pleased to hear that the Wicked Witch had been melted by a bucket of water, and Dorothy at once unlocked the gate of his prison and set him free. They went in together to the castle, where Dorothy's first act was to call all the Winkies together and tell them that they were no longer slaves.

There was great rejoicing among the yellow Winkies, for they had been made to work hard during many years for the Wicked Witch, who had always treated them with great cruelty. They kept this day as a holiday, then and ever after, and spent the time in feasting and dancing.

"If our friends, the Scarecrow and the Tin Woodman, were only with us," said the Lion, "I should be quite happy."

"Don't you suppose we could rescue them?" asked the girl anxiously.

"We can try," answered the Lion.

So they called the yellow Winkies and asked them if they would help to rescue their friends, and the Winkies said that they would be delighted to do all in their power for Dorothy, who had set them free from bondage. So she chose a number of the Winkies who looked as if they knew the most, and they all started away. They traveled that day and part of the next until they came to the rocky plain where the Tin Woodman lay, all battered and bent. His axe was near him, but the blade was rusted and the handle broken off short.

The Winkies lifted him tenderly in their arms, and carried him back

to the Yellow Castle again, Dorothy shedding a few tears by the way at the sad plight of her old friend, and the Lion looking sober and sorry. When they reached the castle Dorothy said to the Winkies:

"Are any of your people tinsmiths?"

"Oh, yes. Some of us are very good tinsmiths," they told her.

"Then bring them to me," she said. And when the tinsmiths came, bringing with them all their tools in baskets, she inquired, "Can you straighten out those dents in the Tin Woodman, and bend him back into shape again, and solder him together where he is broken?"

The tinsmiths looked the Woodman over carefully and then answered that they thought they could mend him so he would be as good as ever. So they set to work in one of the big yellow rooms of the castle and worked for three days and four nights, hammering and twisting and bending and soldering and polishing and pounding at the legs and body and head of the Tin Woodman, until at last he was straightened out into his old form, and his joints worked as well as ever. To be sure, there were several patches on him, but the tinsmiths did a good job, and as the Woodman was not a vain man he did not mind the patches at all.

When, at last, he walked into Dorothy's room and thanked her for rescuing him, he was so pleased that he wept tears of joy, and Dorothy had to wipe every tear carefully from his face with her apron, so his joints would not be rusted. At the same time her own tears fell thick and fast at the joy of meeting her old friend again, and these tears did not need to be wiped away. As for the Lion, he wiped his eyes so often with the tip of his tail that it became quite wet, and he was obliged to go out into the courtyard and hold it in the sun till it dried.

"If we only had the Scarecrow with us again," said the Tin Woodman, when Dorothy had finished telling him everything that had happened, "I should be quite happy."

"We must try to find him," said the girl.

So she called the Winkies to help her, and they walked all that day and part of the next until they came to the tall tree in the branches of which the Winged Monkeys had tossed the Scarecrow's clothes.

It was a very tall tree, and the trunk was so smooth that no one could climb it; but the Woodman said at once, "I'll chop it down, and then we can get the Scarecrow's clothes."

Now while the tinsmiths had been at work mending the Woodman himself, another of the Winkies, who was a goldsmith, had made an axe-handle of solid gold and fitted it into the Woodman's axe, instead of the old broken handle. Others polished the blade until all the rust was removed and it glistened like burnished silver.

As soon as he had spoken, the Tin Woodman began to chop, and in a short time the tree fell over with a crash, whereupon the Scarecrow's clothes fell out of the branches and rolled off on the ground.

Dorothy picked them up and had the Winkies carry them back to the castle, where they were stuffed with nice, clean straw; and behold! here

was the Scarecrow, as good as ever, thanking them over and over again for saving him.

Now that they were reunited, Dorothy and her friends spent a few happy days at the Yellow Castle, where they found everything they needed to make them comfortable.

But one day the girl thought of Aunt Em, and said, "We must go back to Oz, and claim his promise."

"Yes," said the Woodman, "at last I shall get my heart."

"And I shall get my brains," added the Scarecrow joyfully.

"And I shall get my courage," said the Lion thoughtfully.

"And I shall get back to Kansas," cried Dorothy, clapping her hands. "Oh, let us start for the Emerald City tomorrow!"

This they decided to do. The next day they called the Winkies together and bade them good-bye. The Winkies were sorry to have them go, and they had grown so fond of the Tin Woodman that they begged him to stay and rule over them and the Yellow Land of the West. Finding they were determined to go, the Winkies gave Toto and the Lion each a golden collar; and to Dorothy they presented a beautiful bracelet studded with diamonds; and to the Scarecrow they gave a gold-headed walking stick, to keep him from stumbling; and to the Tin Woodman they offered a silver oil-can, inlaid with gold and set with precious jewels.

Every one of the travelers made the Winkies a pretty speech in return, and all shook hands with them until their arms ached.

Dorothy went to the Witch's cupboard to fill her basket with food for the journey, and there she saw the Golden Cap. She tried it on her own head and found that it fitted her exactly. She did not know anything about the charm of the Golden Cap, but she saw that it was pretty, so she made up her mind to wear it and carry her sunbonnet in the basket.

Then, being prepared for the journey, they all started for the Emerald City; and the Winkies gave them three cheers and many good wishes to carry with them.

Chapter 14

The Winged Monkeys

"Why don't you use the charm
of the Cap, and call the Winged
Monkeys to you? They will carry
you to the City of Oz in less than
an hour."

You will remember there was no road – not even a pathway – between the castle of the Wicked Witch and the Emerald City. When the four travelers went in search of the Witch she had seen them coming, and so sent the Winged Monkeys to bring them to her. It was much harder to find their way back through the big fields of buttercups and yellow daisies than it was being carried. They knew, of course, they must go straight east, toward the rising sun; and they started off in the right way. But at noon, when the sun was over their heads, they did not know which was east and which was west, and that was the reason they were lost in the great fields. They kept on walking, however, and at night the moon came out and shone brightly. So they lay down among the sweet smelling yellow flowers and slept soundly until morning – all but the Scarecrow and the Tin Woodman.

The next morning the sun was behind a cloud, but they started on, as if they were quite sure which way they were going.

"If we walk far enough," said Dorothy, "I am sure we shall sometime come to some place."

But day by day passed away, and they still saw nothing before them but the scarlet fields. The Scarecrow began to grumble a bit.

"We have surely lost our way," he said, "and unless we find it again in time to reach the Emerald City, I shall never get my brains."

"Nor I my heart," declared the Tin Woodman. "It seems to me I can scarcely wait till I get to Oz, and you must admit this is a very long journey."

"You see," said the Cowardly Lion, with a whimper, "I haven't the courage to keep tramping forever, without getting anywhere at all."

Then Dorothy lost heart. She sat down on the grass and looked at her companions, and they sat down and looked at her, and Toto found that for the first time in his life he was too tired to chase a butterfly that flew past his head. So he put out his tongue and panted and looked at Dorothy as if to ask what they should do next.

"Suppose we call the field mice," she suggested. "They could probably tell us the way to the Emerald City."

"To be sure they could," cried the Scarecrow. "Why didn't we think of that before?"

Dorothy blew the little whistle she had always carried about her neck since the Queen of the Mice had given it to her. In a few minutes they heard the pattering of tiny feet, and many of the small gray mice came running up to her. Among them was the Queen herself, who asked, in her squeaky little voice:

"What can I do for my friends?"

"We have lost our way," said Dorothy. "Can you tell us where the Emerald City is?"

"Certainly," answered the Queen; "but it is a great way off, for you have had it at your backs all this time." Then she noticed Dorothy's Golden Cap, and said, "Why don't you use the charm of the Cap, and call the Winged Monkeys to you? They will carry you to the City of Oz in less than an hour."

"I didn't know there was a charm," answered Dorothy, in surprise. "What is it?"

"It is written inside the Golden Cap," replied the Queen of the Mice. "But if you are going to call the Winged Monkeys we must run away, for they are full of mischief and think it great fun to plague us."

"Won't they hurt me?" asked the girl anxiously.

"Oh, no. They must obey the wearer of the Cap. Good-bye!" And she scampered out of sight, with all the mice hurrying after her.

Dorothy looked inside the Golden Cap and saw some words written upon the lining. These, she thought, must be the charm, so she read the directions carefully and put the Cap upon her head.

"Ep-pe, pep-pe, kak-ke!" she said, standing on her left foot.

"What did you say?" asked the Scarecrow, who did not know what she was doing.

"Hil-lo, hol-lo, hel-lo!" Dorothy went on, standing this time on her right foot.

"Hello!" replied the Tin Woodman calmly.

"Ziz-zy, zuz-zy, zik!" said Dorothy, who was now standing on both feet. This ended the saying of the charm, and they heard a great chattering and flapping of wings, as the band of Winged Monkeys flew up to them. The King bowed low before Dorothy, and asked, "What is your command?"

"We wish to go to the Emerald City," said the child, "and we have lost our way."

"We will carry you," replied the King, and no sooner had he spoken than two of the Monkeys caught Dorothy in their arms and flew away with her. Others took the Scarecrow and the Woodman and the Lion, and one little Monkey seized Toto and flew after them, although the dog tried hard to bite him.

The Scarecrow and the Tin Woodman were rather frightened at first, for they remembered how badly the Winged Monkeys had treated them before; but they saw that no harm was intended, so they rode through the air quite cheerfully, and had a fine time looking at the pretty gardens and woods far below them.

Dorothy found herself riding easily between two of the biggest Monkeys, one of them the King himself. They had made a chair of their hands and were careful not to hurt her.

"Why do you have to obey the charm of the Golden Cap?" she asked.

"That is a long story," answered the King, with a Winged laugh; "but as we have a long journey before us, I will pass the time by telling you about it, if you wish."

"I shall be glad to hear it," she replied.

"Once," began the leader, "we were a free people, living happily in the great forest, flying from tree to tree, eating nuts and fruit, and doing just as we pleased without calling anybody master. Perhaps some of us were rather too full of mischief at times, flying down to pull the tails of the animals that had no wings, chasing birds, and throwing nuts at the people who walked in the forest. But we were careless and happy and full of fun, and enjoyed every minute of the day. This was many years ago, long before Oz came out of the clouds to rule over this land.

"There lived here then, away at the North, a beautiful princess, who was also a powerful sorceress. All her magic was used to help the people, and she was never known to hurt anyone who was good. Her name was Gayelette, and she lived in a handsome palace built from great blocks of ruby. Everyone loved her, but her greatest sorrow was that she could find no one to love in return, since all the men were much too stupid and ugly to mate with one so beautiful and wise. At last, however, she found a boy who was handsome and manly and wise beyond his years. Gayelette made up her mind that when he grew to be a man she would make him her husband, so she took him to her ruby palace and used all her magic powers to make him as strong and good and lovely as any woman could wish. When he grew to manhood, Quelala, as he was called, was said to be the best and wisest man in all the land, while his manly beauty was so great that Gayelette loved him dearly, and hastened to make everything ready for the wedding.

"My grandfather was at that time the King of the Winged Monkeys which lived in the forest near Gayelette's palace, and the old fellow loved a joke better than a good dinner. One day, just before the wedding, my grandfather was flying out with his band when he saw Quelala walking beside the river. He was dressed in a rich costume of pink silk and purple velvet, and my grandfather thought he would see what he could do. At his word the band flew down and seized Quelala, carried him in their arms until they were over the middle of the river, and then dropped him into the water.

"'Swim out, my fine fellow,' cried my grandfather, 'and see if the water has spotted your clothes.' Quelala was much too wise not to swim, and he was not in the least spoiled by all his good fortune. He laughed, when he came to the top of the water, and swam in to shore. But when Gayelette came running out to him she found his silks and velvet all ruined by the river.

"The princess was angry, and she knew, of course, who did it. She had all the Winged Monkeys brought before her, and she said at first that their wings should be tied and they should be treated as they had treated Quelala, and dropped in the river. But my grandfather pleaded hard, for he knew the Monkeys would drown in the river with their wings tied, and Quelala said a kind word for them also; so that Gayelette finally spared them, on condition that the Winged Monkeys should ever after do three times the bidding of the owner of the Golden Cap. This Cap had been made for a wedding present to Quelala, and it is said to have cost the princess half her kingdom. Of course my grandfather and all the other Monkeys at once agreed to the condition, and that is how it happens that we are three times the slaves of the owner of the Golden Cap, whosoever he may be."

"And what became of them?" asked Dorothy, who had been greatly interested in the story.

"Quelala being the first owner of the Golden Cap," replied the Monkey, "he was the first to lay his wishes upon us. As his bride could not bear the sight of us, he called us all to him in the forest after he had married her and ordered us always to keep where she could never again set eyes on a Winged Monkey, which we were glad to do, for we were all afraid of her.

"This was all we ever had to do until the Golden Cap fell into the hands of the Wicked Witch of the West, who made us enslave the Winkies, and afterward drive Oz himself out of the Land of the West. Now the Golden Cap is yours, and three times you have the right to lay your wishes upon us."

As the Monkey King finished his story Dorothy looked down and saw the green, shining walls of the Emerald City before them. She wondered at the rapid flight of the Monkeys, but was glad the journey was over. The strange creatures set the travelers down carefully before the gate of the City, the King bowed low to Dorothy, and then flew swiftly away, followed by all his band.

"That was a good ride," said the little girl.

"Yes, and a quick way out of our troubles," replied the Lion. "How lucky it was you brought away that wonderful Cap!"

Chapter 15

The Discovery of Oz,
the Terrible

Of course each one of them
expected to see the Wizard in the
shape he had taken before, and
all were greatly surprised when
they looked about and saw no
one at all in the room.

The four travelers walked up to the great gate of Emerald City and rang the bell. After ringing several times, it was opened by the same Guardian of the Gates they had met before.

"What! Are you back again?" he asked, in surprise.

"Do you not see us?" answered the Scarecrow.

"But I thought you had gone to visit the Wicked Witch of the West."

"We did visit her," said the Scarecrow.

"And she let you go again?" asked the man, in wonder.

"She could not help it, for she is melted," explained the Scarecrow.

"Melted! Well, that is good news, indeed," said the man. "Who melted her?"

"It was Dorothy," said the Lion gravely.

"Good gracious!" exclaimed the man, and he bowed very low indeed before her.

Then he led them into his little room and locked the spectacles from the great box on all their eyes, just as he had done before. Afterward they passed on through the gate into the Emerald City. When the people heard from the Guardian of the Gates that Dorothy had melted the Wicked Witch of the West, they all gathered around the travelers and followed them in a great crowd to the Palace of Oz.

The soldier with the green whiskers was still on guard before the door, but he let them in at once, and they were again met by the beautiful green girl, who showed each of them to their old rooms at once, so they might rest until the Great Oz was ready to receive them.

The soldier had the news carried straight to Oz that Dorothy and the other travelers had come back again, after destroying the Wicked Witch; but Oz made no reply. They thought the Great Wizard would send for them at once, but he did not. They had no word from him the next day, nor the next, nor the next. The waiting was tiresome and wearing, and at last they grew vexed that Oz should treat them in so poor a fashion, after sending them to undergo hardships and slavery. So the Scarecrow at last asked the green girl to take another message to Oz, saying if he did not let them in to see him at once they would call the Winged Monkeys to help them, and find out whether he kept his promises or not. When the Wizard was given this message he was so frightened that he sent word for them to come to the Throne Room at four minutes after nine o'clock the next morning. He had once met the Winged Monkeys in the Land of the West, and he did not wish to meet them again.

The four travelers passed a sleepless night, each thinking of the gift Oz had promised to bestow on him. Dorothy fell asleep only once, and then she dreamed she was in Kansas, where Aunt Em was telling her how glad she was to have her little girl at home again.

Promptly at nine o'clock the next morning the green-whiskered soldier came to them, and four minutes later they all went into the

Throne Room of the Great Oz.

Of course each one of them expected to see the Wizard in the shape he had taken before, and all were greatly surprised when they looked about and saw no one at all in the room. They kept close to the door and closer to one another, for the stillness of the empty room was more dreadful than any of the forms they had seen Oz take.

Presently they heard a Voice, that seemed to come from somewhere near the top of the great dome, and it said solemnly:

"I am Oz, the Great and Terrible. Why do you seek me?"

They looked again in every part of the room, and then, seeing no one, Dorothy asked, "Where are you?"

"I am everywhere," answered the Voice, "but to the eyes of common mortals I am invisible. I will now seat myself upon my throne, that you may converse with me." Indeed, the Voice seemed just then to come straight from the throne itself; so they walked toward it and stood in a row while Dorothy said:

"We have come to claim our promise, O Oz."

"What promise?" asked Oz.

"You promised to send me back to Kansas when the Wicked Witch was destroyed," said the girl.

"And you promised to give me brains," said the Scarecrow.

"And you promised to give me a heart," said the Tin Woodman.

"And you promised to give me courage," said the Cowardly Lion.

"Is the Wicked Witch really destroyed?" asked the Voice, and Dorothy thought it trembled a little.

"Yes," she answered, "I melted her with a bucket of water."

"Dear me," said the Voice, "how sudden! Well, come to me tomorrow, for I must have time to think it over."

"You've had plenty of time already," said the Tin Woodman angrily.

"We shan't wait a day longer," said the Scarecrow.

"You must keep your promises to us!" exclaimed Dorothy.

The Lion thought it might be as well to frighten the Wizard, so he gave a large, loud roar, which was so fierce and dreadful that Toto jumped away from him in alarm and tipped over the screen that stood in a corner. As it fell with a crash they looked that way, and the next moment all of them were filled with wonder. For they saw, standing in just the spot the screen had hidden, a little old man, with a bald head and a wrinkled face, who seemed to be as much surprised as they were. The Tin Woodman, raising his axe, rushed toward the little man and cried out, "Who are you?"

"I am Oz, the Great and Terrible," said the little man, in a trembling voice. "But don't strike me – please don't – and I'll do anything you want me to."

Our friends looked at him in surprise and dismay.

"I thought Oz was a great Head," said Dorothy.

"And I thought Oz was a lovely Lady," said the Scarecrow.

"And I thought Oz was a terrible Beast," said the Tin Woodman.

"And I thought Oz was a Ball of Fire," exclaimed the Lion.

"No, you are all wrong," said the little man meekly. "I have been making believe."

"Making believe!" cried Dorothy. "Are you not a Great Wizard?"

"Hush, my dear," he said. "Don't speak so loud, or you will be overheard – and I should be ruined. I'm supposed to be a Great Wizard."

"And aren't you?" she asked.

"Not a bit of it, my dear; I'm just a common man."

"You're more than that," said the Scarecrow, in a grieved tone; "you're a humbug."

"Exactly so!" declared the little man, rubbing his hands together as if it pleased him. "I am a humbug."

"But this is terrible," said the Tin Woodman. "How shall I ever get my heart?"

"Or I my courage?" asked the Lion.

"Or I my brains?" wailed the Scarecrow, wiping the tears from his eyes with his coat sleeve.

"My dear friends," said Oz, "I pray you not to speak of these little things. Think of me, and the terrible trouble I'm in at being found out."

"Doesn't anyone else know you're a humbug?" asked Dorothy.

"No one knows it but you four – and myself," replied Oz. "I have fooled everyone so long that I thought I should never be found out. It was a great mistake my ever letting you into the Throne Room. Usually I will not see even my subjects, and so they believe I am something terrible."

"But, I don't understand," said Dorothy, in bewilderment. "How was it that you appeared to me as a great Head?"

"That was one of my tricks," answered Oz. "Step this way, please, and I will tell you all about it."

He led the way to a small chamber in the rear of the Throne Room, and they all followed him. He pointed to one corner, in which lay the great Head, made out of many thicknesses of paper, and with a carefully painted face.

"This I hung from the ceiling by a wire," said Oz. "I stood behind the screen and pulled a thread, to make the eyes move and the mouth open."

"But how about the voice?" she inquired.

"Oh, I am a ventriloquist," said the little man. "I can throw the sound of my voice wherever I wish, so that you thought it was coming out of the Head. Here are the other things I used to deceive you." He showed the Scarecrow the dress and the mask he had worn when he seemed to be the lovely Lady. And the Tin Woodman saw that his terrible Beast was nothing but a lot of skins, sewn together, with slats to keep their sides out. As for the Ball of Fire, the false Wizard had hung that also from the ceiling. It was really a ball of cotton, but when oil was poured upon it the ball burned fiercely.

"Really," said the Scarecrow, "you ought to be ashamed of yourself for being such a humbug."

"I am – I certainly am," answered the little man sorrowfully; "but it was the only thing I could do. Sit down, please, there are plenty of chairs; and I will tell you my story."

So they sat down and listened while he told the following tale.

"I was born in Omaha – "

"Why, that isn't very far from Kansas!" cried Dorothy.

"No, but it's farther from here," he said, shaking his head at her sadly. "When I grew up I became a ventriloquist, and at that I was very well trained by a great master. I can imitate any kind of a bird or beast." Here he mewed so like a kitten that Toto pricked up his ears and looked everywhere to see where she was. "After a time," continued Oz, "I tired of that, and became a balloonist."

"What is that?" asked Dorothy.

"A man who goes up in a balloon on circus day, so as to draw a crowd of people together and get them to pay to see the circus," he explained.

"Oh," she said, "I know."

"Well, one day I went up in a balloon and the ropes got twisted, so that I couldn't come down again. It went way up above the clouds, so far that a current of air struck it and carried it many, many miles away. For a day and a night I traveled through the air, and on the morning of the second day I awoke and found the balloon floating over a strange and beautiful country.

"It came down gradually, and I was not hurt a bit. But I found myself in the midst of a strange people, who, seeing me come from the clouds, thought I was a great Wizard. Of course I let them think so, because they were afraid of me, and promised to do anything I wished them to.

"Just to amuse myself, and keep the good people busy, I ordered them to build this City, and my Palace; and they did it all willingly and well. Then I thought, as the country was so green and beautiful,

I would call it the Emerald City; and to make the name fit better I put green spectacles on all the people, so that everything they saw was green."

"But isn't everything here green?" asked Dorothy.

"No more than in any other city," replied Oz; "but when you wear green spectacles, why of course everything you see looks green to you. The Emerald City was built a great many years ago, for I was a young man when the balloon brought me here, and I am a very old man now. But my people have worn green glasses on their eyes so long that most of them think it really is an Emerald City, and it certainly is a beautiful place, abounding in jewels and precious metals, and every good thing that is needed to make one happy. I have been good to the people, and they like me; but ever since this Palace was built, I have shut myself up and would not see any of them.

"One of my greatest fears was the Witches, for while I had no magical powers at all I soon found out that the Witches were really able to do wonderful things. There were four of them in this country, and they ruled the people who live in the North and South and East and West. Fortunately, the Witches of the North and South were good, and I knew they would do me no harm; but the Witches of the East and West were terribly wicked, and had they not thought I was more powerful than they themselves, they would surely have destroyed me. As it was, I lived in deadly fear of them for many years; so you can imagine how pleased I was when I heard your house had fallen on the Wicked Witch of the East. When you came to me, I was willing to promise anything if you would only do away with the other Witch; but, now that you have melted her, I am ashamed to say that I cannot keep my promises."

"I think you are a very bad man," said Dorothy.

"Oh, no, my dear; I'm really a very good man, but I'm a very bad Wizard, I must admit."

"Can't you give me brains?" asked the Scarecrow.

"You don't need them. You are learning something every day. A baby has brains, but it doesn't know much. Experience is the only thing that brings knowledge, and the longer you are on earth the more experience you are sure to get."

"That may all be true," said the Scarecrow, "but I shall be very unhappy unless you give me brains."

The false Wizard looked at him carefully.

"Well," he said with a sigh, "I'm not much of a magician, as I said; but if you will come to me tomorrow morning, I will stuff your head with brains. I cannot tell you how to use them, however; you must find that out for yourself."

"Oh, thank you – thank you!" cried the Scarecrow. "I'll find a way to use them, never fear!"

"But how about my courage?" asked the Lion anxiously.

"You have plenty of courage, I am sure," answered Oz. "All you need is confidence in yourself. There is no living thing that is not afraid when it faces danger. The true courage is in facing danger when you are afraid, and that kind of courage you have in plenty."

"Perhaps I have, but I'm scared just the same," said the Lion. "I shall really be very unhappy unless you give me the sort of courage that makes one forget he is afraid."

"Very well, I will give you that sort of courage tomorrow," replied Oz.

"How about my heart?" asked the Tin Woodman.

"Why, as for that," answered Oz, "I think you are wrong to want a heart. It makes most people unhappy. If you only knew it, you are in luck not to have a heart."

"That must be a matter of opinion," said the Tin Woodman. "For my part, I will bear all the unhappiness without a murmur, if you will give me the heart."

"Very well," answered Oz meekly. "Come to me tomorrow and you shall have a heart. I have played Wizard for so many years that I may as well continue the part a little longer."

"And now," said Dorothy, "how am I to get back to Kansas?"

"We shall have to think about that," replied the little man. "Give me two or three days to consider the matter and I'll try to find a way to carry you over the desert. In the meantime you shall all be treated as my guests, and while you live in the Palace my people will wait upon you and obey your slightest wish. There is only one thing I ask in return for my help – such as it is. You must keep my secret and tell no one I am a humbug."

They agreed to say nothing of what they had learned, and went back to their rooms in high spirits. Even Dorothy had hope that "The Great and Terrible Humbug," as she called him, would find a way to send her back to Kansas, and if he did she was willing to forgive him everything.

Chapter 16

The Magic Art
of the Great Humbug

Oz, left to himself, smiled to think of his success in giving the Scarecrow and the Tin Woodman and the Lion exactly what the thought they wanted.

Next morning the Scarecrow said to his friends: "Congratulate me. I am going to Oz to get my brains at last. When I return I shall be as other men are."

"I have always liked you as you were," said Dorothy simply.

"It is kind of you to like a Scarecrow," he replied. "But surely you will think more of me when you hear the splendid thoughts my new brain is going to turn out." Then he said good-bye to them all in a cheerful voice and went to the Throne Room, where he rapped upon the door.

"Come in," said Oz.

The Scarecrow went in and found the little man sitting down by the window, engaged in deep thought.

"I have come for my brains," remarked the Scarecrow, a little uneasily.

"Oh, yes; sit down in that chair, please," replied Oz. "You must excuse me for taking your head off, but I shall have to do it in order to put your brains in their proper place."

"That's all right," said the Scarecrow. "You are quite welcome to take my head off, as long as it will be a better one when you put it on again."

So the Wizard unfastened his head and emptied out the straw. Then he entered the back room and took up a measure of bran, which he mixed with a great many pins and needles. Having shaken them together thoroughly, he filled the top of the Scarecrow's head with the mixture and stuffed the rest of the space with straw, to hold it in place.

When he had fastened the Scarecrow's head on his body again he said to him, "Hereafter you will be a great man, for I have given you a lot of bran-new brains."

The Scarecrow was both pleased and proud at the fulfillment of his greatest wish, and having thanked Oz warmly he went back to his friends.

Dorothy looked at him curiously. His head was quite bulged out at the top with brains.

"How do you feel?" she asked.

"I feel wise indeed," he answered earnestly. "When I get used to my brains I shall know everything."

"Why are those needles and pins sticking out of your head?" asked the Tin Woodman.

"That is proof that he is sharp," remarked the Lion.

"Well, I must go to Oz and get my heart," said the Woodman. So he walked to the Throne Room and knocked at the door.

"Come in," called Oz, and the Woodman entered and said, "I have come for my heart."

"Very well," answered the little man. "But I shall have to cut a hole in your breast, so I can put your heart in the right place. I hope it won't hurt you."

"Oh, no," answered the Woodman. "I shall not feel it at all."

So Oz brought a pair of tinsmith's shears and cut a small, square hole in the left side of the Tin Woodman's breast. Then, going to a chest of drawers, he took out a pretty heart, made entirely of silk and stuffed with sawdust.

"Isn't it a beauty?" he asked.

"It is, indeed!" replied the Woodman, who was greatly pleased. "But is it a kind heart?"

"Oh, very!" answered Oz. He put the heart in the Woodman's breast and then replaced the square of tin, soldering it neatly together where it had been cut.

"There," said he; "now you have a heart that any man might be proud of. I'm sorry I had to put a patch on your breast, but it really couldn't be helped."

"Never mind the patch," exclaimed the happy Woodman. "I am very grateful to you, and shall never forget your kindness."

"Don't speak of it," replied Oz.

Then the Tin Woodman went back to his friends, who wished him every joy on account of his good fortune.

The Lion now walked to the Throne Room and knocked at the door.

"Come in," said Oz.

"I have come for my courage," announced the Lion, entering the room.

"Very well," answered the little man; "I will get it for you."

He went to a cupboard and reaching up to a high shelf took down a square green bottle, the contents of which he poured into a green-gold dish, beautifully carved. Placing this before the Cowardly Lion, who sniffed at it as if he did not like it, the Wizard said:

"Drink."

"What is it?" asked the Lion.

"Well," answered Oz, "if it were inside of you, it would be courage. You know, of course, that courage is always inside one; so that this really cannot be called courage until you have swallowed it. Therefore I advise you to drink it as soon as possible."

The Lion hesitated no longer, but drank till the dish was empty.

"How do you feel now?" asked Oz.

"Full of courage," replied the Lion, who went joyfully back to his friends to tell them of his good fortune.

Oz, left to himself, smiled to think of his success in giving the Scarecrow and the Tin Woodman and the Lion exactly what they thought they wanted. "How can I help being a humbug," he said, "when all these people make me do things that everybody knows can't be done? It was easy to make the Scarecrow and the Lion and the Woodman happy, because they imagined I could do anything. But it will take more than imagination to carry Dorothy back to Kansas, and I'm sure I don't know how it can be done."

Chapter 17

*How the Balloon
Was Launched*

Gradually the balloon swelled out and rose into the air, until finally the basket just touched the ground.

For three days Dorothy heard nothing from Oz. These were sad days for the little girl, although her friends were all quite happy and contented. The Scarecrow told them there were wonderful thoughts in his head; but he would not say what they were because he knew no one could understand them but himself. When the Tin Woodman walked about he felt his heart rattling around in his breast; and he told Dorothy he had discovered it to be a kinder and more tender heart than the one he had owned when he was made of flesh. The Lion declared he was afraid of nothing on earth, and would gladly face an army or a dozen of the fierce Kalidahs.

Thus each of the little party was satisfied except Dorothy, who longed more than ever to get back to Kansas.

On the fourth day, to her great joy, Oz sent for her, and when she entered the Throne Room he greeted her pleasantly:

"Sit down, my dear; I think I have found the way to get you out of this country."

"And back to Kansas?" she asked eagerly.

"Well, I'm not sure about Kansas," said Oz, "for I haven't the faintest notion which way it lies. But the first thing to do is to cross the desert, and then it should be easy to find your way home."

"How can I cross the desert?" she inquired.

"Well, I'll tell you what I think," said the little man. "You see, when

I came to this country it was in a balloon. You also came through the air, being carried by a cyclone. So I believe the best way to get across the desert will be through the air. Now, it is quite beyond my powers to make a cyclone; but I've been thinking the matter over, and I believe I can make a balloon."

"How?" asked Dorothy.

"A balloon," said Oz, "is made of silk, which is coated with glue to keep the gas in it. I have plenty of silk in the Palace, so it will be no trouble to make the balloon. But in all this country there is no gas to fill the balloon with, to make it float."

"If it won't float," remarked Dorothy, "it will be of no use to us."

"True," answered Oz. "But there is another way to make it float, which is to fill it with hot air. Hot air isn't as good as gas, for if the air should get cold the balloon would come down in the desert, and we should be lost."

"We!" exclaimed the girl. "Are you going with me?"

"Yes, of course," replied Oz. "I am tired of being such a humbug. If I should go out of this Palace my people would soon discover I am not a Wizard, and then they would be vexed with me for having deceived them. So I have to stay shut up in these rooms all day, and it gets tiresome. I'd much rather go back to Kansas with you and be in a circus again."

"I shall be glad to have your company," said Dorothy.

"Thank you," he answered. "Now, if you will help me sew the silk together, we will begin to work on our balloon."

So Dorothy took a needle and thread, and as fast as Oz cut the strips of silk into proper shape the girl sewed them neatly together. First there was a strip of light green silk, then a strip of dark green and then a strip of emerald green; for Oz had a fancy to make the balloon in different shades of the color about them. It took three days to sew all the strips together, but when it was finished they had a big bag of green silk more than twenty feet long.

Then Oz painted it on the inside with a coat of thin glue, to make it airtight, after which he announced that the balloon was ready.

"But we must have a basket to ride in," he said. So he sent the soldier with the green whiskers for a big clothes basket, which he fastened with many ropes to the bottom of the balloon.

When it was all ready, Oz sent word to his people that he was going to make a visit to a great brother Wizard who lived in the clouds. The news spread rapidly throughout the city and everyone came to see the wonderful sight.

Oz ordered the balloon carried out in front of the Palace, and the people gazed upon it with much curiosity. The Tin Woodman had chopped a big pile of wood, and now he made a fire of it, and Oz held the bottom of the balloon over the fire so that the hot air that arose from it would be caught in the silken bag. Gradually the balloon swelled out and rose into the air, until finally the basket just touched the ground.

Then Oz got into the basket and said to all the people in a loud voice:

"I am now going away to make a visit. While I am gone the Scarecrow will rule over you. I command you to obey him as you would me."

The balloon was by this time tugging hard at the rope that held it to the ground, for the air within it was hot, and this made it so much lighter in weight than the air without that it pulled hard to rise into the sky.

"Come, Dorothy!" cried the Wizard. "Hurry up, or the balloon will fly away."

"I can't find Toto anywhere," replied Dorothy, who did not wish to leave her little dog behind. Toto had run into the crowd to bark at a kitten, and Dorothy at last found him. She picked him up and ran towards the balloon.

She was within a few steps of it, and Oz was holding out his hands to help her into the basket, when, crack! went the ropes, and the balloon rose into the air without her.

"Come back!" she screamed. "I want to go, too!"

"I can't come back, my dear," called Oz from the basket. "Good-bye!"

"Good-bye!" shouted everyone, and all eyes were turned upward to where the Wizard was riding in the basket, rising every moment farther and farther into the sky.

And that was the last any of them ever saw of Oz, the Wonderful Wizard, though he may have reached Omaha safely, and be there now, for all we know. But the people remembered him lovingly, and said to one another:

"Oz was always our friend. When he was here he built for us this beautiful Emerald City, and now he is gone he has left the Wise Scarecrow to rule over us."

Still, for many days they grieved over the loss of the Wonderful Wizard, and would not be comforted.

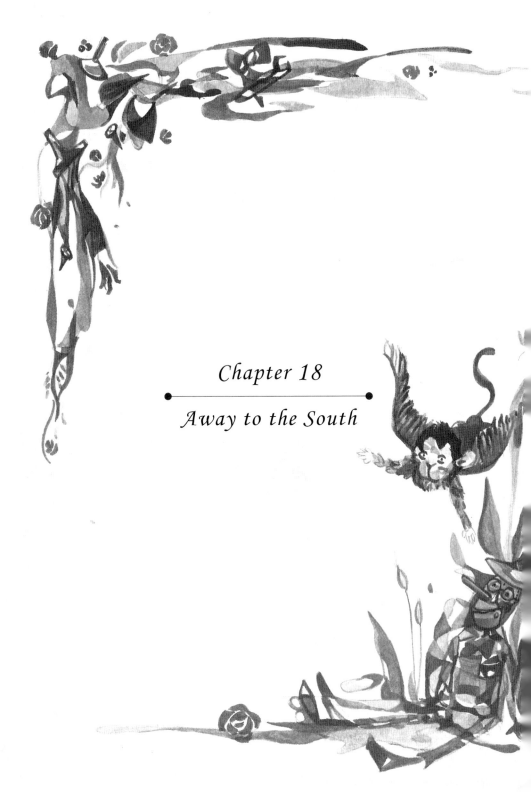

Chapter 18

Away to the South

"The road is straight to the South, but it is said to be full of dangers to travelers. There are wild beasts in the woods, and a race of queer men who do not like strangers to cross their country. For this reason none of the Quadlings ever come to the Emerald City."

Dorothy wept bitterly at the passing of her hope to get home to Kansas again; but when she thought it all over she was glad she had not gone up in a balloon. And she also felt sorry at losing Oz, and so did her companions.

The Tin Woodman came to her and said:

"Truly I should be ungrateful if I failed to mourn for the man who gave me my lovely heart. I should like to cry a little because Oz is gone, if you will kindly wipe away my tears, so that I shall not rust."

"With pleasure," she answered, and brought a towel at once. Then the Tin Woodman wept for several minutes, and she watched the tears carefully and wiped them away with the towel. When he had finished, he thanked her kindly and oiled himself thoroughly with his jeweled oil-can, to guard against mishap.

The Scarecrow was now the ruler of the Emerald City, and although he was not a Wizard the people were proud of him. "For," they said, "there is not another city in all the world that is ruled by a stuffed man." And, so far as they knew, they were quite right.

The morning after the balloon had gone up with Oz, the four travelers met in the Throne Room and talked matters over. The Scarecrow sat in the big throne and the others stood respectfully before him.

"We are not so unlucky," said the new ruler, "for this Palace and the

Emerald City belong to us, and we can do just as we please. When I remember that a short time ago I was up on a pole in a farmer's cornfield, and that now I am the ruler of this beautiful City, I am quite satisfied with my lot."

"I also," said the Tin Woodman, "am well-pleased with my new heart; and, really, that was the only thing I wished in all the world."

"For my part, I am content in knowing I am as brave as any beast that ever lived, if not braver," said the Lion modestly.

"If Dorothy would only be contented to live in the Emerald City," continued the Scarecrow, "we might all be happy together."

"But I don't want to live here," cried Dorothy. "I want to go to Kansas, and live with Aunt Em and Uncle Henry."

"Well, then, what can be done?" inquired the Woodman.

The Scarecrow decided to think, and he thought so hard that the pins and needles began to stick out of his brains. Finally he said:

"Why not call the Winged Monkeys, and ask them to carry you over the desert?"

"I never thought of that!" said Dorothy joyfully. "It's just the thing. I'll go at once for the Golden Cap."

When she brought it into the Throne Room she spoke the magic words, and soon the band of Winged Monkeys flew in through the open window and stood beside her.

"This is the second time you have called us," said the Monkey King, bowing before the little girl. "What do you wish?"

"I want you to fly with me to Kansas," said Dorothy.

But the Monkey King shook his head.

"That cannot be done," he said. "We belong to this country alone, and cannot leave it. There has never been a Winged Monkey in Kansas yet, and I suppose there never will be, for they don't belong there. We shall be glad to serve you in any way in our power, but we cannot cross the desert. Good-bye."

And with another bow, the Monkey King spread his wings and flew away through the window, followed by all his band.

Dorothy was ready to cry with disappointment.

"I have wasted the charm of the Golden Cap to no purpose," she said, "for the Winged Monkeys cannot help me."

"It is certainly too bad!" said the tender-hearted Woodman.

The Scarecrow was thinking again, and his head bulged out so horribly that Dorothy feared it would burst.

"Let us call in the soldier with the green whiskers," he said, "and ask his advice."

So the soldier was summoned and entered the Throne Room timidly, for while Oz was alive he never was allowed to come farther than the door.

"This little girl," said the Scarecrow to the soldier, "wishes to cross the desert. How can she do so?"

"I cannot tell," answered the soldier, "for nobody has ever crossed the desert, unless it is Oz himself."

"Is there no one who can help me?" asked Dorothy earnestly.

"Glinda might," he suggested.

"Who is Glinda?" inquired the Scarecrow.

"The Witch of the South. She is the most powerful of all the Witches, and rules over the Quadlings. Besides, her castle stands on the edge of the desert, so she may know a way to cross it."

"Glinda is a Good Witch, isn't she?" asked the child.

"The Quadlings think she is good," said the soldier, "and she is kind to everyone. I have heard that Glinda is a beautiful woman, who knows how to keep young in spite of the many years she has lived."

"How can I get to her castle?" asked Dorothy.

"The road is straight to the South," he answered, "but it is said to be full of dangers to travelers. There are wild beasts in the woods, and a race of queer men who do not like strangers to cross their country. For this reason none of the Quadlings ever come to the Emerald City."

The soldier then left them and the Scarecrow said:

"It seems, in spite of dangers, that the best thing Dorothy can do is to travel to the Land of the South and ask Glinda to help her. For, of course, if Dorothy stays here she will never get back to Kansas."

"You must have been thinking again," remarked the Tin Woodman.

"I have," said the Scarecrow.

"I shall go with Dorothy," declared the Lion, "for I am tired of your city and long for the woods and the country again. I am really a wild beast, you know. Besides, Dorothy will need someone to protect her."

"That is true," agreed the Woodman. "My axe may be of service to her; so I also will go with her to the Land of the South."

"When shall we start?" asked the Scarecrow.

"Are you going?" they asked, in surprise.

"Certainly. If it wasn't for Dorothy I should never have had brains. She lifted me from the pole in the cornfield and brought me to the Emerald City. So my good luck is all due to her, and I shall never leave her until she starts back to Kansas for good and all."

"Thank you," said Dorothy gratefully. "You are all very kind to me. But I should like to start as soon as possible."

"We shall go tomorrow morning," returned the Scarecrow. "So now let us all get ready, for it will be a long journey."

Chapter 19

Attacked
by the Fighting Trees

The Scarecrow, who was in the lead, finally discovered a big tree with such wide-spreading branches that there was room for the party to pass underneath.

The next morning Dorothy kissed the pretty green girl good-bye, and they all shook hands with the soldier with the green whiskers, who had walked with them as far as the gate. When the Guardian of the Gate saw them again he wondered greatly that they could leave the beautiful City to get into new trouble. But he at once unlocked their spectacles, which he put back into the green box, and gave them many good wishes to carry with them.

"You are now our ruler," he said to the Scarecrow; "so you must come back to us as soon as possible."

"I certainly shall if I am able," the Scarecrow replied; "but I must help Dorothy to get home, first."

As Dorothy bade the good-natured Guardian a last farewell she said:

"I have been very kindly treated in your lovely City, and everyone has been good to me. I cannot tell you how grateful I am."

"Don't try, my dear," he answered. "We should like to keep you with us, but if it is your wish to return to Kansas, I hope you will find a way." He then opened the gate of the outer wall, and they walked forth and started upon their journey.

The sun shone brightly as our friends turned their faces toward the Land of the South. They were all in the best of spirits, and laughed and chatted together. Dorothy was once more filled with the hope of getting home, and the Scarecrow and the Tin Woodman were glad to be of use to her. As for the Lion, he sniffed the fresh air with delight and whisked his tail from side to side in pure joy at being in the country again, while Toto ran around them and chased the moths and butterflies, barking merrily all the time.

"City life does not agree with me at all," remarked the Lion, as they walked along at a brisk pace. "I have lost much flesh since I lived there, and now I am anxious for a chance to show the other beasts how courageous I have grown."

They now turned and took a last look at the Emerald City. All they could see was a mass of towers and steeples behind the green walls, and high up above everything the spires and dome of the Palace of Oz.

"Oz was not such a bad Wizard, after all," said the Tin Woodman, as he felt his heart rattling around in his breast.

"He knew how to give me brains, and very good brains, too," said the Scarecrow.

"If Oz had taken a dose of the same courage he gave me," added the Lion, "he would have been a brave man."

Dorothy said nothing. Oz had not kept the promise he made her, but he had done his best, so she forgave him. As he said, he was a good man, even if he was a bad Wizard.

The first day's journey was through the green fields and bright flowers that stretched about the Emerald City on every side. They slept that night on the grass, with nothing but the stars over them; and they rested very well indeed.

In the morning they traveled on until they came to a thick wood. There was no way of going around it, for it seemed to extend to the right and left as far as they could see; and, besides, they did not dare change the direction of their journey for fear of getting lost. So they looked for the place where it would be easiest to get into the forest.

The Scarecrow, who was in the lead, finally discovered a big tree with such wide-spreading branches that there was room for the party to pass underneath. So he walked forward to the tree, but just as he came under the first branches they bent down and twined around him, and the next minute he was raised from the ground and flung headlong among his fellow travelers.

This did not hurt the Scarecrow, but it surprised him, and he looked rather dizzy when Dorothy picked him up.

"Here is another space between the trees," called the Lion.

"Let me try it first," said the Scarecrow, "for it doesn't hurt me to get thrown about." He walked up to another tree, as he spoke, but its branches immediately seized him and tossed him back again.

"This is strange," exclaimed Dorothy. "What shall we do?"

"The trees seem to have made up their minds to fight us, and stop our journey," remarked the Lion.

"I believe I will try it myself," said the Woodman, and shouldering his axe, he marched up to the first tree that had handled the Scarecrow so roughly. When a big branch bent down to seize him the Woodman chopped at it so fiercely that he cut it in two. At once the tree began shaking all its branches as if in pain, and the Tin Woodman passed safely under it.

"Come on!" he shouted to the others. "Be quick!"

They all ran forward and passed under the tree without injury, except Toto, who was caught by a small branch and shaken until he howled. But the Woodman promptly chopped off the branch and set the little dog free.

The other trees of the forest did nothing to keep them back, so they made up their minds that only the first row of trees could bend down their branches, and that probably these were the policemen of the forest, and given this wonderful power in order to keep strangers out of it.

The four travelers walked with ease through the trees until they came to the farther edge of the wood. Then, to their surprise, they found before them a high wall which seemed to be made of white china. It was smooth, like the surface of a dish, and higher than their heads.

"What shall we do now?" asked Dorothy.

"I will make a ladder," said the Tin Woodman, "for we certainly must climb over the wall."

Chapter 20

The Dainty China
Country

"That would make me very unhappy," answered the china Princess. "You see, here in our country we live contentedly, and can talk and move around as we please."

While the Woodman was making a ladder from wood which he found in the forest Dorothy lay down and slept, for she was tired by the long walk. The Lion also curled himself up to sleep and Toto lay beside him.

The Scarecrow watched the Woodman while he worked, and said to him:

"I cannot think why this wall is here, nor what it is made of."

"Rest your brains and do not worry about the wall," replied the Woodman. "When we have climbed over it, we shall know what is on the other side."

After a time the ladder was finished. It looked clumsy, but the Tin Woodman was sure it was strong and would answer their purpose. The Scarecrow waked Dorothy and the Lion and Toto, and told them that the ladder was ready. The Scarecrow climbed up the ladder first, but he was so awkward that Dorothy had to follow close behind and keep him from falling off. When he got his head over the top of the wall the Scarecrow said, "Oh, my!"

"Go on," exclaimed Dorothy.

So the Scarecrow climbed farther up and sat down on the top of the wall, and Dorothy put her head over and cried, "Oh, my!" just as the Scarecrow had done.

Then Toto came up, and immediately began to bark, but Dorothy made him be still.

The Lion climbed the ladder next, and the Tin Woodman came last; but both of them cried, "Oh, my!" as soon as they looked over the wall. When they were all sitting in a row on the top of the wall, they looked down and saw a strange sight.

Before them was a great stretch of country having a floor as smooth and shining and white as the bottom of a big platter. Scattered around were many houses made entirely of china and painted in the brightest colors. These houses were quite small, the biggest of them reaching only as high as Dorothy's waist. There were also pretty little barns, with china fences around them; and many cows and sheep and horses and pigs and chickens, all made of china, were standing about in groups.

But the strangest of all were the people who lived in this queer country. There were milkmaids and shepherdesses, with brightly colored bodices and golden spots all over their gowns; and princesses with most gorgeous frocks of silver and gold and purple; and shepherds dressed in knee breeches with pink and yellow and blue stripes down them, and golden buckles on their shoes; and princes with jeweled crowns upon their heads, wearing ermine robes and satin doublets; and funny clowns in ruffled gowns, with round red spots upon their cheeks and tall, pointed caps. And, strangest of all, these people were all made of china, even to their clothes, and were so small that the tallest of them was no higher than Dorothy's knee.

No one did so much as look at the travelers at first, except one little purple china dog with an extra-large head, which came to the wall and barked at them in a tiny voice, afterwards running away again.

"How shall we get down?" asked Dorothy.

They found the ladder so heavy they could not pull it up, so the Scarecrow fell off the wall and the others jumped down upon him so that the hard floor would not hurt their feet. Of course they took pains not to light on his head and get the pins in their feet. When all were safely down they picked up the Scarecrow, whose body was quite flattened out, and patted his straw into shape again.

"We must cross this strange place in order to get to the other side," said Dorothy, "for it would be unwise for us to go any other way except due South."

They began walking through the country of the china people, and the first thing they came to was a china milkmaid milking a china cow. As they drew near, the cow suddenly gave a kick and kicked over the stool, the pail, and even the milkmaid herself, and all fell on the china ground with a great clatter.

Dorothy was shocked to see that the cow had broken her leg off, and that the pail was lying in several small pieces, while the poor milkmaid had a nick in her left elbow.

"There!" cried the milkmaid angrily. "See what you have done! My cow has broken her leg, and I must take her to the mender's shop and have it glued on again. What do you mean by coming here and frightening my cow?"

"I'm very sorry," returned Dorothy. "Please forgive us."

But the pretty milkmaid was much too vexed to make any answer. She picked up the leg sulkily and led her cow away, the poor animal limping on three legs. As she left them the milkmaid cast many reproachful glances over her shoulder at the clumsy strangers, holding her nicked elbow close to her side.

Dorothy was quite grieved at this mishap.

"We must be very careful here," said the kind-hearted Woodman, "or we may hurt these pretty little people so they will never get over it."

A little farther on Dorothy met a most beautifully dressed young Princess, who stopped short as she saw the strangers and started to run away.

Dorothy wanted to see more of the Princess, so she ran after her. But the china girl cried out:

"Don't chase me! Don't chase me!"

She had such a frightened little voice that Dorothy stopped and said, "Why not?"

"Because," answered the Princess, also stopping, a safe distance away, "if I run I may fall down and break myself."

"But could you not be mended?" asked the girl.

"Oh, yes; but one is never so pretty after being mended, you know," replied the Princess.

"I suppose not," said Dorothy.

"Now there is Mr. Joker, one of our clowns," continued the china lady, "who is always trying to stand upon his head. He has broken himself so often that he is mended in a hundred places, and doesn't look at all pretty. Here he comes now, so you can see for yourself."

Indeed, a jolly little clown came walking toward them, and Dorothy could see that in spite of his pretty clothes of red and yellow and green he was completely covered with cracks, running every which way and showing plainly that he had been mended in many places.

The Clown put his hands in his pockets, and after puffing out his cheeks and nodding his head at them saucily, he said:

> *"My lady fair,*
> *Why do you stare*
> *At poor old Mr. Joker?*
> *You're quite as stiff*
> *And prim as if*
> *You'd eaten up a poker!"*

"Be quiet, sir!" said the Princess. "Can't you see these are strangers, and should be treated with respect?"

"Well, that's respect, I expect," declared the Clown, and immediately stood upon his head.

"Don't mind Mr. Joker," said the Princess to Dorothy. "He is considerably cracked in his head, and that makes him foolish."

"Oh, I don't mind him a bit," said Dorothy. "But you are so beautiful," she continued, "that I am sure I could love you dearly. Won't you let me carry you back to Kansas, and stand you on Aunt Em's mantelshelf? I could carry you in my basket."

"That would make me very unhappy," answered the china Princess. "You see, here in our country we live contentedly, and can talk and move around as we please. But whenever any of us are taken away our joints at once stiffen, and we can only stand straight and look pretty. Of course that is all that is expected of us when we are on mantels and cabinets and drawing-room tables, but our lives are much pleasanter here in our own country."

"I would not make you unhappy for all the world!" exclaimed Dorothy. "So I'll just say good-bye."

"Good-bye," replied the Princess.

They walked carefully through the china country. The little animals and all the people scampered out of their way, fearing the strangers would break them, and after an hour or so the travelers reached the other side of the country and came to another china wall.

It was not so high as the first, however, and by standing upon the Lion's back they all managed to scramble to the top. Then the Lion gathered his legs under him and jumped on the wall; but just as he jumped, he upset a china church with his tail and smashed it all to pieces.

"That was too bad," said Dorothy, "but really I think we were lucky in not doing these little people more harm than breaking a cow's leg and a church. They are all so brittle!"

"They are, indeed," said the Scarecrow, "and I am thankful I am made of straw and cannot be easily damaged. There are worse things in the world than being a Scarecrow."

Chapter 21

The Lion Becomes the King of the Beasts

"This forest is perfectly delightful," declared the Lion, looking around him with joy. "Never have I seen a more beautiful place."

After climbing down from the china wall the travelers found themselves in a disagreeable country, full of bogs and marshes and covered with tall, rank grass. It was difficult to walk without falling into muddy holes, for the grass was so thick that it hid them from sight. However, by carefully picking their way, they got safely along until they reached solid ground. But here the country seemed wilder than ever, and after a long and tiresome walk through the underbrush they entered another forest, where the trees were bigger and older than any they had ever seen.

"This forest is perfectly delightful," declared the Lion, looking around him with joy. "Never have I seen a more beautiful place."

"It seems gloomy," said the Scarecrow.

"Not a bit of it," answered the Lion. "I should like to live here all my life. See how soft the dried leaves are under your feet and how rich and green the moss is that clings to these old trees. Surely no wild beast could wish a pleasanter home."

"Perhaps there are wild beasts in the forest now," said Dorothy.

"I suppose there are," returned the Lion, "but I do not see any of them about."

They walked through the forest until it became too dark to go any farther. Dorothy and Toto and the Lion lay down to sleep, while the Woodman and the Scarecrow kept watch over them as usual.

When morning came, they started again. Before they had gone far they heard a low rumble, as of the growling of many wild animals. Toto whimpered a little, but none of the others was frightened, and they kept along the well-trodden path until they came to an opening in the wood, in which were gathered hundreds of beasts of every variety. There were tigers and elephants and bears and wolves and foxes and all the others in the natural history, and for a moment Dorothy was afraid. But the Lion explained that the animals were holding a meeting, and he judged by their snarling and growling that they were in great trouble.

As he spoke several of the beasts caught sight of him, and at once the great assemblage hushed as if by magic. The biggest of the tigers came up to the Lion and bowed, saying:

"Welcome, O King of Beasts! You have come in good time to fight our enemy and bring peace to all the animals of the forest once more."

"What is your trouble?" asked the Lion quietly.

"We are all threatened," answered the tiger, "by a fierce enemy which has lately come into this forest. It is a most tremendous monster, like a great spider, with a body as big as an elephant and legs as long as a tree trunk. It has eight of these long legs, and as the monster crawls through the forest he seizes an animal with a leg and drags it to his mouth, where he eats it as a spider does a fly. Not one of us is safe while this fierce creature is alive, and we had called a meeting to decide how to take care of ourselves when you came among us."

The Lion thought for a moment.

"Are there any other lions in this forest?" he asked.

"No; there were some, but the monster has eaten them all. And, besides, there were none of them nearly so large and brave as you."

"If I put an end to your enemy, will you bow down to me and obey me as King of the Forest?" inquired the Lion.

"We will do that gladly," returned the tiger; and all the other beasts roared with a mighty roar: "We will!"

"Where is this great spider of yours now?" asked the Lion.

"Yonder, among the oak trees," said the tiger, pointing with his forefoot.

"Take good care of these friends of mine," said the Lion, "and I will go at once to fight the monster."

He bade his comrades good-bye and marched proudly away to do battle with the enemy.

The great spider was lying asleep when the Lion found him, and it looked so ugly that its foe turned up his nose in disgust. Its legs were quite as long as the tiger had said, and its body covered with coarse black hair. It had a great mouth, with a row of sharp teeth a foot long; but its head was joined to the pudgy body by a neck as slender as a wasp's waist. This gave the Lion a hint of the best way to attack the creature, and as he knew it was easier to fight it asleep than awake, he gave a great spring and landed directly upon the monster's back.

Then, with one blow of his heavy paw, all armed with sharp claws, he knocked the spider's head from its body. Jumping down, he watched it until the long legs stopped wiggling, when he knew it was quite dead.

The Lion went back to the opening where the beasts of the forest were waiting for him and said proudly:

"You need fear your enemy no longer."

Then the beasts bowed down to the Lion as their King, and he promised to come back and rule over them as soon as Dorothy was safely on her way to Kansas.

Chapter 22

The Country
of the Quadlings

"Carry us over the hill to the country of the Quadlings," answered the girl.

The four travelers passed through the rest of the forest in safety, and when they came out from its gloom saw before them a steep hill, covered from top to bottom with great pieces of rock.

"That will be a hard climb," said the Scarecrow, "but we must get over the hill, nevertheless."

So he led the way and the others followed. They had nearly reached the first rock when they heard a rough voice cry out, "Keep back!"

"Who are you?" asked the Scarecrow.

Then a head showed itself over the rock and the same voice said, "This hill belongs to us, and we don't allow anyone to cross it."

"But we must cross it," said the Scarecrow. "We're going to the country of the Quadlings."

"But you shall not!" replied the voice, and there stepped from behind the rock the strangest man the travelers had ever seen.

He was quite short and stout and had a big head, which was flat at the top and supported by a thick neck full of wrinkles. But he had no arms at all, and, seeing this, the Scarecrow did not fear that so helpless a creature could prevent them from climbing the hill. So he said, "I'm sorry not to do as you wish, but we must pass over your hill whether you like it or not," and he walked boldly forward.

As quick as lightning the man's head shot forward and his neck stretched out until the top of the head, where it was flat, struck the

Scarecrow in the middle and sent him tumbling, over and over, down the hill. Almost as quickly as it came the head went back to the body, and the man laughed harshly as he said, "It isn't as easy as you think!"

A chorus of boisterous laughter came from the other rocks, and Dorothy saw hundreds of the armless Hammer-Heads upon the hillside, one behind every rock.

The Lion became quite angry at the laughter caused by the Scarecrow's mishap, and giving a loud roar that echoed like thunder, he dashed up the hill.

Again a head shot swiftly out, and the great Lion went rolling down the hill as if he had been struck by a cannon ball.

Dorothy ran down and helped the Scarecrow to his feet, and the Lion came up to her, feeling rather bruised and sore, and said, "It is useless to fight people with shooting heads; no one can withstand them."

"What can we do, then?" she asked.

"Call the Winged Monkeys," suggested the Tin Woodman. "You have still the right to command them once more."

"Very well," she answered, and putting on the Golden Cap she uttered the magic words. The Monkeys were as prompt as ever, and in a few moments the entire band stood before her.

"What are your commands?" inquired the King of the Monkeys, bowing low.

"Carry us over the hill to the country of the Quadlings," answered the girl.

"It shall be done," said the King, and at once the Winged Monkeys caught the four travelers and Toto up in their arms and flew away with them. As they passed over the hill the Hammer-Heads yelled with vexation, and shot their heads high in the air, but they could not reach the Winged Monkeys, which carried Dorothy and her comrades safely over the hill and set them down in the beautiful country of the Quadlings.

"This is the last time you can summon us," said the leader to Dorothy; "so good-bye and good luck to you."

"Good-bye, and thank you very much," returned the girl; and the Monkeys rose into the air and were out of sight in a twinkling.

The country of the Quadlings seemed rich and happy. There was field upon field of ripening grain, with well-paved roads running between, and pretty rippling brooks with strong bridges across them. The fences and houses and bridges were all painted bright red, just as they had been painted yellow in the country of the Winkies and blue in the country of the Munchkins. The Quadlings themselves, who were short and fat and looked chubby and good-natured, were dressed all in red, which showed bright against the green grass and the yellowing grain.

The Monkeys had set them down near a farmhouse, and the four travelers walked up to it and knocked at the door. It was opened by the farmer's wife, and when Dorothy asked for something to eat the woman gave them all a good dinner, with three kinds of cake and four kinds of cookies, and a bowl of milk for Toto.

"How far is it to the Castle of Glinda?" asked the child.

"It is not a great way," answered the farmer's wife. "Take the road to the South and you will soon reach it."

Thanking the good woman, they started afresh and walked by the fields and across the pretty bridges until they saw before them a very beautiful Castle. Before the gates were three young girls, dressed in handsome red uniforms trimmed with gold braid; and as Dorothy approached, one of them said to her:

"Why have you come to the South Country?"

"To see the Good Witch who rules here," she answered. "Will you take me to her?"

"Let me have your name, and I will ask Glinda if she will receive you." They told who they were, and the girl soldier went into the Castle. After a few moments she came back to say that Dorothy and the others were to be admitted at once.

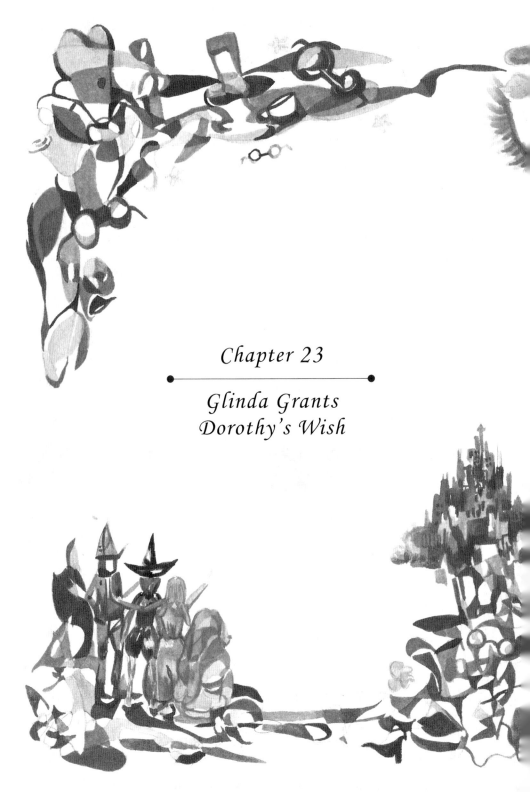

Chapter 23

•————————————•

Glinda Grants
Dorothy's Wish

"Bless your dear heart," she said, "I am sure I can tell you of a way to get back to Kansas." Then she added, "But, if I do, you must give me the Golden Cap."

Before they went to see Glinda, however, they were taken to a room of the Castle, where Dorothy washed her face and combed her hair, and the Lion shook the dust out of his mane, and the Scarecrow patted himself into his best shape, and the Woodman polished his tin and oiled his joints.

When they were all quite presentable they followed the soldier girl into a big room where the Witch Glinda sat upon a throne of rubies.

She was both beautiful and young to their eyes. Her hair was a rich red in color and fell in flowing ringlets over her shoulders. Her dress was pure white but her eyes were blue, and they looked kindly upon the little girl.

"What can I do for you, my child?" she asked.

Dorothy told the Witch all her story: how the cyclone had brought her to the Land of Oz, how she had found her companions, and of the wonderful adventures they had met with.

"My greatest wish now," she added, "is to get back to Kansas, for Aunt Em will surely think something dreadful has happened to me, and that will make her put on mourning; and unless the crops are better this year than they were last, I am sure Uncle Henry cannot afford it."

Glinda leaned forward and kissed the sweet, upturned face of the loving little girl.

"Bless your dear heart," she said, "I am sure I can tell you of a way to get back to Kansas." Then she added,

"But, if I do, you must give me the Golden Cap."

"Willingly!" exclaimed Dorothy; "indeed, it is of no use to me now, and when you have it you can command the Winged Monkeys three times."

"And I think I shall need their service just those three times," answered Glinda, smiling.

Dorothy then gave her the Golden Cap, and the Witch said to the Scarecrow, "What will you do when Dorothy has left us?"

"I will return to the Emerald City," he replied, "for Oz has made me its ruler and the people like me. The only thing that worries me is how to cross the hill of the Hammer-Heads."

"By means of the Golden Cap I shall command the Winged Monkeys to carry you to the gates of the Emerald City," said Glinda, "for it would be a shame to deprive the people of so wonderful a ruler."

"Am I really wonderful?" asked the Scarecrow.

"You are unusual," replied Glinda.

Turning to the Tin Woodman, she asked, "What will become of you when Dorothy leaves this country?"

He leaned on his axe and thought a moment. Then he said,

"The Winkies were very kind to me, and wanted me to rule over them after the Wicked Witch died. I am fond of the Winkies, and if I could get back again to the Country of the West, I should like nothing better than to rule over them forever."

"My second command to the Winged Monkeys," said Glinda "will be that they carry you safely to the land of the Winkies. Your brain may not be so large to look at as those of the Scarecrow, but you are really brighter than he is – when you are well polished – and I am sure you will rule the Winkies wisely and well."

Then the Witch looked at the big, shaggy Lion and asked, "When Dorothy has returned to her own home, what will become of you?"

"Over the hill of the Hammer-Heads," he answered, "lies a grand old forest, and all the beasts that live there have made me their King. If I could only get back to this forest, I would pass my life very happily there."

"My third command to the Winged Monkeys," said Glinda, "shall be to carry you to your forest. Then, having used up the powers of the Golden Cap, I shall give it to the King of the Monkeys, that he and his band may thereafter be free for evermore."

The Scarecrow and the Tin Woodman and the Lion now thanked the Good Witch earnestly for her kindness; and Dorothy exclaimed:

"You are certainly as good as you are beautiful! But you have not yet told me how to get back to Kansas."

"Your Silver Shoes will carry you over the desert," replied Glinda. "If you had known their power you could have gone back to your Aunt Em the very first day you came to this country."

"But then I should not have had my wonderful brains!" cried the Scarecrow. "I might have passed my whole life in the farmer's cornfield."

"And I should not have had my lovely heart," said the Tin Woodman. "I might have stood and rusted in the forest till the end of the world."

"And I should have lived a coward forever," declared the Lion, "and no beast in all the forest would have had a good word to say to me."

"This is all true," said Dorothy, "and I am glad I was of use to these good friends. But now that each of them has had what he most desired, and each is happy in having a kingdom to rule besides, I think I should like to go back to Kansas."

"The Silver Shoes," said the Good Witch, "have wonderful powers. And one of the most curious things about them is that they can carry you to any place in the world in three steps, and each step will be made in the wink of an eye. All you have to do is to knock the heels together three times and command the shoes to carry you wherever you wish to go."

"If that is so," said the child joyfully, "I will ask them to carry me back to Kansas at once."

She threw her arms around the Lion's neck and kissed him, patting his big head tenderly. Then she kissed the Tin Woodman, who was weeping in a way most dangerous to his joints. But she hugged the soft, stuffed body of the Scarecrow in her arms instead of kissing his painted face, and found she was crying herself at this sorrowful parting from her loving comrades.

Glinda the Good stepped down from her ruby throne to give the little girl a good-bye kiss, and Dorothy thanked her for all the kindness she had shown to her friends and herself.

Dorothy now took Toto up solemnly in her arms, and having said one last good-bye she clapped the heels of her shoes together three times, saying:

"Take me home to Aunt Em!"

Instantly she was whirling through the air, so swiftly that all she could see or feel was the wind whistling past her ears.

The Silver Shoes took but three steps, and then she stopped so suddenly that she rolled over upon the grass several times before she knew where she was.

At length, however, she sat up and looked about her.

"Good gracious!" she cried.

For she was sitting on the broad Kansas prairie, and just before her was the new farmhouse Uncle Henry built after the cyclone had carried away the old one. Uncle Henry was milking the cows in the barnyard, and Toto had jumped out of her arms and was running toward the barn, barking joyously.

Dorothy stood up and found she was in her stocking-feet. For the Silver Shoes had fallen off in her flight through the air, and were lost forever in the desert.

Chapter 24

Home Again

"From the Land of Oz," said
Dorothy gravely. "And here is
Toto, too. And oh, Aunt Em!
I'm so glad to be at home again!"

A unt Em had just come out of the house to water the cabbages when she looked up and saw Dorothy running toward her.

"My darling child!" she cried, folding the little girl in her arms and covering her face with kisses. "Where in the world did you come from?"

"From the Land of Oz," said Dorothy gravely. "And here is Toto, too. And oh, Aunt Em! I'm so glad to be at home again!"

(THE END)

國家圖書館出版品預行編目(CIP)資料

綠野仙蹤 / L・法蘭克・包姆著；盛世教育西方名著翻譯委
員會譯. -- 初版. -- 臺北市：笛藤, 2017.08　面；　公分
中英對照雙語版
譯自：The Wonderful Wizard of Oz
ISBN 978-957-710-697-1(平裝附光碟片)

874.59　　　　　106011071

2017年8月22日　初版 第1刷　定價 380 元

綠野仙蹤

The Wonderful
Wizard of
Oz

中英對照雙語版

情境配樂
英文朗讀
MP3

著　　　者	L・法蘭克・包姆
翻　　　譯	盛世教育西方名著翻譯委員會
插　　　圖	VIVIANWANG
封 面 設 計	王舒玗
總 編 輯	賴巧凌
編　　　輯	林子鈺
發 行 人	林建仲
發 行 所	笛藤出版圖書有限公司
地　　　址	台北市重慶南路三段1號3樓-1
電　　　話	(02)2358-3891
傳　　　真	(02)2358-3902
總 經 銷	聯合發行股份有限公司
電　　　話	(02)2917-8022・(02)2917-8042
製 版 廠	造極彩色印刷製版股份有限公司
劃 撥 帳 戶	八方出版股份有限公司
劃 撥 帳 號	19809050

本書為世界圖書出版上海有限公司
授權八方出版股份有限公司（笛藤出版）
在台灣地區出版發行的繁體字版本